The Turbulence of Migration

For Teodor

The Turbulence of Migration

Globalization, Deterritorialization and Hybridity

Nikos Papastergiadis

Polity Press

First published in 2000 by Polity Press in association with Blackwell Publishers Ltd.

Editorial office:
Polity Press
65 Bridge Street
Cambridge CB2 1UR, UK

Marketing and production:
Blackwell Publishers Ltd
108 Cowley Road
Oxford OX4 1JF, UK

Published in the USA by
Blackwell Publishers Inc.
Commerce Place
350 Main Street
Malden, Massachusetts 02148, USA

A catalogue record for this book is available from the British Library.

Library of Congress Cataloging-in-Publication Data
Papastergiadis, Nikos, 1962–
    The turbulence of migration : globalization, deterritorialization and hybridity / Nikos Papastergiadis.
        p.   cm.
    Includes bibliographical references and index.
    ISBN 0-7456-1430-2 (hb.).— ISBN 0-7456-1431-0 (pb.)
    1. Emigration and immigration.   2. International economic relations.
    3. Cultural relations.   4. Immigrants—Social conditions.   I. Title
    JV6032.P34   2000
    325—dc21   99-27521
                                                                                CIP

Typeset in 10 on 12 pt Times by Ace Filmsetting Ltd, Frome, Somerset
Printed in Great Britain by TJ International, Padstow, Cornwall

This book is printed on acid-free paper

Contents

Acknowledgements

I began writing this book in 1993 when, with my first ever laptop computer, I headed out to Australia. After having 'keyed in' half of my first draft I experienced the now legendary 'hard disk failure'. In retrospect, I am grateful for this little catastrophe for it punctured all my illusions about the infallibility of modern technology and alerted me to the pitfalls of writing on the road. Over the next five years this book slowly emerged in the form of long essays, many of which were prodded along by other editors. I would like to acknowledge the encouragement offered by Diana Nemiroff, Gilane Tawadros, Pnina Werbner and the editorial team of the *Arena* journal. This book would not have found its present shape without the incisive and helpful comments from Tony Giddens, John Thompson and Lynn Dunlop at Polity Press. The reader's reports from John Solomos and John Rex were invaluable.

The breadth and texture of this book is mostly due to the different worlds in which I live and work. This is an attempt to bring them together, or at least to demonstrate that conversations that began in one place can be resumed in another. I am especially grateful to Scott McQuire, Bill Papastergiadis, Peter Ash, Rita Armstrong, John Berger, Victoria Lynn, Peter Lyssiotis, Constanze Zikos, Rasheed Araeen, Gillian Bottomley, Guy Brett, Ron Benner, Ann Brydon, Pavel Buchler, Anne Daniel, Jean Fisher, Helena Guldberg, Sneja Gunew, Jamelie Hassan, Richard Hylton, Vivian Kondos, Lois McNab, Don Miller, Stephen Snoddy, Gayatri Chakravorty Spivak, Nick Tsoutas, Liz Turnbull and Leon Van Schaik.

My greatest debt lies with my friends and colleagues at Manchester University. This book reflects the lively debates, conversation in corridors and long lunches that made me think through the connections between political economy and cultural theory. In particular, I would like to thank Teodor Shanin, Huw Beynon, Helen Sampson, Steve Quilley, Sheila Rowbotham, Simon Miller, Peter McMylor, Fiona Divine, Paul Kelemen, Mike Savage, David Morgan, Rod Watson, Rosemary Mellor, John Hutnyk, Anna Grimshaw, Peter Halfpenny, Jeff Henderson, Patrick Joyce, Marcia Poynton, Andrew Causey and Katherine Isaacs, who once gave me an invaluable piece of advice: 'When you are in a hole, stop digging.'

1

Introduction: The Turbulence of Migration

The subjects of history, once the settled farmers and citizens, have now become the migrants, the refugees, the *Gastarbeiter*, the asylum seekers, the urban homeless.

Neal Ascherson, *The Black Sea*

Migration, in its endless motion, surrounds and pervades almost all aspects of contemporary society. As has often been noted, the modern world is in a state of flux and turbulence. It is a system in which the circulation of people, resources and information follows multiple paths. The energy and barriers that either cause or deflect the contemporary patterns of movement have both obvious and hidden locations. While nothing is utterly random, the consequences of change are often far from predictable. For the most part, we seem to travel in this world without that invisible captain, who can see ahead and periodically warn us to 'return to our seats and fasten our security belts'. The journey nowadays is particularly treacherous, with financial storms which can break out in Hong Kong and have repercussions in New York, acid rains generated in the north drifting south, the global emission of CFC gases directly affecting the growth of the hole in the ozone layer above the Antarctic, the threat of atomic fallout looming larger as the nuclear arsenals of thirty or more countries are positioned along jagged lines of brinkmanship, and the systemic flooding of the ranks of the unemployed as the chilling technology of economic rationalization bites into every locale. These are just some of the known sources of fear. There may be other storms on the horizon which we cannot name, let alone control, that force people to move.

The turbulence of modern migration has destabilized the routes of movement and created uncertainty about the possibilities of settlement. The scale and complexity of movement that is occurring currently has never been witnessed before in history, and its consequences have exceeded earlier predictions. To take account of this excess, migration must be understood in a broad sense. I see it not just as a term referring to the plight of the 'burnt ones', the destitute others who have been displaced from their homelands. It is also a metaphor for the complex forces which are integral to the radical transformations of modernity. The world changes around us and we change with it, but in the modern period the process of change has also altered fundamental perceptions of time and space. Countless people are on the move and even those who have never left their homeland are moved by this restless epoch.

These changes have a profound effect on the way we understand our sense of belonging in the world. It is impossible to give an exact location and date for the emergence of modernity. Modernity has had multiple birthplaces. Giddens's general definition of modernity, as referring to the institutional changes that took place somewhere around the eighteenth century, is about as accurate as one can get.[1] Throughout the modern period, most people have understood their sense of belonging in terms of an allegiance to a nation-state. This task of conferring clear and unambiguous forms of belonging was never a straightforward operation. Nation-states were from the outset composed of people with different cultural identities. Among the central aims of the project of nation-building was the unification of these diverse peoples under a common identity, and the regulation of movement across their territorial borders. However, the complex patterns of movement across national boundaries, and the articulation of new forms of identity by minority groups that emerged in the past couple of decades, have destabilized the foundations of the nation-state.

This book seeks to examine the interconnected processes of globalization and migration and to explore their impact on the established notions of belonging. It seeks to question the dominant forms of citizenship and cultural identity which defined belonging according to national categories and exclusive practices of identification, by exploring the emergent forms of diasporic and hybrid identities. There is a great urgency in our need to rethink the politics of identity. If the historical and cultural field that shapes contemporary society is increasingly diverse and varied, then we can no longer exclusively focus on the traditions and institutions that have taken root in a given place over a long historical period. The identity of society has to reflect this process of mixture that emerges whenever two or more cultures meet.

The political will to adopt such an approach towards migrant communities and minority groups has not been readily forthcoming. While there is a growing recognition that we are living in a far more turbulent world, a critical language and affirmative structures to address these changes have been lagging behind. A haunting paradox lurks at the centre of all claims to national autonomy: while the flows of global movement are proliferating, the fortification of national boundaries is becoming more vigilant. Every nation-state is at once seeking to maximize the opportunities from transnational corporations, and yet closing its doors to the forms of migration that these economic shifts stimulate. New pressures and new voices have emerged in the cultural and political landscape. Even countries like Germany and Japan, which have boasted of their ethnic homogeneity and aggressively restricted the right to citizenship, are increasingly confronted with the inevitability of seeing themselves as multi-ethnic societies. As nation-states are losing more and more of their power to regulate activities within their territory, they are becoming increasingly aggressive about the defence of their borders. Tougher laws against asylum-seekers, the rounding up of gypsies and ruthless eviction of 'economic migrants' are some of the ways in which governments vent their frustration in a world where they have seemingly lost control but dare not admit it. The need for global action to address local issues has never been more necessary, but there are few signs of supranational co-operation, nor any new agencies with the powers and responsibilities to address human needs on a global scale.

New concepts for a turbulent world

The twin processes of globalization and migration have produced changes in the geopolitical landscape that have compelled social scientists to rethink their conceptual frameworks. Since the 1970s, there has been a growing legitimacy of multicultural perspectives in places like Canada and Australia, which have questioned the dominant political categories for defining citizenship according to birthplace and residence within a nation-state. Previously, most of the literature on migration was staked between the automatic assimilation and the gradual integration of the migrant into the host society. As 'ethnic elites' gained authority within the cultural and political circles of the dominant society, they began to argue in favour of new models for representing the process of cultural interaction, and to demonstrate the negative consequences of insisting upon the denial of the emergent forms of cultural identity. Multicultural perspectives on political rights and cultural exchange thus began to have a dynamic role in the reshaping of contemporary society.

Since the 1980s, especially in the American and French academic communities, the concept of class had come under scrutiny. Conservative scholars like Francis Fukuyama saw the collapse of the Soviet Union as the ultimate triumph of liberalism, and the 'end of history' in terms of class struggle. Samuel Huntington took a more pessimistic view of the global picture, noting the ascendance of Islam, the rising influence of the east, and predicted cataclysmic 'clashes of civilization'. Structural changes were definitely occurring, the imperial orders were being dismantled and reconfigured, multi-ethnic societies were becoming the norm, and in contradistinction to these patrician scholars, I believe that the more sober reappraisal of the fundamental social divisions was offered by the new intellectual movements of feminism and postcolonialism.

The concept of space, which in the 1990s was given greater theoretical significance by British geographers like Doreen Massey, added a crucial dimension in the rethinking of the relationship between migration and globalization. In the past there was a tendency to discuss migration in the mechanistic terms of causes and consequences. Space was often seen as a vacant category, reduced to a neutral stage upon which other forces were at play in the narratives of migration. Space was rarely seen as an active part in the field of identity formation. However, it is increasingly evident that contemporary migration has no single origin and no simple end. It is an ongoing process and needs to be seen as an open voyage. Departures and returns are rarely, if ever, final, and so it is important that we acknowledge the transformative effect of the journey, and in general recognize that space is a dynamic field in which identities are in a constant state of interaction. This would enable us to shift the discourse on migration from merely an explanation of either the external causes or the attribution of motivation to an examination of the complex relationships and perceptual shifts that are being formed through the experience of movement. Just as in science there is the new consensus that every entity is composed of interacting forces, there is now an emerging debate in the humanities and social sciences that agency is in a state of mutual transformation with its surrounding structures. Hence, the cultural identity of the migrant will need to be seen as being partly formed by and in the journey, or on what Paul Virilio calls the 'trajective', and not as a locked item that preceded the very act of movement.

These political transformations and intellectual debates on nationalism and multiculturalism, class and agency, and space and time provide the broad horizons of this book. More specifically my aim is to explore the parameters of three questions. First, what are the available models for mapping migration and explaining social change? Second, how is migration linked to the broader social changes associated with globalization? Third, how do concepts like deterritorialization, translation, recognition and hybridity expand our understanding of identity and culture in plural societies?

Throughout this book the term 'turbulence' appears. I have adopted it from James Rosenau's work in international relations in order to break out of the mechanistic models for explaining migration. Turbulence is not just a useful noun for describing the unsettling effect of an unexpected force that alters your course of movement; it is also a metaphor for the broader levels of interconnection and interdependency between the various forces that are in play in the modern world. The flows of migration across the globe are not explicable by any general theory. In the absence of structured patterns of global migration, with direct causes and effects, turbulence is the best formulation for the mobile processes of complex self-organization that are now occurring. These movements may appear chaotic, but there is a logic and order within them. An analogy can be drawn with phenomena that were once thought to lack any structure, like turbulent flows, and which are now understood as possessing intricate patterns of interconnection. As Manuel de Landa noted, 'a turbulent flow is made out of a hierarchy of eddies and vortices inside more eddies and vortices.'[2] The internal structures of migration have often gone unnoticed. Both the drag effect that is produced on migrants as they are caught in the flow of movement, and the complex linkages that are generated to sustain a momentum, are often overshadowed by the attention given to external forces. I am concerned with the interrelationship between the energy for movement and the effects on its surroundings. What I aim to offer in this book is an account of how the experience of movement has produced novel forms of belonging and stimulated shifts in our understanding of contemporary culture.

To address the contemporary problematic of migration requires a new cross-disciplinary approach. Migration studies are no longer confined to the domain of sociology, demography, politics and economics. Key contributions have also been made by anthropology, history, psychology, geography, philosophy, cultural studies and art criticism. Disciplines like literary theory and political economy, which a decade ago were considered to be poles apart, have now discovered new borders of interest. These new studies have increasingly drawn attention to the complex links between diffuse levels of experience and deep structural changes. For instance, concepts like deterritorialization and hybridity do not reside exclusively in any particular discipline, they have served as 'bridging concepts', extending the parameters of analysis and highlighting a mode of explanation which is alert to the role of difference and contingency in contemporary society.

The critical debates on globalization have also significant implications for both migration studies and the classical sociological and anthropological definitions of the boundaries of society and culture. From the moral questions of how judgements are posed across the boundaries of cultural difference,[3] to the political debates on the future of the nation-state and the institutions of governance in a globalized world,[4] there is now an extensive programme of rethinking conceptual frameworks. Migration, in its contemporary form, also needs to be understood as an interminable and multifarious process. It could be seen as both the all too visible problem and the invisible catalyst in what Habermas called 'the incomplete project of modernity'.[5] Thus the aim of chapters 2 and 3 is to establish a conceptual framework which challenges some of the conventional definitions of migrants and seeks to present broader categories of belonging in modernity.

The twin processes of globalization and migration have shifted the question of cultural identity from the margins to the centre of contemporary debates. Cultural identity, in one form or another, preoccupies the construction of the public sphere. The definition of a criminal code, the provisions for public housing, the rules for immigration, the services established within health and welfare programmes, conception of madness and disability, the understanding and evaluation of artistic production, the formulation of academic curricula, are all issues which can no longer be addressed without some reference to the discourse of anti-racist discrimination, equal opportunity and affirmative action. Increased recognition and negotiation of cultural difference has challenged the very foundations of almost every institution or practice that shapes the contours of social life.

Both the excesses of political correctness, and the ethnocentric backlash against multiculturalism, are symptoms of a deeper uncertainty about how to measure and manage the viability of cultural differences within a given social space affected by globalizing forces. The structures of the local are increasingly formed by elements and ideas from distant sources. As ideas are rapidly imported from elsewhere and membership of local institutions is altered, the identity of society is subjected to new pressures.

Globalization, as I argue in chapter 4, has raised new questions about the institutions of governance and exposed the limits of the nation-state. The influence of transnational corporations, the integration of financial services within the networks of the global stock markets, the ceding of political power to supranational bodies like the European Union, the deregulatory pressures of global competitiveness in the labour market, the emergence of new social movements to tackle global ecological issues, have all, for good or ill, undermined the legitimacy and putative autonomy of the nation-state. While the modern nation-state demanded the undivided loyalty of its subjects, insisted on sovereignty over its territory, and sought to define the identity of its community in singular terms, it remained intrinsically resistant to the rights of ethnic minorities and diasporic subjectivities. Migration may have spawned new diasporic communities and facilitated the critique of the nation-state, but this in itself has not necessarily produced greater levels of freedom and cross-cultural understanding. For, if it was difficult to secure the terms by which minorities could find democratic forms of representation within the political system of the nation-state, it now seems infinitely more precarious under the conditions of globalization.

The 'chaos' of global migration

The current flows of migrant labour are now fundamentally different from earlier forms of mass migration. There have been dramatic shifts in the destinations of migration, restrictions on residency and strict limitations on settlement. The great metropolitan centres of the north and west, New York, Paris, London – in terms of migrant influx – have been eclipsed by the capitals of the east and south. Is this because the prospects of work are better elsewhere, or are there other reasons? There are currently more construction cranes in operation in the new economic zones of China than anywhere else in the world. The world's tallest building is neither a cathedral in Europe, nor an office block in New York, but the twin towers of Kuala Lumpur. Mexico City is swelling at a rate that is stretching its urban infrastructure to breaking-point. After the Chernobyl nuclear disaster over 400,000 people were displaced; the ecology of their homelands ruined for centuries to come. Today people are on the move for a variety of reasons. NAFTA (North American Free Trade Area) agreements force peasants to be on the move across the Americas; political and ethnic clashes have displaced millions from their homes in Africa; some of the most educated women in the Philippines accept exploitative contracts to work as housemaids in the Gulf States. Do all these people fit under the term migrant?

The early mappings of international migrations were predominantly Eurocentric. They were defined either in relation to the colonial ventures from the sixteenth to the nineteenth century, or to the processes of industrialization and rapid urbanization in the late nineteenth and twentieth century. Between 1500 and 1850 approximately 10 million slaves were transported from Africa to the Americas. Between 1815 and 1925 over 25 million Britons were settled in predominantly urban areas of the colonies. The 'classical period' of migration referred to the trajectory of peasants from the peripheral rural-based societies to the core industrial countries of western Europe, the United States, Canada and Australia.

For many migrants the first sight of their new country was caught from the deck of their ship. After the First World War, most migrants heading for the United States would have probably disembarked and gone through immigration procedures on Ellis Island, just off New York. The dock and hall of Ellis Island are now part of a museum. At the end of the twentieth century, the aeroplane has become the dominant means of mass transport. Today, migrants mostly arrive by descending into what Marc Auge calls the 'non places' of modern airports.[6] The journey from a Third World village to a First World city can now be calculated in terms of hours. The greater levels of mobility in modernity, however, have not been reciprocated by more hospitable forms of reception.

The current trends of global migration reveal a far more multidirectional phase. In this context, migration is neither directed to, nor exclusively generated by, the needs of the north and the west. The vast majority of migrants are no longer moving exclusively to the north and the west, but also between the new industrial epicentres within the south and the east. While for the earlier periods of migration, movement was generally mapped in linear terms, with clear co-ordinates between centre and periphery, and definable axial routes, the current phase can best be described as turbulent, a fluid but structured movement, with multidirectional and reversible trajectories. The turbulence of migration is evident not only in the multiplicity of paths but also in the unpredictability of the changes associated with these movements. However, this has not meant that the pattern of movement is random and the direction totally open-ended. There are also strict barriers and firm counter-forces which either resist or exploit the flows of human movement, just as there are 'passengers' who carefully control their journeys rather than being swept towards unknown destinations.

The relationship between work and migration has always been unstable and ambivalent. During the colonial period migrants from the 'mother country' were selectively encouraged to 'settle' in the 'new' societies. The rapid urban expansion and industrialization in the nineteenth century also demanded that some migrants were recruited when certain needs arose, and expelled when their services were no longer deemed necessary. However, in the current geopolitical climate these relationships have become even more jagged. Where migration is now regulated through contractual or negotiated terms, the civil and work rights of migrants are severely limited. Where migration is permitted for temporary periods, policing is extremely draconian and the abuse of human rights is rife. An increasing number of migrants are taking employment and entry into countries on an illegal basis. The migrant in all these circumstances effectively lives in a police state – susceptible to exploitation and constantly in fear of punishment and deportation.

Along with the shifts in global geopolitics there have been profound changes in the patterns of economic and cultural exchanges. The revolution in information technology, which has coincided with the restructuring of capitalist markets and the dismantling of the socialist command economies, has had a drastic impact on the forms of migrant labour. The new dogma of 'flexibility' in the workplace has meant that working-class communities can no longer assume that employment can be guaranteed in their particular locale. Declining public transport and congested roads have also meant that the journey from home to work is often increasing. Commuting times of two to three hours a day are not uncommon in Los Angeles and Moscow. Meanwhile politicians across the world are instructing their labour forces that, in order to be competitive in a global market and in a technologically advancing world, they must accept the inevitability of both the mobility of the workplace and the redundancy of traditional skills.

The emergence of global media industries has also meant a greater degree of cultural interpenetration. Ideas developed in one place are increasingly promoted and circulated on a global scale. While this has not necessarily meant that the patterns of reception and identification with the global media forms have been homogeneous, it has implied that each locale has both to mediate signs at a greater rate and also to confront a wider variety of codes. Contemporary cultural systems are criss-crossed by signals from diverse sources, with the result that a culture can no longer be understood as merely reflecting the particular practices which emerge within a specific territorial zone. Certain cultural practices may be concentrated or intensified within a given territory, but the politics of cultural ownership and the practices of dissemination are often extended beyond their territorial boundaries. It is from this perspective that globalization and migration have led to what I describe in chapter 5 as the deterritorialization of culture.

Migration, it must be stressed, is not a unique feature of our modern times. From the perspective of the frantic mobility of the present it is tempting to imagine the past as a stable and relatively isolationist period. Yet, people have travelled vast distances throughout history. Examples of cross-cultural exchanges, complex networks of trade and translocal identities are ever-present throughout history. Anthropologists have painstakingly examined how different communities borrow religious symbols from each other and develop rituals for integrating different types of strangers. These strategies for internalizing difference have been remarkably elastic, varying from the incorporation of the 'prized' bride of a neighbouring community, to the introduction of a liminal position for the anthropologist. All cultures seem to have mechanisms for making a limited space for others, or for selectively absorbing strangers as 'one of their kind'. Archaeologists have also mapped extraordinary trading routes in ancient history. For instance, the discovery of traces of silk and cocaine in Egyptian tombs has suggested possible links between the Mediterranean, China and South America. Our knowledge of the extent of ancient sea travel is still very crude. Even with Thor Heyerdahl's brave reconstructions of the ancient techniques for transatlantic and cross-Pacific routes, we have only begun to gain a glimpse of the persistence and breadth of pre-modern forms of long-distance navigation:

> We do not know when the Egyptian influence on the islands began but the Phoenicians gradually took over. We know little of the origins of the Phoenicians or of the kind of ships they first constructed. Reed boats were originally used among their nearest neighbours east and south, and even west; for an engraved ring from ancient Crete shows a crescent-shaped reed boat with transverse lashings, mast and cabin . . . No one will ever be able to retrace the routes of all these vessels or reconstruct the relationships between all these diversified civilizations, intimately interlocked and yet clearly different as they were, partly imposed on earlier local cultures, and nourished by different rulers, in different geographical environments. Who will ever identify the mariners of the fourth century BC who carried a jar of gold and copper Mediterranean coins to Corvo Island in the outer Azores, a point nearer to North America than to Gibraltar? Seeking fortune or refuge, thousands of ships left their home ports during antiquity, leaving no written records . . .True, the people of America had not seen ribbed ships of wooden planks before the arrival of Columbus, but the people of Morocco and of the entire Mediterranean and of Mesopotamia had seen reed boats, like those that survive in America.[7]

However, until the invention of the 'tall ships', the railway, steamships, automobiles and ultimately the aeroplane, the frequency of movement, the volume of migrants, and the distance that could be crossed, were restricted. Today there are over 100 million international migrants and 27 million stateless refugees. This means that there are more people living in places that are outside their homeland than at any previous point in history. The turbulence of migration is not only evident in the sheer volume of migrants, but also by the emergence of new subjects, communication networks and forms of economic dependency. The modern migrant no longer conforms to the stereotypical image of the male urban peasant. Women in manufacturing, electronic assembly lines and domestic workers are now at the front line of global migration. Over 65 per cent of the migrants from Sri Lanka and 78 per cent from Indonesia are women.[8] The value of remittances sent to the homelands of foreign workers has been estimated as being over $10 billion. These transfers of payments are second in value to the trade in crude oil. In places like the Philippines and Albania the major contribution to the national economy is accredited to the earnings of foreign workers.[9] The paradigm of the nation-state as the principal anchor in the conferment of identity has also blinkered our understanding of migrant flows.

Modernity and migration

This book does not seek to track the migration patterns of a specific group, nor does it measure the impact of migration on a particular society. The main concern is to examine the interrelationships between modernity and migration. Thus the flows of movement are not identified in terms of their effects on a given time and place. Most studies on migration are also examinations of the boundaries and structures of belonging to a nation-state. While there are many studies which have demonstrated the significant role of migrants in establishing 'new societies', few have made the larger claims that migration is a central force in the constitution of modernity. The significance of migration is neither confined to the modest contribution of individual migrants, nor captured by the monumental structures of upheaval, but needs to be understood in a broader framework. The tension between movement and settlement is constitutive of modern life. As Derrida noted, the condition of exile is at the centre of the nation's culture.[10] By not confining the significance of migration in terms of the paths into and alterations within the nation-state, I am not denying the value or relevance of this body of scholarship. The nation-state is still an active force in the regulation of migration. We do not live in a borderless world. The significance of migration in the formation of nation-states has only begun to gain its proper recognition. My concern with the broader patterns of global migration is not driven by indifference to or ignorance of such tasks, but is motivated by a parallel need to outline the general context in which migration is occurring and to evaluate the available concepts for representing this phenomenon.

The precise nexus between migration and modernity is still unclear. The metaphor of the journey, the figure of the stranger and the experience of dis-placement have been at the centre of many of the cultural representations of modernity. Migrant artists and writers like Picasso and Joyce are among the most celebrated and perplexing figures of modernism. In chapter 6, I have at-tempted to expand the investigation into the relationship between an exilic con-sciousness and the modern sensibility, by looking at the contemporary aesthetic practices of borrowing and translation. Artists are not only among the most mobile members of a community, but they are often outriders of the transfor-mations between the local and the global.

Within social theory, however, the links between the experience of migra-tion and the vision of modernity have remained obscured owing to a tendency to conceptualize change as an external force. Throughout the twentieth century the 'sociological imagination' has manifested a tendency to become trapped within a mechanistic paradigm that, while preoccupied with the institutional and structural forces, lost sight of the subtle intersubjective processes of every-day life. It is important to stress a number of broad characteristics and changes that were initiated by modernity: the uneven transformation in the relationship between the urban and the rural, the valorization of technology over tradition, the oscillation between the social values of secularism and religion, the conflict between individuality and collectivity. Studies on modernity, whether empiri-cal or interpretative, have been primarily investigations of the transition be-tween these positions. Social scientists sought to measure change, to identify the co-ordinates or the symbols that mark the passage out of one stage and the emergence of another. But this attention to the beginnings and ends of the journey has often obscured the interminable process, the unending journey of modernity.

Movement is not just the experience of shifting from place to place, it is also linked to our ability to imagine an alternative. The dream of a better life and the nightmares of loss are both expressed by the metaphor of the journey. It is not only our 'life narrative' but the very 'spirit of our time' which seems to be haunted by this metaphor. The journey of modernity – which sought to base action on the solid foundations of reason, which sought to build a rational order that would supersede all previous forms of waste, folly and mystification, which believed that truth and proof could substitute for dogma and religion – has turned out to be an endless march into the unknown. The future, which was filled with such promises of progress, liberation and emancipation, is now dark-ened by fear and insecurity. Zygmunt Bauman, one of the most astute and sober critics of the transformations of modernity, argues that the pre-set destination of modernity is now unattainable and that there has been a break in the vision of progress and control. His account of postmodernity is not an apocalyptic dec-laration of ending, nor a naive proclamation of succession, but a bitter-sweet appraisal of the way modernity has lost its direction and driving force. The measurement of modernity against its own goals has revealed that its aspirations and promises can no longer be plotted on to a linear graph, or situated in a privileged location. At this juncture, modernity does not seem to follow a clear path; progress drifts and tumbles. As Bauman noted, the distinctive feature of postmodernity is that while it can no longer predict what lies ahead, there is still the insistence that it is better to keep moving.

> Modernity is what it is – an obsessive march forward – not because it always wants more, but because it never gets enough; not because it grows more ambitious and adventurous, but because its adventures are bitter and its ambitions frustrated. The march must go on because any place of arrival is but a temporary station. No place is privileged, no place is better than another, as from no place the horizon is nearer than from any other. This is why the agitation and flurry are lived out as a forward march; this is, indeed, why the Brownian movement seems to acquire a front and a rear, and restlessness a direction; it is the detritus of burnt-out fuels and the soot of extinct flames that mark the trajectories of progress.[11]

The restless trajectories of modernity can also be witnessed through the transformations in the representations of identity. Bauman notes that the modern construction of the human subject as a peripatetic being has shifted from a pilgrim to a tourist.[12] This shift in subjectivity is not only linked to a destabilization of the cultural codes that distinguish between places of origin and reverence, but to a broader rupture in the sense of belonging and the perception of destiny within an individual's life-narrative. Home and shrine are no longer defined in terms of fixed location or within ritually bounded zones. All the co-ordinates of transition and destination in a life's passage are now defined as if everything is suspended along an infinite stage. From a moral perspective, we seem to be in a situation that says a great deal about where we have come from, a little about where it is we would like to go, but demonstrates almost no knowledge of why we are moving in the first place, or what it is that drives us on and away.

The dynamic of displacement is intrinsic to migration and modernity; however, the links between them have been largely overlooked. Migration was often interpreted as a transitional phase within modernity. As a consequence, the earlier sociological models, which shared the founding assumptions of modernity, have tended to represent migration in terms of trauma and disruption. The emphasis given to tracking the harsh economic, desperate political or brutal military forces that push people away from their homes has often obscured the less tangible desires and dreams for transformation which give migration its inner heading. Since the pioneering work of sociologists like Stephen Castles and Jean Martin in the 1970s, there has been an unequivocal demonstration of both the central role played by economic and political structures in the regulation of migration, and the distorted levels of cultural exchange caused by the migrant's socio-economic inferiority within the host society. While the sociological mainstream emphasized the levels of stratification and integration, the critical schools stressed the contradictions and conflicts, but both positions understood the social as a total system. Migration was thus seen as either a necessary addition or an unwelcome burden to this system. The impact of migration was reduced to a temporary feature, rather than an ongoing constitutive process within modernity. However, as the postmodern critiques of the social have attempted to redefine the boundaries and processes which shape society, there has been a further opportunity to reconceptualize the relationship between migration and modernity.

By turning my attention to the forms of cultural survival, I have not sought to ignore the crucial role of bureaucratic and institutional networks which have influenced the possibility of minority groups gaining an economic and political grounding. I am keenly aware of the inequalities that cut into the position of migrants. Nevertheless my overriding aim is a critique of the kinds of identities and affiliations that emerge in and despite the polarization and conflict of globalization. There is no desire to join in with those facile and sponsored choruses which celebrate the vitality of cultural diversity while detaching it from all socio-economic references; rather there is an attempt both to theorize the small acts of cultural defiance and to articulate the degrees of residual incommensurability which the dominant frameworks render inchoate and invisible. As I argue in chapter 7, the points of difference between competing cultural codes and the concepts which remain untranslatable matter a great deal, for they reveal not just a differing set of priorities, but also the seeds of rival world-views.

The stranger in modernity

Of all the classical social theorists who identified the significance of migration, Georg Simmel was exceptional because he appreciated both the predicament and the sensibility of the stranger. However, even his account of the stranger does not provide us with a universal model for representing all the forms of estrangement generated by global migration. Simmel's representation of the stranger is limited in two fundamental ways. First, there is an almost imperceptible elision between the figure of the stranger and the process of estrangement as a trope for creative and critical thinking. This ambiguous relationship between the figure of the stranger and the trope of estrangement has caused much confusion, especially in the recent debates on sexual and cultural difference. Second, Simmel's construction of the stranger is embedded within a series of dichotomies, us–them, modern–traditional, insider–outsider; and while the stranger oscillates between these positions, it presupposes that these prior positions are fixed and counterposed according to a binary logic. In the current phases of global migration there is a need for a more complex framework of differentiation, one that is capable of addressing the shifting patterns of inclusion and exclusion.

It is now commonplace for our neighbours to be strangers from distant countries, our security in the workplace to be dependent on the priorities of transnational corporations, and our cultural knowledge to be formed through the interaction of signs taken from a variety of places. Our sense of identity is neither immune to nor above these transformations, but it is inextricably linked to them. However, the representation of identity has often been cast in far more narrow and restrictive terms. In particular, the identities of peasants, migrants and minorities were confined to traditional categories, reflecting primordial values and embodying exclusionist practices. Identity was defined in terms of a unique essence. Difference was presented in oppositional terms maintaining a convenient boundary between migrants and settlers. That model of representation and those boundaries are untenable in contemporary society.

As I argue in chapter 8, there are now a number of contributors to the debates on identity who demonstrate the need to shift the conceptual framework in terms of an ongoing process of negotiating differences that cross and ground our life's narrative, rather than the rigid performance of a predetermined script. Identity is not about determining a singular path that constantly closes down the horizons of becoming by pulling back everything to a single point of origin. While the role of the past is a significant force in the shaping of any identity, it does not have the exclusive power to determine all the possibilities for shaping identity in the present. Today the stereotypical images of the stranger as asylum-seeker, gypsy or refugee often precede the arrival of migrants, proliferating on the screens of media networks, which in turn unsettle colonial poles of centre and periphery. The identity of the stranger is thus crucially affected by the media and its use of stereotypes. In this context the ambivalence that is projected against the stranger can take more extreme forms.

What is also overlooked in many of the recent debates on identity politics is the relational aspects of identities. While it is necessary to recognize the specific contexts within which identities are constituted there must always be a concurrent process of connecting identity to a broader social consciousness. Edward Said has been particularly critical of the tendency towards exclusivism in identity politics. He argues that the politics of ethnic affirmation have been driven by the logic of displacement where one form of ethnic particularity competes with another for the position of authority. To counter this ingrown and defensive vision, Said offers a mode of being that he calls 'worldliness', which is a form of identity that emerges through the practice of connecting individual meanings of cultural differences within the 'large, many-windowed house of human culture as a whole'.[13]

Hybridity has become one of the most useful concepts for representing the meaning of cultural difference in identity. In the work of Homi Bhabha and Stuart Hall identity is defined as hybrid, not only to suggest that origins, influences and interests are multiple, complex and contradictory, but also to stress that our sense of self in this world is always incomplete. Self-image is formed *in*, not prior to, the process of interaction with others. This interpretation of identity as hybrid is a direct challenge to earlier quasi-scientific claims that hybrids were sterile, physically weak, mentally inferior and morally confused. The colonizing fantasies of the 'master race' as culturally and eugenically superior were underscored by a stigma that was projected on hybrids. This stigma has now been converted into a positive gain. In many of the recent applications of this concept, the figure of the hybrid is extended to serve as a 'bridging person', one that is both the benefactor of a cultural surplus, and the embodiment of a new synthesis. However, this benign view of hybridity has a number of limitations. By stressing the hybrid's positive achievement of reconciliation between cultural differences it blurs the very relational process that hybridity ought to highlight. In the rush to find an alternative to aggressive and chauvinistic forms of identity, the concept of hybridity has frequently been promoted to the position of a new form of global identity. This celebration of identity as hybridity has failed to pay sufficient attention to the deeper logic of accumulation and consumption that frames modern identity. In a society where the principle that dominates social relations is not reciprocity but consumption, hybridity is often reduced to the occasional experience of exotic commodities which can be repackaged to sustain the insatiable trade in new forms of cultural identity. Hybridity, as a metaphor for identity formation, can only function critically when the dual forces of movement and bridging, displacement and connection, are seen as operating together. It is only when there is a consciousness of this oscillation between different positions and perspectives, that hybridity can offer a new understanding of identity.

Communities of difference

In the final chapter of this book I conclude that the significance of migration for modern society will not be grasped if its meaning is confined to conventional definitions of physical movement and social settlement. As a consequence of the restless dynamism in modern society, the boundaries of community, as well as the more general sense of belonging, have changed radically. We need to understand the flows of cultural change from at least two perspectives: the movement of people, and the circulation of symbols. However, as noted earlier the introduction of foreign symbols and different cultural practices is no longer dependent on the physical presence of strangers. As new channels of communication travel are established across borders, new forms of cultural displacement can occur without the movement of people.

This transformation in the cultural politics of belonging is clearly linked to the expansion of media technologies. Benedict Anderson astutely tracked the influence of the invention of the printing press and the mass literary projects that led to what he called the 'imagined community'.[14] Once texts could be reproduced in greater volume and circulate across vast distances, new affiliations between people could be formed. Communities were established with less regard for geographic proximity and more attention to a common language and shared ideals. People felt a belonging through a communion of certain structures of belief, rather than by the obligations and responsibilities that are drawn from day-to-day and face-to-face contact.

The revolution initiated by 'print capitalism', which altered the sense of 'togetherness' as it magnified the possibilities for disseminating narratives of 'us' and 'them', has taken a further turn with the ascendancy of camera and computer-based telecommunications. The increased domestic access to telephones, faxes and electronic mail, the diversity of uses for television screens from pleasure and information to security and surveillance has led collectively to a proliferation of images and messages. These technological advances enabled optimists, like Marshall McLuhan, to prophesy over the birth of a new communitarianism. However, as McLuhan also noted, the essential drive of telecommunication is interruptive: 'Nothing can be further from the spirit of the new technology than "a place for everything and everything in its place". You can't go home again.'[15] For him, this radical transformation of our relationship to space was meant to mark a liberation from the 'tyranny of distance', and provide the network for a single and integrated society that would occupy the whole planet.

Such enthusiasm has not been shared by all the commentators on the new technologies of telecommunication. For Guy Debord, the promise of a global village was warily perceived as either a mirage or a new form of totalitarian surveillance. The illusion that home was everywhere in the spectacle was, for Debord, underscored by the haunting feeling of being at home nowhere. He predicted that the access to the new media technologies would be highly selective, and their uses reflect the vested interests of existing holders of power.[16] Whether or not we agree that the increasing role of the media has led to political emancipation or cultural enrichment, it is now beyond doubt that, for those who are 'hooked' into these circuits, there has been a series of transformations in the modalities of individual perception and collective memory. Paul Virilio also claimed that, as the screen dominates the post-industrial interior, the moral density of civic society is eviscerated:

> At the end of the 20th century, urban space loses its geopolitical reality to the exclusive benefit of systems of instantaneous deportation whose technological intensity ceaselessly upsets all of our social structures. These systems include the deportation of attention, of the human face-to-face and the urban vis-à-vis encounters at the level of human/machine interaction. In effect, all of this participation in a new 'post urban' and transnational kind of concentration.[17]

The links between modernity, migration and the media have remained relatively undertheorized. However, Scott McQuire's recent work has excavated many of the deep philosophical and cultural paths that intersect at the junction of camera technology, modernization and displacement.[18] The age of the camera not only coincides with modernity but heightens our attention to the anxieties of the 'homeless subject'.

The limits of explanation

Throughout the 1960s and 1970s, and even in the early 1980s, there were vigorous debates within sociology over how migration could be explained. It was presumed that migration does not just happen; it has to be caused by something. There were two prevailing models. First, the voluntarist perspective which defined the movement in dual terms of an internal *push out* (due to the stagnation at home), and an external *pull up* (from the promise of greater opportunity elsewhere). Second, the structuralist political-economy perspective, which charted migration according to the global division of central industrialized capitalist societies in the west and north, and peripheral peasant-based societies in the east and south. There were inherent limitations to both of these perspectives, with the former overly stressing the individual's decision as rational calculation, while the latter resulted in a form of economic determinism that subordinated race and gender under the heading of class.

These social divisions and their relationship to migration have now been addressed in a new series of debates on agency. However, despite a period of intensive theoretical contestation, the debates about the paradigms for understanding the causes of migration have lulled. Most contemporary accounts of migration are now either more empirical, or present an eclectic theoretical model composed of both voluntarist and structuralist concepts. The presentation of a new general theory of migration, or even an extension to the previous theoretical debates, is lacking. This has left a serious gap in our knowledge of the turbulent dynamics of migration. For by continuing to explain migration purely in terms of cause and consequence of other forces, the social scientists have remained dependent on an outdated mechanistic universe. Both the conservative-functionalist and the progressive-Marxist models have tended to explain human movement in terms of a water-pump system. The energy for movement was confined to the flows that were generated by the engines of industry and regulated by the valves of state policies. As industry demanded labour, governments turned valves, and the flow of migrants either contracted or expanded. This crude model is unable to accommodate what I call the auto-dynamics and multi-vectorial flows in this turbulent phase of migration.

The social scientist's version of the water-pump model of equilibrium assumed that something will emerge only if there is an attending force to displace something else, or if there was a pre-existing vacuum from which it could be drawn. Such structuralist models were also transposed on to the subjectivities or the life-narratives of migrants. To construct the stereotype of the 'migrant as victim' a number of social forces were given priority over the agency of the individual. Translated into cultural politics, this means that the identity of the migrant was extracted from the fixed repertoire of stereotypes associated with the place of origin, that the space for the representation of different perspectives in modernity was finite, that the resources for mutual understanding amongst strangers were limited, and that the success of one interest was always at the expense of another. Narratives of migration in the social sciences have thus repeated the territorial competitiveness and binary oppositions that they were meant to critique. One of the crucial aims of this book is to present alternative models for conceptualizing cultural exchange.

The task of rethinking the social, with cultural difference as a constitutive feature, is only just beginning. This task will need to proceed on at least two levels: one which can attend to the changes in the configuration between the local and the global, and the other which develops a broader conceptual framework for representing the processes of cultural transformation. Given the enormity of this task, it might be worthwhile to begin by noting the steps that have already been taken. Many scholars have commented on the problems associated with administering the social policy of multiculturalism on a national basis. There is also growing debate about the contradiction in the political trajectories and the poverty of the philosophical framework for representing cultural difference. However, while the issues emerging from cultural difference may seem complex and intractable within the context of the nation-state, how much more demanding do they become when viewed from a global perspective? What framework will structure the negotiation of cultural differences in the age of globalization? Under whose jurisdiction and with which tribunals will the rights of minorities be represented? The aim of this book is not so much to complete this task of rethinking cultural identity in the context of global migration, but to lay down a number of tracks that will assist in the understanding of the changes that are taking place all around us.

The urgency of such a task is particularly evident in multicultural nation-states like the United States and Australia. Three decades after the civil rights movement, political leaders are now being compelled to confront the entrenched divisions and unacknowledged crimes perpetrated along the lines of cultural difference. While the indigenous peoples of Australia struggle with the legacy of genocide, one of the highest infant mortality rates in the world, countless unexplained deaths of young men while held in custody, the pursuit of land rights through the courts and compensation for the stolen generation of children taken away from their families in order to be assimilated into white society, the Prime Minister John Howard vacillated over his own moral duties. He responded to these burning claims by insisting that the current regime should not bear the burden of the past. Meanwhile he pursues a path of consolidating the interests of mining companies and pastoral leaseholders at the expense of the indigenous people. Across the Pacific Ocean, the University Regent of California Ward Connely, who is black, and must surely be aware of the bitter statistic that for every black male that completes a university degree one hundred are sent to prison, dismissed President Bill Clinton's attempt to initiate a 'great and unprecedented conversation about race', because he claimed that 'where the American people want to go is beyond this whole issue of race.'[19]

Within what sort of framework is it possible to get beyond race and rethink the issues of cultural difference? There is little evidence of success so far. The practices of exposing institutionalized racism are in themselves but the first steps towards dismantling the structures and categories of domination. New techniques and strategies are necessary for critiquing the hierarchies of power and justice. The liberal principles of equal opportunity seem inadequate to the task of achieving social equality and often conflict with their intrinsic claims of cultural neutrality. Should there be one form of identity which is central and dominates others? Does a minority position threaten the cohesion of the social? These questions have intensified as the multicultural debates begin to consider who defines the parameters of the social, the limits of tolerance, and what sort of identities are considered compatible with the codes of modern society.

While not a new phenomenon, migration has never been as multidirectional, and the experience of displacement has never been as multidimensional as it is today. When the performance artist and founding member of the Border Arts Workshop, Guillermo Gomez-Pena, asked himself the question: 'Who am I?' his response – an itinerary of multiple and mixed places of origin – was not presented as a sign of an exotic biography, but as a metaphor for the contradictions and complexities of belonging:

I wake up as a Mexican in US territory. With my Mexican psyche, my Mexican heart and my Mexican body, I have to make intelligible art for American audiences that know very little about my culture. This is my daily dilemma. I have to force myself to cross a border, and there is very little reciprocity from the people on the other side.

I physically live between two cultures and two epochs. I have a little house in Mexico City, and one in New York, separated from each other by a thousand light-years in terms of culture.

I also spend time in California. As a result, I am a Mexican part of the year, a Chicano the other part. I cross the border by foot, by car and by airplane.

When I am on the Mexican side, I have strong artistic connections to Latin American urban pop culture and ritual traditions that are centuries old. When I am on the US side, I have access to high-technology and specialized information. When I cross back to Mexico, I get immersed in a rich counter-culture: the post-earthquake movement of opposition. When I return to the US, I am part of the inter and cross-cultural thinking emerging from the interstices of the US's ethnic milieus.

My journey not only goes from South to North, but from the past to the future, from Spanish to English and from one side of myself to another. [20]

Cultural identity is increasingly in excess, or excluded from the traditional political categories of exclusive membership to a singular nation-state. But then, how to represent an identity that does not correspond to some form of national origin? The difficulty of grasping this complexity is linked to a series of fundamental questions which theorists are now confronting simultaneously: What is the future of the nation-state? What are the boundaries of society? How do cultures survive? How do we understand agency?

We now need new models not only because the density, velocity and multidirectionality of current migration flows have baffled analysts and discredited earlier theories, but because they also need to be related to the economic and cultural phases of globalization. The decentring and dematerialization of economic activity have summoned the spectre of 'placeless capital' and the 'homeless subject'. Vital decisions that affect local economies are increasingly made elsewhere. We have entered an era which Lash and Urry call the 'end of organised capital'.[21] This turbulent state should not be confused with an evocation of so-called 'postmodern indeterminacy'. It simply means that the nodal points of economic and social activity are neither integrated within the spatial co-ordinates nor synchronized according to the temporal rhythms of the nation-state. The neat binarisms and linear oppositions of the colonialist and nationalist expansions are no longer the appropriate grids within which the contemporary flows can be plotted and mapped. The flows that these new formations have stimulated need to be mapped in terms of multi-variate circuits.

In this context, the experience of migration may well be even more precarious than we have yet been able to imagine. Despite the rhetorical appeal of multiculturalism and the intellectual popularity of concepts like diaspora and hybridity, the horizon of the migrant's imaginary is increasingly filled with experiences of itinerancy, ghettoization and illegality. Displacement is not only a more common but also a more complex experience. Both the normative boundaries and the physical location of members within communities are on the move. Following from Derrida it may be worthwhile for the social sciences not only to map the trajectories and consequences of human movement, but to ask such fundamental questions as: What gives the movement its start?[22] A different look at our turbulent times may also bring into question the available models of explanation, and expand our understanding of change beyond the mechanistic frameworks of causation and consequence. In an age of global migration we also need new social theories of flow and resistance, and cultural theories of difference and translation. We need a mode of investigation which can track these dispersed and reflexive practices of empowerment and negotiation. Migrant forms of belonging are rarely the mere duplication of traditional forms, or the blind adoption of modern practices. Through their actions and decisions migrants enter into a constant dialogue between past and present, near and far, foreign and familiar. A dialogical approach, rather than the monological and progressivist narratives which dominated the social sciences, may assist our future understanding of the complex ways migrants participate in and reshape the social worlds within which they move. Perhaps it is time for social scientists to face the more complex representation of reality that an artistic sensibility yields. In the early 1970s, just as the mass migration schemes in Europe were grinding to a halt, John Berger wrote these words:[23]

A man's resolution to emigrate needs to be seen within the context of a world economic system. Not in order to reinforce a political theory but so that what actually happens to him can be given its proper value. That economic system is neo-colonialism. Economic theory can show how this system, creating underdevelopment, produces the conditions which lead to emigration: it can also show why the system needs the special labour power which the migrant workers have to sell. Yet necessarily the language of economic theory is abstract. And so, if the forces which determine the migrant's life are to be grasped and realized as part of his personal destiny, a less abstract formulation is needed. Metaphor is needed. Metaphor is temporary. It does not replace theory . . .

Yet his migration is like an event in a dream dreamt by another. As a figure in a dream dreamt by an unknown sleeper, he appears to act autonomously, at times unexpectedly; but everything he does – unless he revolts – is determined by the needs of the dreamer's mind. Abandon the metaphor. The migrant's intentionality is permeated by historical necessities of which neither he nor anybody he meets is aware. That is why it is as if his life were being dreamt by another. *(pp. 41, 43)*

2

Mapping Global Migration

Migration patterns have changed dramatically over time. Stories of migration, while having many features in common, differ significantly. The narratives of global migration are structured differently from the earlier narratives of the slave trade and the movement of the peasantry from the country to the city. People have moved from one place to another for a variety of reasons: out of fear of invasion, in search of better pasture, to establish new commercial links, or in pursuit of a vision to recreate a new mode of society. Images of people on the move, as colonizers, invaders, convicts, nomads, adventurers and dissenters, are frequent in western consciousness. Mass migration and even long-distance migration are not a new phenomenon. Narratives of exile have been recorded on Egyptian papyri, and with the Virgilian epic and Judaeo-Christian myths of exodus it could be argued that much of our contemporary understanding of migration is still framed by a universal notion of displacement.[1] Yet along with its seemingly continuous history, the story of migration needs to be told in all its specificity. Each movement of people has its unique features. Not only do the geographic co-ordinates of home and exile shift, but the meanings and causes of displacement change.

Neil Ascherson's account of the Pontic diaspora illustrates how deep and resilient are the cultural links to a homeland. Over three thousand years ago Greek colonists passed through the Bosporus to settle and set up trading posts around the Black Sea. Major cities like Trebizond were established and a kingdom formed, and further migration spread into the Caucasus, Crimea and the land around the Sea of Azov. The Pontic culture and language, as it incorporated the influences of the Genoese, Venetian, Turkish and Russian Empires, came to diverge from its Greek origin. Yet in 1923 with the proclamation of the

Turkish republic and the forcible expulsion of the Greek peoples, 164,000 Pontians were 'returned home'. Since 1991, with the collapse of the Soviet Union, another 200,000 Pontians have 'returned' to a country which is practically alien to them. Despite being displaced across the Black Sea, with formal links long since severed, the enforced return of the Pontians to their Greek homeland suggests a historical consciousness of origin that has either survived or been successfully reinvented after nearly three millennia.[2]

Such examples provoke profound consideration of the interconnections between the meanings of home and migration. In some periods there are clear axioms which seem to guide movement. During colonialism the flows of human traffic were ruthlessly directed by the priorities of the colonial centre. Subsequent social and economic developments meant that there were places from which people seemed desperate to leave, and others which they were anxious to enter. In the late nineteenth and early twentieth century, the rural economies of Ireland and southern Italy were vastly depleted as people rushed towards the industrial centres of western Europe and North America. Such passages, whether they were across the Atlantic or from south to north, presented distinct patterns of movement. The vast literature on migration in the humanities and the social sciences has drawn attention to the multiple factors that generate movement. In this chapter I shall review this literature and present a mapping of the major patterns of migration. It will begin by examining a number of phases of migration where the direction of movement could be represented, to a large extent, in terms of one-way arrows, and where the expectations of settling were relatively open-ended. These linear flows from rural to industrial economies, and the histories of resettlement in the New World, contrast sharply with the turbulent and multidirectional patterns of present movements.

Although this chapter covers a vast period of migration, and considers examples of movement from a number of diverse places, it does not aim to give any detailed historical analysis or sociological account of the specific causes and consequences of migration for a particular time or place. My focus will be on mapping the general flows of people. From this perspective the difference between the turbulent flows in contemporary migration can be contrasted with the more structured patterns of earlier historical movements. Earlier patterns of movement, such as the transatlantic slave trade, or the international labour migration in the first phase of industrialization, could be coherently plotted on a map. However, the pattern of migration associated with globalization, while perpetuating many of the structured inequalities that were characteristic of earlier movements, has been further complicated. The routes of global migration involve a decoupling of the historical paths. There has been a fundamental shift away from the traditional destinations, an expansion in the types of people who embark on migration, and the imposition of more restrictions on the conditions of entry settlement.

The diversity of paths, and the complexity of forms of migrations, have meant that it is now almost impossible to map movement with a series of arrows, on a flat two-dimensional representation of the world. There would be a greater number of arrows going in multiple directions, and also the time scale would have to be so contracted and irregular that the map would lose its objective of representing movement. Looking for patterns in such maps would be like looking for order in chaos theory. While the form of global migration may be incoherent, the scale of the phenomenon is unmistakable. Migration has become such a regular feature of modern life that it can no longer be considered as the exceptional event in the otherwise long historical process of settlement. The mobility of people has reached unprecedented levels. As ever, the experience of migration varies from the traumatic to the opportunistic. However, given that migration, directly or indirectly, touches the experiences of most people on a constant basis, and that our understanding of society has been irreversibly altered by it, it is also necessary to develop a broader conceptual understanding of the patterns of movement.

The theoretical models that have been utilized to explain mass migration will also be examined in this chapter. As the sociological literature has become more attentive to the complex forms and ongoing dynamics of migration in modern society, there has been a growing awareness that migration is rarely a phenomenon that can be explained by monocausal models. The unhelpful opposition between structuralist and voluntarist accounts, which dominated the social science debates during the 1970s and 1980s, seems to have waned. It is no longer tenable to confine migration to the study of labour movement, as if the questions of race and gender were either secondary or marginal. Nor can the general flows of global migration be plotted according to the binary coordinates of the colonial centre and the colonized periphery, or the developed First World versus the underdeveloped Third World. The models which had plausible explanatory power in the past are not only in need of re-evaluation, but the whole mechanistic paradigm – within which the forces of causation and consequence were modelled – needs to be critiqued.

Where theorists once relied on metaphors like 'waves' to describe the linear flows of migration, they may now need to reconsider the complex dynamics that determine the shape and strength of waves, as well as the rips and crosscurrents that can flow within them. Just as the cause of a great wave is considered to be the peculiar *conjunction* of a distant storm, a great oceanic tide flowing over a unique seabed, as well as the gravitational pull of the moon, so too the metaphors of global migration will need to suggest both the volatility as well as multidirectionality of current flows.

Contemporary migration scholars tend to adopt a variety of theoretical approaches which incorporate elements from political economy as well as acknowledging the significance of cultural agency and gender. Grand theorizing about the fundamental causes has given way to the more empirically oriented approaches of measuring the complex consequences of migration. However, this shift still avoids the most demanding theoretical task: understanding the processes of migration.

What poets have known all along, that 'In dreams begins the journey',[3] sociologists still have difficulty grasping. Tracing the primal causes, or predicting the final outcomes, is a labyrinthine task. Migration is never a spontaneous gesture. It presupposes some knowledge of the other side, a guide, a map or, at least, a rumour. The obvious difference between the places of departure and arrival, as well as the tangible distance between them, belies the complexities of motivations and hopes that fuel these journeys. In the age of global media the call to migration will take even more unexpected turns.

Historical patterns of migration: slavery and colonialism

Mass migration, either through the transportation of captured slaves or the practice of large-scale colonization, was a notable feature of the ancient world. Greeks established new city-states throughout the Mediterranean, Romans granted special rights to citizens, and Arabs achieved extraordinary expansion through conquest and slave trading.[4] However, the sixteenth century is the most commonly accepted starting-point for the survey of global migration. For during this period, the unique technical and mercantile achievements of western capitalism not only restructured the circulation of commodity trade, but also revolutionized the patterns of migration. The invention of 'tall ships' and improvements in cartography and navigation made transoceanic trade and migration more viable. Power and influence were no longer measured by territorial conquest alone, but through the regulation of trade, and control over the new technologies of transport. The emergence of the Venetian and British Empires provides telling examples of how global domination was increasingly linked to control over mercantile ports and shipping routes, rather than the consolidation of a land base through territorial expansion. Shipbuilding and armaments were the crucial factors that enabled new levels of expansion.[5] The outward search for trade along the coastal ports of the colonies, unlike the incremental spatial advance of feudal empires, was to generate global patterns of migration. These patterns were never uniform, but they can be distinguished from the earlier movement of people.

Three distinct phases are commonly identified. First, the European colonial regimes, which from the sixteenth century developed expansionist programmes and colonial ventures. In the name of creating new capitalist markets and bringing civilization to the New World, large numbers of Europeans were transferred to settle or administer the colonies. The principal routes for trade and colonization were between western Europe, the west coast of Africa and the

Americas. This transfer of Western goods to Africa, African slaves to the Americas, and produce from the Americas back to Europe, formed the co-ordinates of the infamous transatlantic triangle. Central to this enterprise was the genocide of indigenous peoples, and the forced migration of slaves and indentured labourers. It was common for a ship to leave, for instance, from the port of Liverpool, loaded with manufactured goods or guns; this cargo could be exchanged in Accra for slaves, who would then be transported to Virginia; and the same ship would eventually return with raw cotton or sugar for production and consumption in Britain. The transportation of slaves was central to western capitalism. Between 1500 and 1850 approximately 10 million slaves were transported from Africa to the Americas.[6] Parallel to this was the forced settlement of convicts in America and Australia.

Through their superior technologies in navigation and naval power, the colonizing states of western Europe were able to expand outwardly and conquer the coastal areas of other continents. Ports were established to administer their interests, and regulate the new forms of production. The colonized territories were exploited either by extracting their mineral resources, or through the establishment of new plantations. Indigenous people were coerced into labour or threatened with genocide as settlers arrived to take advantage of the New World.

During the period of colonialism, migration was predominantly forced and coercive. Vast numbers of people were not only geographically displaced from their homeland, but they were sentenced to work under a new regime. The transfer of populations was thus inextricably linked to the social and economic transformations that colonialism introduced. Third World Marxist theorists were the strongest critics of the interdependence between western capitalism, colonialism, slavery and coercive migration. Samir Amin represented the global and structural transformations, that were ushered in by colonialism, in terms of centre and periphery. This model represented migration not in terms of individual decisions about opportunity, but through the binary structures that differentiated between a process of independent development at the centre, and dependent development on the periphery. Labour migration was thereby linked to the twin axioms of capitalist development: commodity exchange and capital accumulation. According to Samir Amin, capital accumulation and exchange relationships are characterized by a bi-polar and uneven formation: there is the 'capitalism of the centre' and the 'capitalism of the periphery'.[7] In this schema the centre is not only dominant but also exclusive, that is, its socio-economic formation has accumulated a superior volume of capital, replaced all pre-capitalist modes of production, and integrated all the mechanisms of capitalist production.

The periphery, in contrast, lacks this level of integration, for while capitalist modes are the emergent dominant, there are still pre-capitalist modes which operate in contradiction with each other. As the centre concentrates the dominant forms of production within its region, it not only makes the periphery dependent upon it, but also blocks the periphery's process of development. The periphery provides the raw materials, the centre processes them, firstly for its own internal market, and then exports it back to the periphery. The centre accumulates and the periphery donates. It effectively 'donates', because it is buying back its own resources, at a price, which in itself is blocking its own industrial and technological development.

Migration and the industrial contracts

In the first phase of mass migration European colonizers administered the transportation and exploitation of the colonized, slaves and indentured labourers. The direction of movement was singularly determined according to the needs of the imperial centres in western Europe. During the second phase western Europe is once again the epicentre of migration. Millions of Europeans were now to begin their exodus from their homelands to settle in the New World. This process of settlement was to lead to the first challenge to western Europe's hegemony over the direction and flow of people.

The second phase needs to be broken down into two related processes. First, the process of industrialization and depeasantization of the west. This involved the massive transfer of population from rural communities, to the new urban centres of the industrializing nations of Europe. As this process was largely a form of internal rather than international migration, I will not discuss it in detail. Second, the colonization and industrialization of the New World. From the early nineteenth to the mid-twentieth century there is what is widely referred to as the 'classical period' of migration. For instance, between 1815 and 1925 over 25 million people left Britain, mostly heading for the colonies.[8] Prior to this period, free white settler colonization was only a fraction of the uprooted population. Migrants from throughout Europe headed for South Africa, Australia, New Zealand, South America, Canada, but with the vast majority going to the United States of America.

By the end of the nineteenth century the United States of America had already become the greatest industrial power in the world. Millions of workers who could find means of escape from stagnant economic regions or repressive regimes headed for the United States of America. This 'Great Migration' to the New World was coeval with the industrial revolution and rapid urbanization in the Old World. As Teodor Shanin pointed out, industrialization in urban areas occurred along with the depeasantization of rural societies. Peasants abandoned their traditional links to the land, leaving behind important skills and social networks, to move to new urban centres. It was in the new industrial cities that primary material and machinery were concentrated to form new sites of production. Thus, as Shanin argued, a crucial factor in industrialization is the mobilization of the peasantry.

The image of the land-bound and static peasantry is an urban stereotype. Peasants have always moved in times of crisis, overpopulation or economic opportunity. For instance, both the farming practices and the process of extensive subdivision made migration a constant feature of peasant culture. In the nineteenth century Ireland's economy was inextricably dependent on the British. After planting their crops, peasants made seasonal migrations to Britain in order to gain supplementary cash income. As the process of social and industrial change accelerated in Britain, and small-scale farming became untenable, Irish migration intensified.[9] Although similar patterns can be observed across Europe, it could not be said that the peasantry acted as a homogeneous class. The programmes of movement were as diverse as the cultural characteristics of the peasantry. Yet, if it were not for the peasantry's willingness to leave their villages, permanently or temporarily, the project of industrialization would not have been able to get off the ground:

> The availability of peasants, to be 'structurally disintegrated' and squeezed, has been central to industrialization/capital accumulation in that it offered cheap, hardened manual labour eminently exploitable and with the expenses of its reproduction charged elsewhere (i.e. carried by their own villages). 'Enclosing' peasant lands, the expansion of markets through the destruction of crafts, and the squeeze of cheap raw materials out of the colonial peasantry were also highly relevant here. But it was the peasant labour input which seems decisive, for it could rarely be substituted.[10]

Peasants were willing to move to the cities, but not always to remain there. At the end of the nineteenth century it was estimated that up to 47 per cent of the migrants who went to the USA from Europe returned home.[11] Often to build their own new 'American' house in their old village. This display of wealth and 'modernity' in itself tended to stimulate further emigration. The undeniable feature of capitalism is that its large industrial factories and manufacturing plants periodically required new pools of labour. Russel King has noted that both emigration and immigration allowed industrialization to take the rapid course that it took in the nineteenth century. Immigrants, and the general increases in population, could be absorbed in the industrial centres of western Europe, but, as he concludes,

> the dramatic increase in the rate of economic growth in Europe in the nineteenth century was only sustained by using emigration as an 'escape hatch'. The exodus of 50 million people allowed Europe in the nineteenth century to create a mix of the factors of production – land, labour, capital, industrial raw materials, enterprise – which promoted record growth, without having that growth swallowed up by population increase.[12]

From the late nineteenth century, and well into the twentieth, a large proportion of migrants were being lured to foreign places, not by imperial dictates or explicit political upheaval, but by the suggestions and solicitations of their own kin. As migrants found prosperity or opportunity for themselves, they would often send for their relatives, or by their return home stimulate the need to emigrate in others. Chain migration often led to the formation of clusters of migrants from the same region, who shared the same background and provided new employment opportunities for each other. During the nineteenth century, the idea of migration had become a 'craze'.[13] Migration had entered the popular imagination as the cure to all ills. Just as the idea of revolution promised an alternative to the misery of the 'here and now', emigration represented the possibility of 'rebirth and salvation elsewhere'. Chain migration relied, not only on the new means of long-distance communication, and the speed and security of travel that the steamship introduced, but most crucially it depended on the authority and enthusiasm in the reports of life in the New World from friends and family members. They would not only pass on practical information for securing the passage, but also provide loans for the journey and assistance in resettlement. In this way, whole villages would often follow the path of one migrant. The travel writer Patrick Leigh Fermor often found himself impressed by the degree of historical specialization in the different regions in Greece, but utterly puzzled by their transplantation and re-employment in distant places:

> Villages, towns, regions and islands all over the country have cornered professions. The dwellers along the banks of the Hebrus cut the reeds and strip and bind them into brooms . . . There are interesting reasons why Chios became so prominent in international banking; good reasons, too, for the allegiance of Crete, Epirus and the Mani to the blood-feud. But why were the cotton fortunes of the Nile amassed by villagers from Mt. Pelion and Vlach emigrants from Thessaly? . . . History accounts for Hydra and Spetsai being almost entirely populated by admirals; but why was Hydra, and why is Kalymnos today, the home of most of the sponge-fishers on the Libyan reefs and in Florida?[14]

As industrialization expanded further in the post-Second World War period, employers found it necessary to supplement national labour resources, and to arrange for the entry of workers from other states.[15] In this phase, the flow of migration is the reverse of the colonial phase of migration. Colonialism was still the base of much of the movement in this period. However, the majority of migrants were no longer Europeans leaving for the New World, but migrants arriving in Europe from the peripheral spaces of the colonies. Britain, for instance, recruited workers from Ireland, the West Indies, India and Pakistan. France drew immigrants from its colonies in North Africa. Germany, which had lost control over its colonies in the First World War, was forced to establish recruitment programmes from the semi-industrialized or peripheral countries of southern Europe.

Throughout this period, migrant movements were generally seen to be by people who moved freely, for their own economic benefit. However, from the late nineteenth century, and well into the post-Second World War period, a vast proportion of migrants were contract labourers. The USA, western Europe, Australia, Canada, and more recently the Gulf States, Japan and the newly in-dustrializing countries of south-east Asia have all employed contract labour schemes. These schemes systematically recruit labour from abroad to perform specific tasks for a limited duration. Employers bear no obligation for extend-ing the same welfare and social rights as they do to the indigenous labour, nor do the participating states make provision for settlement and citizenship. In fact, clear restrictions are imposed on these contract labourers to inhibit any expectation of legal settlement.

The contract-labour migration schemes have to be seen as a form of 'unfree labour', whereby state agencies and companies collaborated to secure a source of cheap labour that could be readily exploited and controlled, and in time of surplus deported. The US Bracero programme and the 'guest-worker' system in western Europe are two examples of how social costs and workers' rights were minimized, by schemes which restricted the political and social rights of migrant labour. These practices have been extended in Asia, where, once again, migrants have been selected to perform specific tasks, prohibited from bringing their families, and expelled whenever the state, or their employer deemed it necessary. By the mid-1970s these schemes had ended in western Europe, Aus-tralia and the USA. Stephen Castles has argued, that this cessation was partly due to the very emergence of migratory flows, and patterns of settlement, which the governments had intended to prevent.[16] Despite the formal constraints, mi-grants had begun to find ways to bring their wives, in some instances as co-workers, and then, with the birth of their children, complicated questions about the rights to citizenship, and the politics of diasporic communities took form. Those very restrictive 'routes', which sought to secure that migration remain a temporary feature of economic life, were laying down 'roots' for a form of permanent social change.

The sociological theories of migration

The theoretical models that were proposed to explain the migration patterns in the classical phase of migration can be separated into two perspectives: voluntarist and structuralist. The voluntarist perspective is best exemplified by the 'push–pull' model. According to this model, migration is always caused by twin and counterbalancing forces: people were 'pushed' out of stagnant rural peasant economies, and 'pulled' up towards industrial urban centres. This 'push–pull' model tended to see migration as being caused by the individual calcula-tion of economic opportunity. However, it was also possible to explain migratory flows by the predominance of one force, either the pull effect of unsatisfied markets in the receiving country, or the push effect of unsatisfied labour in the donating country. The more sophisticated versions of this theory recognize the existence of underlying, medium-term, personal and enabling factors, within the push–pull dynamic.[17] For instance, push factors can be broken down to underlying forces, like population growth and repressive political regimes, while medium-term crises come with the downward turn of economic cycles. Enabling factors include the changes in the technologies of transport, such as the shift from tall ships to steamships. The routinization of shipping and the reduction in transportation costs was undoubtedly a major enabling factor in global migration. Pull factors vary, from the preferential immigration policies offered by a state, economic benefits in the forms of state incentives or greater opportunity, to personal contacts which can secure the passage, and assist in resettlement.

This push–pull model, which attributes migration to the decision of individual actors, has been largely discredited in current theory. Critics of this model have claimed that the binarism of receivers and donors presumes an untenable degree of homogeneity and interchangeability in the labour forces. The rationale of economic calculation that this model presupposes is also too limited to embrace the complex motivations of migrants. It presumes that, ultimately, the labour market is free, the only constraints upon freedom being the differential resources of the individual and the imposition of state regulation. According to the push–pull model, it is these external constraints which determine the directions and flows of migration. By being able to calculate their finances and identify the opportunities in the immigration policies of the host country, migrants are regarded as being in a position to choose and compare their options. The choices most frequently made by migrants, however, do not conform to the rationale of this model. If income differentials were the strongest pull factor, it would be difficult to explain why migration patterns are not higher as economic polarization intensifies, and also why people from intermediate social positions, rather than the poorest, are those most likely to migrate. Similarly, the tendency of migrants to follow earlier patterns of movement, for instance Indians moving to Britain, says more about the persistence of historical links forged under colonialism than it does about the economic calculation to move to the nearest available job.

As a general model for explaining migration the push–pull model is also premised on a narrow definition of individualism. The emphasis on the individual choice of destination, as a process that is only constrained by, rather than related to, economic and socio-political factors, seriously limits the explanatory scope of the theory. Even more recent accounts, which have rejected the monocausal models, and attempted to address the role of labour market segmentation within a broader and variable schema of push–pull effect,[18] subordinate the role of agency to the driving force of income differentials. The model is still incapable of explaining why migration occurs when the rates of economic growth are high at home, and unemployment increasing in the receiving country. Nor can it adequately accommodate the forms of migration that are generated by political struggles. The limitations of this model have been acutely noted by structuralist feminist critics. As Janet Abu-Lughod argued, the local and international political conflicts in the Middle East generated forms of migration which defy the central objectives of this model.[19] Similarly, the emergence of women as a major force in global migration could not have been anticipated by this model. Anne Phizacklea has also argued that the push–pull model remains blind to gender and cultural differences.[20]

One of the most influential representatives of the structuralist perspective is Stephen Castles. In his early work, especially his exemplary account of post-war European migration, he argued that these movements were better explained by a model drawn from political economy.[21] The specific trajectories of migrants were situated within the context of global and national economic systems. These trajectories were explained, not by a voluntarist perspective which stressed the individual and singular choices of migrants, but in terms of the economic differentials between developing and industrialized countries. Migration was no longer seen as a 'one-off' event, but rather as a dynamic process, whose size and direction were influenced by the dual forces of state regulation and industrial development. He stressed the linkage between state-driven immigration policies and the structural forces of capitalist expansion.

In the literature that developed from these studies, priority was given to understanding structural laws, forms of social segregation, and the institutions that regulated movement. The agency of the migrant was largely seen as subordinate to, and determined by, the structures of 'state capitalism'. The primary forces in the political-economy model of immigration were the 'state' and 'capital'. The 'state' in its development of immigration policies, the administering of settlement and the policing of undesirables, was perceived as responding to the needs of the economy. As the economy in the post-war period began to expand, and there was greater need for industrial workers, the state was obliged to recruit new pools of workers to fill labour shortages. Most Marxist writers saw this relationship between the state and capital purely in instrumental terms. The state by regulating the flows of migrant labour was, to use the often quoted phrase, 'basically underwriting the interests of capital'. It was the conduit by which capital could draw a supply of cheap labour in times of need, and also the valve that could constrict flow in times of economic recession and stagnation. Migrants were seen as the 'reserve army of labour' that could be strategically manoeuvred to fill the 'dirty' gaps and fortify the 'dangerous' positions that indigenous workers had refused to hold.

Central to the structuralist theory of migration is the concept of the 'reserve army', which is drawn from Marx's account of the relationship between employment opportunity and the cycles of capitalist expansion and contraction. A precondition to expanding industrial expansion is the availability of cheap and dispensable labour. As profits are invested in new technologies, or as demand drops, labour requirements can vary. Marx identified three forms of the 'reserve army': first, the floating surplus population, workers in industry who were dismissed in times of recession but reintroduced in times of expansion; second, the latent surplus, displaced labourers from the rural sector who seek work in the new industries; third, the stagnant surplus, being the most marginalized workers. According to Castles this typology helps to explain the relationship between the structural position of the migrant worker and the general patterns of migration that developed under western capitalism.

This pattern of exploitation of migrant labour was often seen as being analogous to the uneven exchange that was highlighted in the earlier centre–periphery model. Migrant labour symbolized the enduring patterns of dependent development in the periphery. The migration of labour represented not only an escape from super-exploitation in the periphery, but the centre's gain of cheap labour without incurring the burden of social costs. In this exchange the periphery is doubly undermined: not only does it lose the most dynamic members of its labour force, but it also bears their 'reproduction costs'. Buroway has criticized the economistic models of migrant labour not for the conceptual limitations of this approach, but for its failure to calculate the real costs of the system. He rejects the dependency thesis which sees migrant labour as an organic part of capitalism at a particular stage in its development, and argues that 'it is a conjunctural feature which acts as a functional substitute for other modes of organising labour.'[22] Given that the costs of administering and policing migration are borne by the state, Buroway stresses that the introduction of migrant labour cannot be purely explained by the inevitable progression of capitalism. The volume of migrant labour is thus once again linked to the state's calculation of economic benefit, but the equation is determined by the reduction rather than the externalization of social costs. It also suggests that the co-ordination between state and capital is not as harmonious as is often stressed by the structuralist model.[23]

Economics is such a dominant factor in the sociological studies of international migration, that the very language of analysis tends to marginalize social or cultural factors. Migrant studies still tend to focus on single major factors and track the consequences of dominant structures rather than attend to obscure networks or subtle processes. Hence, the focus has been predominantly on institutional transformations, such as governmental policies and bilateral agreements on migration quotas and exchange programmes; foreign investment; industrial development and urban development; mechanization of agriculture and rural transformation.

This concentration on the public and objective factors within the sociological literature on migration has not facilitated a break in the long-standing conceptual bottleneck between race and class. For while considerable insight has been gained into the institutionalization of racism, the relationships between racial and class behaviour have been relatively undertheorized. Throughout the debates in British sociology between the 1960s and the 1980s the concept of class was privileged over race. Weberians like John Rex defined 'race relations' as a category of class relations, whereas Marxist writers such as Robert Miles constructed 'blacks' as a class formation.[24] Both positions gave primacy to the concept of class over race, thereby exaggerating the power of economic factors in determining social and political relations. For instance, it is not entirely accurate to see migration as the transferral, of one group of proletarians, from the periphery to the centre, as does Anthony King in *Global Cities*, where he argues that 'subproletariats previously located in the colonies are now relocated in previously working class or lower middle class areas (such as Bengalis in the East End and West Indians in South London).'[25]

The social history of migrant communities has often focused on their experience of victimhood.[26] While immigrants have faced considerable hostility, their identity and cultural practices cannot be restricted to mere defensive reactions against the negative pressures exerted against them. Michael Piore has noted a number of limitations in the models which stress the primacy of economic structures, and those paradigms which reduce the agency of the migrant to the victim-proletarian.[27] Firstly, as he argues, there is no correspondence between the characteristics of the migrants and the demands of migrant labour. Only a small minority of migrants who have found work in manufacturing or heavy industry have any prior experience or skills in these areas. Secondly, considering the income differentials, why is the pressure to migrate not stronger? Thirdly, how does the economy, in times of inertia and stagnation, continue to absorb further inputs of migrants?

To understand the diverse motivating forces, and the complex transformations that emerge in migration, Piore stresses the concept of status. He draws attention to a correlation between migration and mobility, and thereby suggests that migration is not just a 'step out', but also a 'step up'. In this sense, the migrant is, by definition, also an agent involved in the broader process of cultural transformation, and not just in pursuit of economic rewards. Piore, while acknowledging that the migrant is more exposed to the fluctuations and closures in the economy, argues that it is this awareness of flux and vulnerability that also makes the migrant more willing to enter the secondary sector of the labour market. Piore thereby proposes a model based on the dualism and flux, as well as the specific concentrations and structured divisions in the marketplace. This partially explains why migrants endure the hardship and the deskilling in the workplace, as well as their resilience in times of economic recession and inertia.

This view has been supported by Goldsheider, who argues that consciousness of social change is linked to the economic structures of migration. Practical knowledge of routes and opportunities often follows tracks established within cultural circuits rather than through class affiliations. As a consequence, the patterning of social relations by migrants does not always neatly repeat the hierarchies of class, or conform to the strict opposition between tradition and modernization:

> Migration may be viewed as a vehicle or mechanism of moving 'traditional' people into contact with 'modernity'. When the focus is on the urban area, the issues tend to be these: How 'traditional' are rural immigrants to the city and how 'modern' are city residents?[28]

There is no simple relationship between migration and social class. Both the voluntarist 'push–pull' and the structuralist 'centre–periphery' model presuppose an underlying mechanistic understanding of social change. The real force which causes migration is always seen as being external to the actions of the migrants. Whether migrants are seen as being pulled up, or pushed out of their traditional homes, by the invisible hand of modernization, or being displaced by the restless drives of capital, their own agency, in the process of social transformation, is always rendered secondary to, or determined by, these external forces. There has been little attention to the way the patterns of migration are in a dynamic relationship to the actions and understandings of individual migrants.

To understand the complex dynamics, through which the broad cultural patterns are inscribed within specific individual actions, would require a break with the mechanistic paradigms of social change. We would need to think more about the processes of flux and flow, rather than fixing solely on the causes or consequences of single trajectories. From this perspective, migration would be seen as a multi-vectorial phenomenon. Change would be understood more broadly as being generated by the very process of interaction, rather than the imposition of external forces on predefined subjects. Within a non-mechanistic perspective, which acknowledges the relative autonomy of culture, the identity of the migrants is not subordinate to external categories, but formed out of their own experience of movement and settlement. In the growing literature on migration within the discipline of cultural studies, there is greater emphasis on understanding the complexities of representing migrant subjectivity.

Recent historical research on post-war British immigration policies has also called for a broader theoretical framework.[29] In these studies the traditional frameworks, which emphasized the category of class over race, have been found wanting. For instance, it has been noted that in the post-war period the British government took an active role in resolving labour shortage in certain sectors of the economy by undertaking the costs of recruitment, transport and repatriation of migrant labour. The sources of labour were located predominantly in Europe. Displaced persons languishing in refugee camps were targeted. Following health checks, they were contracted to enter Britain with limited labour rights, and prohibitions on the entry of their dependants. It was assumed that these workers might eventually assimilate and behave as 'worthy members of the British community'.[30] After the First World War restrictions on entry into Britain were both tightening and being structured according to racialized anxieties. British subjects from the West Indies and India were increasingly subjected to discriminatory regulations. Thus post-war migrant labourers arriving from these colonies were treated in a manner significantly different from the Europeans. This differential practice in labour recruitment implied that there was a colour code on the reserve army thesis.

These new historical findings have revealed that the British government's practice of regulating immigration was never driven by purely economistic policies that would neatly deliver workers to the needs of capital. For when the British government was faced with the prospects of black immigration, they were more concerned with the racialized anxieties around miscegenation, preoccupied with reports about the potentialities of black criminality, threatened by the fears of black sexuality, and swayed by claims of idleness and mental inferiority. In short, the government's perception of black immigrants was not as a new category of proletarians, but as, in the words of one spokesman, the 'dark strangers' that posed a threat to public and national culture.[31]

Drawing on this new body of historical research, Ali Rattansi has argued that the British government's responses to black immigration from the colonies, and the administrative practices that were established to select or discourage their arrival, and then to police their settlement, were framed by the twin forces of racial typologies that had been developed in the course of empire, and based upon the self-belief that their role in world politics was dependent on being seen as the figurehead of a strong and united Commonwealth. These concerns were not always complementary to the needs of industry and capital. The fears that immigration would lead to the construction of spaces like a 'new Harlem in Liverpool', or that the black men's 'superb sense of rhythm and their natural ease of keeping time with music'[32] would seduce white women by leading them back to a more primitive time, were expressive of a discourse in which racialized and sexualized anxieties not only competed with capital, but were overriding the considerations of class. The conventional structuralist and voluntarist models would be unable to explain these practices. A broader conception of the relationship between migration and social change is necessary. It is clear that economistic calculations are not the sole criteria for policy formation on immigration levels, just as wage differentials are not the sole motivating factor for migrants.

The 'postmodern frame' that Rattansi proposes would dispense with any universalist pronouncement of class as a determining category, and replace this with a mode of analysis which demonstrates how the concepts of race, class and gender are intertwined in the complex operation of policy formation and social relations. It is far too simplistic to see migration patterns as being regulated by either economic forces or public opinion, and the role of the state being confined to a mere instrument which reacts to these demands. We need to see more clearly how the role of the state, in defining policy, is actively involved in the ideological context within which migrants have to operate, but also to understand that, in turn, these policies are formed in the complex interaction of broader social changes and the ongoing patterns of migration.

To develop this broader approach Rattansi turns to Foucault's insight into the operation of 'bio-politics'. This concept refers to the way the modern western states sought to manage the 'social body'. The practices and functions that were mobilized by the state were formed by the production of the knowledge–power networks, which were implemented in specific institutions like immigration offices or factories, and articulated by professionals in fields as diverse as medicine and architecture. These new forms of knowledge for the representation of the 'social body' and the new techniques of organization and policing were far from being consistent and unisonant. The contradictions between these racialized typologies and the pure economistic calculations of labour are nowhere as evident as they are in the discourses and practices for regulating migration. For instance, the criteria for entry can be read as an index of what the social body should or should not look like. In determining these images, government policies which sought to manage the process of social and cultural interaction according to racialized categories did not privilege class considerations. Throughout this century, the patterns of migration have constantly exceeded, or disrupted, the crude monocausal or essentialist models of social change.

Globalization and dispersal

The most recent literature on global migration has drawn more attention to the conceptual difficulty in distinguishing between different forms of movement, in particular, the distinction between political refugee and labour migration. The third phase is thus linked to the complex structural changes in the new international division of labour, and the uneven geopolitical transformations that are associated with globalization. In 1973/4 the guest-worker schemes were halted – the oil crisis being cited as the reason. However, this was also the forerunner to a period of stagnation and restructuring in Europe. Similarly entry quotas into the USA were tightened. The increasing social cost of labour and environmental regulations were seen as constraints on industrial expansion in the western states. The end of organized recruitment of manual workers by advanced industrialized countries led to a fundamental restructuring of the labour process and the world economy. Capital-intensive stages of production, control of finance, research and design remained in the west, while rapid patterns of industrialization have occurred in south-east Asia and in the Arab states.

In western states, migration is no longer exclusively linked with economic expansion in the primary sector, but more related to the less centralized processes of succession in the new service industries, and in catering for the consumption patterns that have emerged as a consequence of migration itself. These profound shifts in the global economy and society have led theorists like Stephen Castles, who previously subordinated the cultural effects of migration to the base–superstructure and centre–periphery model, to abandon the strict polarities of the economistic framework. Castles acknowledges, in his most recent work, that even if one gives primacy to economic motivation in migration, one still needs to understand the *dual pattern* of changes that flow from it: 'workforces become multinational within each country due to migration; they become multinational on the global level as transnational corporations dot their worksites around the world.'[33]

By the early 1980s the manufacturing base of the global economy had clearly shifted to the Pacific Rim. This shift in industrial concentration has stimulated new directions of migration. These economic transformations have also coincided with new forms of political crises which in themselves stimulated a shift in migration patterns. The political fragmentation of the USSR and the increasing instability in Latin America have unleashed great numbers of migrants: from Soviet soldiers being returned to their home bases, to peasants fleeing from assassination squads – the political dimensions of migration have been sharply brought into focus.[34] Even in these circumstances, migration is not just about fleeing. The necessity to flee is crucially linked to that complex nexus between political aspiration and cultural practice which defines an ethnic identity. When political divisions are structured along ethnic lines, migration patterns, and nation-building projects become explicitly fused.

Alexandra Korol's study of the resilience of Ukrainian ethnicity throughout the Soviet period, where saints' days figured more deeply than the officially sanctioned May Day, and where Ukrainian was considered a 'mother tongue' even by those who were fluent only in Russian, revealed the underlying tensions between public and private definitions of national identity. This cultural and political tension found a powerful rallying point with the Chernobyl nuclear disaster. The devastation and displacements associated with Chernobyl finally brought Soviet hegemony to the brink of its demise and galvanized the Ukrainian independence movement.[35] In Latin America the ideological persecution and economic suffering inflicted by the ruling dictatorships led to more than 2 million migrants. The wars in former Yugoslavia and Africa have presented us with a new addition in the vocabulary of displacement: 'ethnic cleansing'. Ecological disasters in China and the creeping desertification of previously arable lands have also displaced people.

At the close of the twentieth century, as the media increasingly link human movement with political instability, we have become witness to unprecedented levels of migration and displacement. Both the scale and the diverse forms of migration have compelled a closer understanding of the dynamics that link the changes occurring in one region with structural shifts that cause turbulent re-verberations across the globe. If the work of Stephen Castles can be read as an indicator of the new methods for mapping and explaining global migration, then it can be noted that the relationship between migration and social change is more complex than in any other historical phase. The theoretical models that are now being utilized are both more loosely defined and predisposed to multi-causal accounts. As the migration process becomes global in character, Stephen Castles and Mark Miller have argued that it also possesses a relative autonomy – being more or less impervious to either restrictive measures in the country of arrival or development in the country of origin.[36] The increasing pervasiveness of global culture and the growth of cross-border movement of capital, com-modities and people have also demanded a rethinking of the models and the-ories for explaining social change. The simple binarisms between centre and periphery or First World and Third World are no longer adequate for mapping the co-ordinates and explaining the processes of global migration.

Contemporary patterns of migration

The proliferation in the directions of movements, the restrictions in settlement, the diversification in the identity of migrants and the widening variation in their resources have made the patterns of migration so complex that no general model has been proposed to explain the flows of global migration. There are signs of old forms of contract labour in the Arab states and trade in 'sex slaves' from eastern Europe coexisting with new forms of 'bi-locality' across the Pacific and temporary migration in Asia and Africa. Illegal migration continues to grow despite the existence of even more draconian laws in the United States and the Arab states. The feminization of the migrant labour force has also contradicted the earlier patterns of movement and confounded prior theories. The link be-tween the flows of capital and labour is no longer represented in isomorphic terms. These new patterns of mobility, along with the shifts in geopolitical borders and immigration policies, have added such complexity to the field of migration studies that it now demands a fundamental rethinking of the concep-tual frameworks in which the process of movement can be considered.

The decoupling of the traditional linkage between migration and industrial expansion in the west has impelled a rethinking of global migration patterns. However, the new narratives of global migration are often superimposed upon crude explanations of the decentring of industrial expansion. Migration is thereby, once again, subordinated to broader structural changes. The driving forces in these accounts are again implicitly defined within a mechanistic model. Claiming that, as labour regulations, immigration controls and social and eco-logical demands made industrial expansion more difficult in the traditional cen-tres of the west, capital moved production to locations where labour and social costs could be kept to a minimum. Capital made the simple calculation that it was more profitable to locate industry where labour was cheaper, political culture was most compliant, and environmental responsibilities were minimal. It was simply much cheaper to relocate production to the periphery than to recruit new forms of cheap labour from the periphery. This reversal meant that it was no longer labour that was migrating to the centres of industry in the west, but rather, it was western and non-western machinery and capital that were being moved closer to the periphery of cheap labour.

The decline in the need for factory workers, and the dismantling of the family reunion schemes for foreign workers in the west, have, however, stimulated new flows of illegal migrants and coincided with the more restricted forms of migration in the non-west. For instance, American computer software designers and Filipino sex workers may now share the same flights to Japan, but they occupy opposite ends of the spectrum of 'contract worker'. Their patterns of mobility and their motivation for movement are vastly different. Furthermore, as Mike Douglass has noted, many migrants do not always move primarily for work, but on arrival often enter the labour market. Students and tourists who overstay their visas often pick up casual work, while refugees and asylum seekers who are waiting for their cases to be heard are effectively forced to take work in the dirty and dangerous sectors of the labour market.[37]

The link between globalization of the economy and the international labour market is not a clear one. Deregulation in one area does not automatically imply a loosening of restrictions in the other. The one form of international migration which does resemble the new flows of capital is the circulation of 'skilled transients'.[38] There is now a significant flow of corporate managers, consultants and technicians who are highly mobile. They frequently move between countries with minimal restrictions, or find themselves being relocated according to the needs of a transnational corporation. Intra-company transfers and the attraction to global cities for 'skilled transients' is now exerting a significant economic and political role in the global migration systems.

At the other end of the socio-economic spectrum there is not such a direct link between patterns of mobility and economic production. The tragic stories of women being lured to the west with the promise of marriage, only to find their passports confiscated, their children abducted, and themselves coerced into working as prostitutes, are no longer uncommon. According to Anita Gradin, the European Union Justice Commissioner, between 200,000 and 500,000 women, mostly from Asia, Africa, Latin America and the former Eastern bloc, have become victims of traffickers in sex slaves.[39] On the promise of work or marriage, they have been drugged, beaten and condemned to work for pimps across Europe. They are sold from brothel to brothel, fetching from $500 to $5,000.[40] Their earnings and movements monitored by ruthless pimps, forced into living and working in appalling conditions, these women have few rights and are often too intimidated to call for help. Their pimps not only threaten them with reprisals but also convince them that they would be severely punished by the state if they were caught working illegally as prostitutes. A further strategy is the possession of humiliating videotapes which they threaten to show to their families back home.

Pimps are conscious that they can exploit the ignorance of the law and are also aware that few countries have laws which explicitly prohibit the smuggling of human beings. In most countries the smuggling of sex slaves is not even a criminal offence. Until 1998 smuggling of sex slaves was under Australian law a mere misdemeanour in immigration regulations. Apart from Belgium, the Netherlands and Austria, no other country has modified its laws to deal with this horrendous crime. This crime has reached such proportions that smuggling of human beings is considered less risky and more profitable than the drug trade. According to senior Frankfurt police officer Bernhard Kowalski, a pimp can earn 30,000 marks a month from one slave-prostitute.[41] It has been estimated that since the 1970s, some 30 million women and children have fallen victims to the traffickers in human flesh, generating an income of $7 billion a year. While drugs and guns are sold only once, a trafficker can sell a woman's services over and over.[42] The foreign prostitutes in many countries outnumber nationals. In Germany, foreign prostitutes make up about 75 per cent of the total. In Austria, some 85 per cent of women working in bars and brothels are from abroad, mostly from the ex-communist states of eastern Europe. The European report on the trafficking in women also noted that criminal groups earmarked women from certain countries for particular destinations. Women from the Dominican Republic often end up in Spain or Italy, while Thai women are targeted for the Netherlands. In New York's Brighton Beach, where there is the largest concentration of Russians in the USA, there are countless 'second-storey businesses' like marriage brokers and dating services which are fronts for prostitution brokers.

As the scale of trafficking increases, the role of state officials has also been brought to public attention. In 1991 it was estimated that in Pakistan there were over 200,000 Bangladeshi women who had been forced into prostitution, and yet not a single trafficker was arrested or convicted in that year. In Japan, where there are over 70,000 Thai women working in indentured servitude as 'hostesses', who are being sold for an average of $14,000 to clubs run by yakuza gangsters, there have been recorded instances where officials, have not only been indifferent to the plight of these women but have even returned escapees to the gangsters.[43] These activities are proceeding in a legislative vacuum. As Ludmila Bojkava has noted, drastic political changes are needed to address this issue:

We need more information directed at young women in the east and we need financial incentives for these women to return home. But let us be realistic. The women can earn so much more working in the west. They will go on doing it until the west does the only thing it knows how to do: put up the walls of Fortress Europe. Then no one will get in, just like during the cold war.[44]

The plight of contemporary 'sex slaves' could be read as an index of the turbulent patterns in the new global (dis)order. There are further moral and political grounds that should prevent us from drawing analogies between the rights of workers and the flows of capital, for that would imply that labour can be reduced to its commodity value. However, there is now considerable evidence to suggest that, while nation-states are attempting to regulate the flows of labour in contradictory ways to capital, capitalism is defining labour costs not according to local needs but from the position of the lowest global cost. Richard Appelbaum's analysis of the garment trade provides a relevant illustration of the flows of global capitalism and the mobility of the manufacturing industry. The garment industry, which once relied on the Third World only for the supply of primary materials, and concentrated manufacturing as well as research and design in the First World, has now shifted the low-wage and labour-intensive levels of production to distant sites across the world. In 1959 only 6.9 per cent of the US consumption in the clothes trade consisted of imports; by 1981 it was over half.[45] The example of the Nike sportswear company, with $3 billion sales in 1991, is telling. While designers, advertising consultants and marketing managers all work in US offices, the company does not own a single link in its chain of commodity production. Nike is the front-line company of global manufacturers without factories. Benetton has also reached global success by managing its image and product but without owning any of the outlets that carry its name and exclusively sell its products. All production and handling is subcontracted. Responsibility for the levels of wages and the social costs of labour is transferred elsewhere. However, against the flow of this outgoing tide, Appelbaum also observes a contrary stream: 'Alongside the explosion of low-wage factory jobs in what were once peripheral countries has come the reperipheralization of the core. The coming home of sweatshops to take advantage of the home markets and cheap immigrant labour.'[46]

In his case study of the Los Angeles garment industry Appelbaum has noted the resurgence of small-scale manufacturing operated by ethnic minorities who employ migrant women. At least a quarter of these are illegal immigrants. Wages are at sub-minimum levels and working conditions are crude. These women, who have mostly come from Mexico, are effectively competing with women in China who have also left their villages but are working in modern large-scale factories. The globalization of this industry has had the effect of feminizing labour worldwide and stimulating the informal economy in the First World. The spatial location of Los Angeles in relation to low-wage immigrants from Central America, and the concentration of industry-related professionals, may explain why the industry has experienced considerable growth in this area, while the traditional sites in the north-eastern United States continue to decline as factories are subcontracted out to the peripheries. Similar patterns have been identified in Europe with the shift of clothing manufacture back into the urban centres by ethnic entrepreneurs.[47]

Do these transformations in global capitalism conform to the structures established in the early stages of industrialization? Can the input of low-wage immigrant labour be represented as the 'reserve army' of the global proletariat? Is the ascendancy of Hong Kong and Singapore simply a realignment of the centre–periphery dependency relations? If we presume, with Appelbaum, that despite the new international division of labour, in which the production of goods and services has been spread across many countries, and control and responsibility for the commodity are not directed back to any single country, the nation-state remains sovereign, and the exploitation of labour is the principal source of wealth for the nation, then the preceding questions can be answered within the paradigm of industrial society. However, the logic of this argument underestimates the extent to which global transformations have not only intensified and diversified the structures of production, but also created new modes of relation between the traditional co-ordinates of power. To develop a clearer understanding of the changes associated with globalization may well depend on a remapping of the patterns of migration.

The clearest mapping of the relationship between migration and social transformation is the one suggested by theorists who drew on Marxist models of capital circulation. Within these maps and models the flows of capital have been periodized in the following stages. Nineteenth-century liberal and colonial circuits operated through the interconnection of various and dispersed localities and regions. The second phase, twentieth-century capitalism, saw the integration of production, consumption and investment within the boundaries of a national economy. Markets and labour collectives were organized nationally. Towards the end of the twentieth century we have witnessed the ascendancy of more fragmented and flexible types of production accompanied by a vast expansion in the deregulated sector of financial services. Capital now circulates with greater velocity and with less commitment to any given national economy. This era and this process of capital circulation have been described by Lash and Urry as 'disorganized capitalism'. Like the turbulent patterns of migration, the circulation of capital flows across greater distances and with higher speeds. However, unlike the mobility of capital, the right of labour to cross boundaries has become more restricted. The harsh conditions that new migrants are forced to endure have imposed new burdens and created tensions with the already established migrant communities. In many states the regulation of migrants is conducted by policies that explicitly forbid them to form communities and exclude any possibility of permanent settlement.

The relationship between movement and settlement has become increasingly jagged. The contrast between earlier policies of migration, which were motivated by selective resettlement, and the current phase, which is driven by economic advantage can also be illustrated by the shifts in attitudes in places like Australia. Until the early 1960s the Australian government offered British people assisted passage schemes to encourage 'white immigration'. Fares were heavily subsidized, and preferential opportunities for housing and work were made available. These racialized policies were eventually dismantled only to be replaced with new criteria which predominantly linked entry to economic benefit. The most notable example of this policy is the creation of special 'fast tracks' for citizenship to attract wealthy Asian entrepreneurs. Yet, owing to the circuitous loops of global speculation, the money that is brought in to secure citizenship rarely trickles down to the national economy. Shifting in no longer implies a commitment to stay.

The ability of certain Asian entrepreneurs to buy citizenship in a second and sometimes third country presents a different image from the conventional category of the migrant as victim. These new middle-class migrants have a far greater flexibility in their ability to move and in their selection of destination. Countries like Canada and Australia now actively compete with each other in offering inducements that bypass the current restrictions on immigration from Asia. However, as some commentators have noted, the integration of the entrepreneurs within the new host country has created hostility from members of the established Asian immigrant communities, as well as stimulating broader resentments from the hegemonic groups in the host societies.

The commitment of these immigrants has also been questioned as their relationship to place has been described in terms of 'bi-locality'. The flow of movement is not one-way. There is a high rate of return as well as many forms of ongoing exchange. For political or educational reasons children and older members of the family are often 'parachuted' into one country while the 'astronaut' breadwinners continue to commute across the Pacific. Decisions over the spatial location of the family are often made in terms of security and economic opportunity, and given their resources, the decision to move on to another country is not a difficult one. These transnational migrants, who use different locations to create the optimal conditions for their own prosperity and family security, have forced commentators to rethink the 'classical' factors of migration. In these instances, the model of push–pull fails to address the patterns of mobility and the decisions for integration into a host society. Given the complexity of high finance and flux in political security, sociologists have gained very little insight into the forms of agency that operate in these forms of migration.

Although these complex patterns of movements have no doubt heightened the exchange of ideas and transferred skills and wealth in a two-way system, there is not much sociological knowledge on the social impact of these movements. Little is known of the sense of community that develops among people who, for instance, split their time between Melbourne as a place of study for the children, Hong Kong as the family home and Vancouver as the location of the parent's business. Chan and Ong have noted the limitations of earlier models in explaining these new patterns, and have stressed that the agency of migrants must be seen as engaging in what Giddens calls a 'dialectic of control'.[48] Emerging from these observations are trends which, they argue, reveal the migrant as developing complex and dynamic strategies of mobility, and expressing motivations which are collectivistic in nature. The availability of new forms of telecommunication, along with the possibility of 'commuting' across the Pacific, has led to the emergence of new forms of the spatially extended migrant family. Separation is, in this instance, not so much an indication of loss and deprivation as the strategic luxury of economic optimization and risk minimization.

The prior linkage between regulated migration and industrialization in the west has virtually come to a halt. Western Europe has effectively frozen all formal programmes of mass immigration. Although the European union has dramatically relaxed the laws for the movement of citizens between member states, and while North America moves towards the creation of a free-trade zone, the borders of the regions have been increasingly tightened. Étienne Balibar's wry observation of the relocation of the barriers between Europe and its Other returns our attention to the linkage between racism and the crisis in Europe's identity problem, 'the future "iron curtain" and the future "wall" threaten to pass somewhere in the Mediterranean, or somewhere to the south-east of the Mediterranean, and they will not be easier to bring down than their predecessors.'[49]

In many western countries the balance between emigration and immigration has shifted. Countries like Italy and Greece, which traditionally were thought of as emigrant societies, are now becoming either the destination or the transitional zone for a new range of immigrants.[50] In Britain, despite populist phobias of being 'swamped' by foreigners, and the exceptional period between 1958 and 1963, emigration has consistently exceeded immigration.[51] In the past decade, multicultural states like Australia, Canada and the United States have developed more restrictive policies for labour migration and tightened the opportunities for family reunification. The migration that is occurring within the west in this phase is therefore mostly unregulated and generated by a vast number of micro-agencies and personalized networks. In the post Reagan–Thatcher era of unregulated markets and the attack on nationally protected economies, we can see all the more how the 'south grates up against the borders of the north, and bleeds'.

The greater flows of migration are now directed towards and within non-western locations. On 1 May 1984 there were said to be more planes flying above the Pacific than the Atlantic.[52] This statistic has often been interpreted as one of the signs of the turbulence in the new global (dis)order. If we tried to map current movements, it would be impossible to lay them out with a set of linear arrows pointing to identifiable nodal positions. It is clear that the Atlantic axis linking North America with Europe and the north–south axis are being significantly overlaid by a number of other lateral movements as well as the major shifting of power over the Pacific. As Ronald Skeldon argues,

> Over the last twenty-five years we have seen a major shift in the global systems of international migration. From a system dominated by movement out of Europe across the Atlantic and to Australasia, there has been a shift to trans-Pacific move-

ment out of Asian countries to the traditional destinations for European settlement. These trans-Pacific flows of the twenty-first century could easily come to rival the trans-Atlantic flows of the late nineteenth and early twentieth centuries.[53]

Movement is also now taking place in a criss-crossing pattern across and within eastern Europe, Africa, Asia and Latin America. The Arab states are unique in that they have conducted extensive and tightly regulated structures of labour recruitment. Over 70 per cent of the workforce in Saudia Arabia are non-nationals, and in places like the United Arab Emirates the proportion can be as high as 90 per cent. Migrants are heavily concentrated in the construction, manufacturing and service industries. While these states have imposed strict procedures for the administering of labour permits, and enforce draconian measures in the deportation of migrants with expired or invalid permits, the illegal entry and overstay of migrants are growing at a faster rate than the legal arrivals.[54]

The earlier markers of migration as a set of movements from rural and pre-modern spaces to industrial and modern cities has now been blurred, as most migrants are from other urban centres. The changes in migration flows have also been marked in a change in the orientation and the intensity of migrants. Not only are more migrants heading towards new industrial projects within the Third World, but their means and purpose have changed. The legal settlement of migrants has been replaced by the temporary and clandestine arrival of migrants. Rather than the construction of segmented mono-ethnic communities or the formation of new multicultural diasporas, migration is now encouraging single men and women who are forced to work in foreign environments and live in isolated ghettos.

The prospects for migrants to develop mechanisms for overcoming isolation, and to generate new communities that affirm common values and provide social support, are becoming more precarious.[55] The symbiosis between dominant and minority communities does not presuppose the wholesale transplantation of cultural structures, but we still must ask the question: what forms of alliance, cross-cultural dialogue or community-wide organization are possible when the predicament of the migrant is increasingly threatened by deportation, exploitation and discrimination? If migration continues to be framed by solitude, itinerancy and illegality, and if migrants are excluded from experiencing solidarity even amongst themselves, then future multicultural societies will be even more politically and socially fractured than they are at present.

Borders and flows

The degree to which migrants can move varies considerably. In most cases it depends on the status and resources of the migrant and, in some instances, it relates to the degree to which territorial boundaries are actively policed. In some regions communities are either settled across borders or move freely between them. The Lapps in northern Scandinavia and the loosely guarded borders of West Africa are examples where political regulations are not a restraint on movement. However, the majority of nation-states in the world are increasingly tightening entry and exit from their territories. There is a temptation to relate the movement of migrant labour with the broader flows of capital and information across the world. To make such a connection would certainly draw attention to the links between demographic, economic and cultural changes. Yet there can be no direct correspondence between the circulation of money with the movement of people. The tracks on which they move and the barriers imposed on them are often contradictory.

A more useful way of thinking of borders and flows in the contemporary migration patterns is from a dual perspective, one which focuses on both regional political regulations and specific cultural prohibitions, while also recognizing the global pressures and motivations for movement. No nation-state can completely close its borders. All borders are both permeable and selective. Certain categories of migrants will be encouraged at given times; and at all times, if the inducements for migration are strong, some people will find other ways to bypass the official border controls. This dual perspective will need to acknowledge the effectiveness of some states in regulating movement across their borders, as well as being cognizant of the ways in which migrants target their destinations and on arrival develop new expectations of settlement. Neither the historical routes established by colonial links, nor the proximity of neighbouring states, provide the main clues for the paths that future migrants will take. Sociologists have underestimated the extent to which migration is based on the transmission of ideas, stories told by other migrants, rumours of opportunity, the strutting of returnees, as well as the more conventional practices of recruiting agencies and the complex levels of influence exerted by the media, collectively stimulating the thought that life is better elsewhere. The directions and sources of migration have multiplied dramatically, and these can only be accounted for by taking a perspective which draws attention to both the global perception of mobility and the local strategies of selectivity across borders.

It is perhaps necessary to think of migratory movements beyond the binarism of either long-term resettlement, or short-term contracted labour. Both at the level of skilled and unskilled, legal and illegal workers, migration has generated new relationships between place and belonging. During the period of the 'classical migration' to the New World, the stereotypical vision of the migrant was either as the young man who left to make his fortune and return as a hero, or as the man who left to set up a home and enterprise in a new country. Migration was either a one-way trip, or a temporary sojourn. It represented the opportunity to start a new life elsewhere, or to provide the resources for getting a better foothold in the original homeland.

The self-image of settler societies in the New World was built on the unacknowledged genocide of the indigenous people and the ambivalent promise that a new nation could be built by migrants from other nations. Not all migrants were granted the same privileges, but there was the underlying assumption that a selective form of diversity was a positive force in national unity. In countries like the United States, Canada, Australia and New Zealand the formation of a new national culture was premised at first on the assimilation of the minorities to the hegemonic Anglo-Celtic culture, and then redefined in terms of pluralist models of cultural integration. Given that the foundational scars of genocide have far from healed in these countries, and the promise of equality under the policies are far from the daily realities of the diasporic communities in these countries, there is little confidence that the west can furnish a universal model for managing the future of global migration.

The driving motivation for contemporary migrants is rarely expressed in the masculinist narrative of the pioneer that dominated the hopes and sentiments of settlers in the New World. The experiences of Third World women, a key force in the international labour market, cannot be described in such pioneering terms. Their presence in the national imaginary of their host country is confined to cheap and temporary labour. There is no social space which beckons the migrant as a positive and permanent feature. According to the United Nations Population Division (1990), women make up half the world's migrants. In countries like the Philippines, women account for up to 80 per cent of the migrant population. The restructuring of the global economies with a demand for services in the First World, and the increasing feminization of manufacturing industries in the Third World, have led to a dramatic realignment of gender relations. These women are often seen as double victims. Shouldering inherited family debts and exploited by the agencies that contract them to overseas companies, they have no opportunities to create a new sense of community in their migrant homes. They have short-term contracts and live, for the most part, in isolation from other migrants with whom they could form social bonds. Yet their experience of alienation is often accompanied by a broader rethinking of their identity and social position. In places like Britain, immigrant women, particularly from the Indian subcontinent, have been at the forefront of initiating cultural change. But these cultural and political initiatives in Britain have to be seen in the context of extended migration and the complexities of multicultural policies.[56] The position of immigrant workers in Britain is significantly different from the contract workers in the Gulf States.

Across Europe and Asia we see new patterns of migrants entering countries both legally and illegally for limited periods. Despite the existence of strict border controls, vast numbers of migrants oscillate between their homeland and workplace(s). The scale of illegal migration has grown dramatically in the 1990s. In the USA illegal migrants tend to settle for more extensive stays. Skeldon estimates that the smuggling of people into the USA is a business worth $3 billion a year.[57] In 1993 the General Accounting Office reported that there were from 3.4 to 5.5 million illegal workers in the USA.[58] This growth in illegal migration reflects the broader inequalities and turbulent phase of global politics. However, as Mark Miller argues, the pattern of movement of illegal migrants cannot be explained by a neat binarism which presupposes that illegals are impelled to move because of economic stagnation and political crisis in the homeland, and then lured by the high wages and prosperity of the host country:

> Rarely, however, does it suffice to account for illegal immigration in such bald terms. A great deal of illegal immigration occurs between developing countries and fits poorly into a south to north schema. Indeed, two of the most striking points to be made about the late twentieth century illegal migration are its globalization, with transportation and communication advances facilitating migration that was scarcely possible several decades earlier, and its decoupling from historically set patterns.[59]

The historical links forged under colonialism still provide some of the axial routes of migration. Algerians continue to head for France, while Pakistanis try their luck in Britain. However, the recent trends reveal that migrants, in particular those from the former Eastern bloc countries, are heading for new destinations on the basis of covert agencies, or messages sent along complex information chains that link friends and families across diverse locations. The diversity in the sources of migration implies that there are more limited possibilities for migrants to form ethnic bonds. The established immigrant communities can be as foreign to them as the hegemonic community. Despite the growing militarization of national boundaries to ward off illegal migration, the more draconian visa restrictions and the possible penalization of employers who fail to check the status of their workers, the international battle against migration is far from won. How can a state defend itself against a process which is so deeply implicated within its own development? With a rapid feedback system that informs potential migrants about the various means of entry, how do immigration officials develop clear rules that will legitimately distinguish the legal from the illegal migrant?

> Thus while restricting the entry of aliens for permanent settlement, states may simultaneously encourage or even promote the entry of tourists, business men, artists, social workers, scientists, skilled workers, students, diplomats, or even a certain number of unskilled workers. In addition, the entry of refugees, though generally not encouraged, may be tolerated for humanitarian reasons. Consequently, unless external controls are reinforced by strong and effective internal controls, illegal migration is likely to emerge as a relatively viable option for a person denied access to *bona fide* migration opportunities.[60]

Government policy in terms of the relationship between globalization and migration can be characterized as contradictory. Deregulation and casualization in the workforce may make the labour markets more competitive on a global scale, but they also stimulate the informal economy, towards which migrants gravitate with greater intensity than the indigenous labour force. The evisceration of inner cities and the dismantling of welfare services have also created more hostile and more divided urban spaces. Urban planning is now more concerned with surveillance and segregation than with inspiring any form of civic integration. The decline of local economies and social services has fuelled a new dimension of scapegoating within the racist ideologies that proliferate in these inner cities. This tense environment of conflict and competition could produce far more explosive and exploitative forms of social relations than political leaders anticipate. Global cities like New York, London and Sydney often proudly parade the vitality of 'their' multiculturalism, by displaying variety at the level of ethnic cuisine. Yet this gastronomic boast would have greater social credibility if it were matched by a commitment to promote the conditions by which different cultures are sustained and new cultural forms articulated. What would a multicultural workplace look like? How do urban planners accommodate cultural differences in domestic situations? Who will judge, when there is a legal conflict between competing cultural codes? Global migration has heightened the urgency of such questions, as it has cleaved open the gulf in the political rhetoric, which seemingly endorses multiculturalism, but also denies the need to rethink the terms of social inclusion and spatial belonging:

> Cities and communities are increasingly conflicted about immigration. Residents often do not mind including those who fit into the self-image of a prosperous, technologically innovative and democratic society, but wish to exclude the workers who are, in fact, necessary for the reproduction of society. Immigrants are more likely to belong to the excluded. But the groups are more closely bound together than they think: the corporate elite profit from illegal immigrants, and the prosperous suburbanites use the labor of poorer immigrants they find so threatening. It is out of this contradiction and multi-layered character of the post-modern city that its enormous energy, its cultural dynamism, and its innovative capability emerge.[61]

Before these changes, government agencies respond in conflicting ways. They seek to strike the impossible balance between satisfying the global interests of capital as well as protecting the local needs of labour. The patterns of migration that emerge from these contradictory aspirations are so multiple and of such a complex nature that it is now impossible either to generalize about the logic which determines its causes, or to map its flows according to the binary co-ordinates of departure and destination. Migrants have become more mobile and the story of migration is even more jagged. Flexibility in the marketplace has not meant more diversity in the workplace, but has only stretched the capacity of labour to endure insecurity and to see opportunity in displacement. A current map of global migration would have to be as complex as all the migrant biographies.

3

The Ability to Move: Defining Migrants

Never before our time have so many people been uprooted. Emigration, forced or chosen, across national frontiers or from village to metropolis, is the quintessential experience of our time.

John Berger, *And Our Faces, My Heart, Brief as Photos*

At the close of the twentieth century, the experience of displacement is becoming both more commonplace and more complex. Across the First World, the media and politicians are anxiously redefining the levels of acceptable immigration, and calling for the end of 'unproductive' immigration. There is no country which is actively recruiting migrants, but many which are declaring that migrants are a threat or burden to the state. Throughout these debates immigration is increasingly linked to the destabilization of traditional communities, and migrants are being blamed for the unsettling changes in social relations. Today the term 'migrant' has a looming presence. It has an ambivalent association. For some it suggests a positive image of cosmopolitanism and adventure. To others it issues a defensive reaction against the so-called 'dirty' foreigners and 'bogus' asylum-seekers who, according to some commentators, unfairly abuse the limited welfare resources of the nation-state.

In the context of globalization such a display of hostile stereotyping not only requires political refutation, but must inspire a deeper rethinking of the relationship between the stranger and the citizen. There is a danger that the ubiquity of migration effects will render the term 'migrant' politically dangerous and conceptually useless. If we are all, to some extent, the product of migration, then how do we distinguish between one story and another? Are we really equally displaced? Clearly some people's suffering, caused by political displacement, cannot be compared with the pleasures of tourism. As the means for long-distance travel increase, and as the time necessary to cross vast distances diminishes, more and more barriers are constructed to screen movement. Never has the transfer of capital been so rapid and the movement of labour so regulated. Despite the popular self-image of the west as a place where you are free to move as you please, our ability to move is not a natural right. The image of the Soviet border guard was, throughout the Cold War, the archetypal image of a repressive totalitarian system. Yet the irony of 'fortress Europe' blocking the passage of aspirants after the disappearance of the 'iron curtain' was barely noted. Movement in the modern world is regulated by an ever-tightening matrix of economic, political, sexual and cultural factors.

Questions of identity are always posed in relation to space. Migrants find such questions particularly poignant. By this I do not mean that 'true' identity is rooted in the given place of either origin or present position. Rather, we need to ask how certain socio-political flows and barriers, that constitute spatial configurations, also constitute and reflect the formations of identity. The dynamics of our movement in space, our ability to move, speak more about the form of our identity than the conventional answers to the questions: Where are you from? Where do you belong?

Space is neither a flat stage upon which subjects perform their historical tasks, nor a predefined volume through which they pass. Space is both a transformative force and a field that is transformed by the interactions that occur within it. Doreen Massey has argued, that the recognition of the politicization of the spatial, within the social sciences, has led to the further understanding, 'that the social and the spatial are inseparable and that the spatial form of the social has causal effecticity'.[1] Not only are spatial arrangements constructed through the social divisions of race, class and gender, but the concept of space is itself often represented through a gendered distinction. A recent body of feminist criticism has set out to challenge the dualism of time and space, whereby the latter is defined in opposition to, or as the lack of, the former. The concept of space and woman has often served as the subordinate position upon which the dynamic concept of time and man rests. Massey has argued that this dichotomy is 'related to the construction of the radical distinction between genders in our society, to the characteristics assigned to each of them, and to the power relations maintained between them'.[2]

The radical task is not simply to invert or reverse the dichotomies between time and space; man and woman; foreigner and familiar, but to rethink the imbrications between these different positions. Space and identity must be understood as dynamic concepts which are constituted through interactions. The specific position of women and the dynamics of spatial trajectories have been overlooked in the majority of studies on migration. Women were not seen as active agents in the great migration stories; they were either left behind, or taken along as part of the man's family. Similarly, the engine of history was represented as the driving force of migration. Frontier and border crossings were merely the stages that had to be passed as part of the grander temporal narrative of the migrant story. The 'new land' was just the setting for a new beginning, a rebirth in time. This limited perspective has both obscured the presence of women and failed to grasp the nature of change. In the context of increasingly polarized debates about the relationship between gender and estrangement, it is necessary to proceed with the broad claim that all identity is formed through dislocation. Identity cannot be confined within a polarity, which defines one set of identities as either lacking or damaged, only to be contrasted with another set which is supposedly fixed in a privileged place, or imbued with eternal traits.

In this chapter I would like to outline the scale of migration, and then draw attention to the difficulties in defining this phenomenon. Although migration had been recognized as a critical force within classical social theory, our understanding of the phenomenon has been limited by two factors. First, the identity of migrants has been restricted by the inherited gender blindness of the 'founding fathers'. Second, migration as process has been largely confined to those spatial trajectories which can be mapped according to the binary opposites like traditional versus modern, country versus city, or by the geographical coordinates of national boundaries. I will argue that a broader understanding of the spatial and gendered forms of migration is a necessary precondition for understanding the dynamics of migration in contemporary social relations.

Defining migrants

The right to travel, or move in search of work, has never been a given in history. However, the regulation of movement intensified during the eighteenth and nineteenth centuries. At the same time, the remapping of geopolitical space according to interlocking national boundaries, and the invention of the passport after the First World War, made movement from one place to another more difficult. The mechanisms for policing human movement also employed began to resemble a military operation. Migrants increasingly found themselves at the hard end of the most brutal contradictions of nationalist ideologies. Traditional notions of allegiance and belonging were transformed, as territories were defined by national boundaries, and subjects identified according to national citizenship. In this period borders replaced frontiers.[3] The concept of the border is in itself a constitutive feature of the nation-state. All nation-states have at least attempted to impose strict limits on the flows of migration across their borders. No nation-state has openly declared that immigration is free and unchecked. These regulating policies have invariably been formulated according to the principle that the national community needs protection and regulation like a body. The national border becomes like the skin of the community. The principles of inclusion and exclusion – who could enter a given space, who should be assimilated in order to stay, and who needed to be excluded – were influenced by a series of organicist metaphors which underpinned the new national ideologies. The question of origin, and the determination of the national boundary, became the most contested zones, and produced some of the most bloody outcomes of recent history. In the era of the nation-state, migration has been understood as the process of human movement across national boundaries. Citizenship and exile are the dual categories that determine either inclusion or exclusion from a nation-state.

In 1990, according to the International Organization for Migration, there were 80 million people who were defined as international migrants.[4] If we define migrants as those people who were born outside the country in which they live, then there is no country where migrants are more than 10 per cent of the total population.[5] This may suggest that migrants are only a minority of the world's population. In 1995 the United Nations High Commission on Refugees also estimated that there were 27 million refugees. This is regarded as the greatest number of stateless people in history. For the last twenty years the number of refugees has quadrupled every decade. To illustrate the scale of these numbers, the wretchedness of the refugee's trajectory, and also the foot-dragging response of the world community, the spokesperson of UNHCR has stated that 'every day, every week, every month last year 10,000 more people became refugees outside their own countries.' By 1997 the number of refugees worldwide increased by another 4 million to stand at 31 million. These calculations do not include the 24 million people displaced by violence and persecution and who have become homeless *within* their own countries. The plight of refugees who have not crossed international borders has also raised questions as to whether their predicament needs to be considered under the international conventions of human rights, or according to the respective national laws on minority rights.

The issues facing refugees have never been adequately addressed, in the sociological literature on migration, because of the prior complexity of ascribing a national origin to all the people of the world. It has been estimated that the number of self-defined peoples exceeds the number of nation-states by a proportion of five to one. The sociological debates on migration, which define national identity through the binarism of citizenship and exile, have difficulties in facing these complex and multiple quests for a homeland. The modern use for the word 'homeland' is predicated on the existence of a nation-state. It is presumed that since everyone is a member of a national community, they are also at home there. However, this overlooks the vast number of people who have become homeless, because they have either taken flight from their own nation, or for historical reasons their homeland was never constituted as a nation-state. If, for instance, Kurdistan will never be a nation, where do all the Kurdish people go, when they are told to return 'home'? The ruptured sense of belonging of indigenous peoples, like the Australian aborigines, who have remained within the boundaries of the nation, but have been displaced from their traditional homeland, also needs to be addressed seriously.

Given that the political leaders of the west, have sought increasingly restrictive interpretations of the 1950 Geneva Convention on asylum-seekers, and that the potential 'invasion' of migrants is repeatedly represented as a threat to social order by the media, it is surprising that the discipline of sociology has not been more concerned with challenging the prevailing definitions of the migrant. A more subtle vocabulary on migration is necessary, one which may attend to what Janet L. Abu-Lughod has noted is a clear lacuna in the sociological imagination. For as she notes, in regard to the plight of the Palestinian people, there is 'no concept to describe the phenomenon of "exile" without moving'.[6]

Neither the strict definition of 'the migrant' as anyone who lives outside of their country of birth, nor the alarming statistics of escalating numbers of displaced people, adequately addresses the scope and complexity of global migration. Families are often excluded from the calculation of international migrants. These 'objective' definitions fail to grasp the ongoing and subjective associations with migration. For instance, if the term 'migrant' is confined to those who were born outside the country in which they live, then why, for instance, are the children and grandchildren of migrants in Australia referred to as second- or third-generation migrants? The identification with migration often continues long after the physical act of movement is over. A more extreme example of the limitation of the conventional definition of migrants is the failure to accommodate refugees who are stateless, or the indigenous people who have been displaced from their traditional territories. Given the political complexity in defining the migrant, and the ongoing cultural dimensions of migration, two commonplace assumptions need to be questioned from the outset. First, the migrant can no longer be represented solely within the sociological typology of the 'marginal man'. Second, migration cannot be seen as either a temporary or purely negative process in modern society.

At the crux of the problematic of defining the migrant is also the issue of the effectiveness of the nation-state as a regulator of entrants across its borders. There are no reliable records on the total number of illegal migrants or refugees. Some nations are buckling under the pressure of the rising flows of refugees and migrants. Iran is presently host to the greatest number of refugees, over four million. The collapse of the civil order in one region impacts on the resources of another as refugees flee for safety. The burden of the most recent conflicts is often carried by states which are least equipped to bear it. African states like Malawi, Ethiopia and Kenya have been far more 'generous' than any of the affluent western states. While it was the western states which, at the end of the Second World War, had the perspicacity to define the rights of refugees and the responsibilities of the world community, according to the United Nation's High Commissioner for Refugees it is these very states which are closing their doors to refugees, imposing more barriers to deflect flows, and forcibly repatriating asylum-seekers.[7]

Despite the growing awareness that certain social problems have a global impact, the dominant political responses to migration and asylum are invariably proposed to fit national priorities. In the face of global migration and the complex forms of displacement, national policies on immigration controls and asylum quotas, no matter how they are justified in terms of protecting the economic interests of their own communities, can appear as both unjust and ultimately unsustainable. Under what terms should one community offer hospitality to a stranger? Derrida has argued that the principle of hospitality should not be premised on the prior identity of the stranger. Hospitality should not be confined to 'those' whom 'we' already deem worthy because 'they' are already familiar to 'us', or 'we' find 'them' potentially useful. Their identity or utility should not be determined in advance, for the stranger comes, in Jacques Derrida's words, 'as an absolute arrival'. Their admission should not be based on the necessary assumption of assimilation. The condition of hospitality ought to be extended without the expectation of integrating the stranger into proper membership, or from the hope of gaining a return:

> What I have been saying about the absolute arrival cannot generate a politics in the traditional sense of the word: a policy which could be implemented by a State-nation. But whilst I realize that what I have been saying about the event and the arrival is impracticable and unpolitical from the point of view of this concept of politics, I still want to claim that any politics which fails to sustain some relation to the principle of unconditional hospitality has completely lost its relation to justice.[8]

As racist ideologies against migrants and refugees gain ascendancy in many western countries, political leaders increasingly avoid any moral considerations in determining their national policies on migration quotas. There is the persistent belief that government policies should reflect national economic interests, rather than the ideals of morality and justice. Protecting local communities from global problems has been a feature of political practice which may appear as legitimate, even if it involves making decisions which contradict the principles of justice. The crippling burden of debt in the Third World clearly benefits the banks in the First World, but also by stimulating new lines in global migration indirectly places greater pressures on the policing of national boundaries. No nation has ever been able totally to control its own borders. Every attempt to restrict the flows only produces more innovation and resilience in the the illegal methods. Senior immigration and police officers in the United States and Australia have recently acknowledged that the ability of the state to discern the motivations of tourists, or students entering legally but intending to overstay their visas, to anticipate the tactics of organized syndicates which smuggle in migrants, to ensure that their agents are upholding and applying their directives, or have the ability to perceive new loopholes, is looking less and less effective. Migration has made Raymond Williams's prophecy, that nation-states are now too small for the big problems of contemporary life, and too big for the small problems, appear more and more accurate.[9]

Old routes and new borders

In the vast sociological literature on migration the predominant factor in the calculus of movement has been economic benefit. The motivation for the movement of people, from one place to another, is primarily attributed to the possibility of generating greater economic profit. Employers see migrants as a cheap source of labour, and migrants supposedly leave their homelands in search of greater prosperity. The identity of the migrant has thus been tied to this economic calculation of opportunity over exploitation. Before we accept that this equation is a satisfactory definition of the identity of the migrant, a few more probing questions are necessary. What distance needs to be covered before we speak of migration? Are there other 'invisible' boundaries that must also be crossed before the migrant approaches the national borders? Is economic survival at the centre of migration, or is the journey the first step in the pursuit of a personal dream of cultural progress? Do migrants leave home out of necessity or do they head out for new opportunities? These questions of geography and cultural transformation problematize the distinction between voluntary and involuntary movement. For, if economics is not the only factor that stimulates migration, then the sociological literature on migration must also be read in conjunction with the debates in the disciplines of politics, cultural studies and psychology.

The parameters of choice and coercion in migration are difficult to define. Is the decision to leave made out of individual aspiration or collective needs? Do migrants go to foreign countries to offer economic assistance to their parents, or to provide their children with greater educational opportunities? The constraints of the past and the possibilities of the future are carefully weighed in every decision to migrate. From such a perspective the question of personal choice may simply seem like the wrong question. It gives too much attention to the individual's present action, and blurs the complex networks of responsibilities that link a person to the past and future.

The distinction between voluntary and involuntary need not be determined purely by the relative absence or presence of coercion. A broader understanding of displacement would also allow us to see a relationship between the people who have felt compelled to leave their homeland, and those who have been expelled. Phillip Corrigan has convincingly argued, that while the words 'slavery' and 'migration' connote separate worlds, these forms of displaced labour should not be conceptualized as exclusive categories operating in distinctive time frames. It is unhelpful to confine the brutality of slavery to an irrational and earlier social system, just as it is misleading to stress the freedom and mobility of the individual migrant. Both the terms, 'slave' and 'migrant', could be seen as expressing different technologies for the exploitation of unfree labour, and as located along a continuum of 'coercive circulation'.[10]

Stephen Castles has also stressed that the category of migrant needs to be defined in relation to other traditional terms like indentured labourer, refugee and exile, as well qualifying and distinguishing the various modern forms of these terms.[11] Migrant workers have always been exposed to the sharpest edges of the contradictions in the ideology of the free-market economy. There is little about their conditions of work which they are 'free to choose'. They have fewer legal and welfare rights, are often subject to limited terms of contract, and excluded from certain professions. It is therefore not inappropriate to compare labour migrants with the various forms of 'unfree labourers' ranging from colonial slaves, bonded labourers in the industrial workhouses, forced labourers in concentration camps and the ghettoes of apartheid.

Any current definition of the migrant must also address a complex array of sexual, political, economic and cultural forms. The political realignments of the so-called new world order, the shifts in production patterns due to globalization, and the restructuring of gender-and-global development projects, have stimulated both new patterns of movement and created new obstacles. Collapsing empires and emerging power blocs like NAFTA and the EU, deindustrialization in the west and outsourcing in the periphery, international feminism and micro-credit schemes to third world women, have all challenged the conventional categories by which we defined migrant workers.[12] How do we now measure the distance between legal and illegal immigrants; permanent settlers versus temporary migrants who move backwards and forwards across borders; economically privileged entrepreneurs and manual guest-workers; émigrés who have left their homeland out of a perceived sense of lack of cultural opportunities and the corporate itinerants who seek professional enhancement abroad. Similarly, the forms of coercive displacement that force refugees to flee must include factors like ecological disaster and 'ethnic cleansing'.

Attention to the complex forms of migration is necessary because an examination of the paths of movement, and the rights of entry and exit, may give further insight into the uncertain world we are living in. The difference between being defined as an economic migrant, as compared to a political refugee, can mean either deportation or asylum. The legality of migration has once again become a volatile issue. Politicians anxious to impress a confused electorate would sooner draw on a rhetoric of vilification than elaborate national responsibilities to minorities and asylum-seekers undertaken in the international conventions on human rights. For instance, Margaret Thatcher's notorious remark that Britain was being 'swamped' was echoed and amplified almost a decade later by a whole chorus of ministers from the Tory cabinet in the 1993 Blackpool convention. Michael Portillo, Michael Howard and Peter Lilley unashamedly mimicked foreign accents for cheap laughs, mocked foreigners for speaking the language of thieves and accused resident Europeans of being scroungers on 'Crook's Tours' of British benefits.[13] This discourse of blame and punishment is symptomatic of both the racist projection onto vulnerable individuals, and the anxieties caused by loss of control over policy and regulation that occurred in the context of the European Union. Migration only becomes illegal when new laws are made to restrict movement. As Britain takes an ever more aggressive role in tightening the gates of 'fortress Europe', the migrations that were legal in the times of the Commonwealth are now deemed illegal.

Just as the intellectual distinction between legal and illegal migration has become more difficult to make, the jurisdiction of both national and international courts has also been contested. Decisions to restrict migration are consistently made in the face of the glaring uneven development and the prevailing historical links between places. As Britain moved towards higher levels of political integration with Europe, this produced conflicting responses on immigration policies and border controls. For instance, in 1995 the British Home Secretary Michael Howard was in almost continuous conflict with the High Court as he sought to restrict the flow by publishing a list of countries from which Britain would not consider claims for asylum, and others which were deemed to be safe third countries to which asylum-seekers would be returned; increasing visa restrictions; placing legal burdens and policing functions upon employers; and removing the right to an oral hearing to establish the case for asylum.[14] As one legal commentator noted, the criteria that he specified had become so severe that had Howard's own father, who was a post-war Jewish refugee, tried to gain asylum under the current terms, he would have been refused entry.

Globalization has propelled people in uncertain directions. It has also made us more aware of the interconnections between places. Our consciousness of how space may be open or closed has been heightened by these transformations. The concept of the border has thus come to the centre of theoretical discussion.[15] Borders can no longer be seen purely as those permanent and natural geographic markers of territory. They are socially constructed lines from which we can identify different political and cultural constituents. Borders are flexible. Historically they have both shifted in order to make sense of changes in social relations, and been dismantled by sheer force. The German borders, for instance, have shifted on no less than five occasions since 'unification' in 1871. It is the presence of a border which distinguishes 'us' from 'them'. National identity is mostly defined through this artificial opposition. Clarity is sharpened by this process of exclusion. The identity of the citizen presupposes the other, the migrant, the exile. Identity emerges, not just from the identification of the common characteristics for those who are included within the nation, but from the more visible difference of those excluded. The national question: 'Who are we?' is largely answered by declaring: 'We are not them.'

The regulation of movement across borders is always selective. Borders are never rigidly closed or totally open, they remain relatively porous. Borders are like invisible lines that separate nation-states, but are also like firm contracts that connect them. The difficulties of defining territorial demarcations are often linked with confused definitions of citizenship and foreignness.[16] The problem of citizenship has remained unresolved since the birth of democracy. Citizenship in the ancient Greek polis presupposed a common lineage, language and cultural experience amongst its members. While the concept of blood descent has been incorporated through *ius sanguinis* into the definition of citizenship rights in many modern nation-states, notably Germany, the most inclusive laws of citizenship, as defined by the French in 1889 by *ius soli* were those which defined nationality in terms of place of birth.[17] The laws of citizenship in Germany give preference to the 'blood' of subjects over their place of birth. The *Gastarbeiter*, guest-workers recruited to work on industrial projects since the 1960s, have always lived under a spiral of discriminatory laws. Not only are they restricted from certain professions and civic responsibilities, but they are liable to deportation at the end of their contracts, or at any time the state deems them a burden. Children of the *Gastarbeiter,* though born in Germany, have no automatic rights of citizenship and can, at best, eventually qualify for limited rights of residence. Whereas people of the Germanic diaspora, who had been dispersed across eastern Europe, and may no longer speak the German language, or have had any contact with the state for generations, are entitled to full citizenship and are offered welfare packages to encourage their 'return' to the motherland. For those with Germanic blood, citizenship is an automatic right, whereas for foreigners who legally reside in the country, and their German-born children, 'naturalization' is the exception. In 1974 immigration by recruitment was banned, and, according to Blaschke, since the 1980s the left, the right and the Green party have all agreed that 'the immigration boat in Germany was indeed full and that it was time one admitted openly that immigrants could be allowed in only within the bounds of quotas.'[18]

The political discourse on the formation of nation-states conceives of the border primarily as a protective device. It seeks to screen the passage of people and goods in order to defend the interests of its own economy and political structures. However, these regulations are constantly undergoing selectivity and intensification. Passages across borders are checked by the power differentials and historical links between neighbouring states, as well as the perceived economic value, cultural status and linguistic skills of individual migrants. For instance, well after Britain and France had ceded control over their colonies, the most significant flows of migrants to these countries were still being driven by the legacy of colonialism. Global migration, although not confined to these established paths, continues to follow geographic routes and rely on socio-economic systems of exploitation that have been in place since the fifteenth century. Lydia Potts has argued that there is a continuum between the rationale behind the various forms of forced migration of slaves and coolies, and the modern cost-benefit analyses which motivate the movement of 'free wage labour':

> Between the colonial phase of the world market for labour power and the second phase, which extends into the present day and encompasses the import into the metropole of living labour, there have been a number of developments of a continuous nature. Present-day labour migration and the brain drain, like the slavery and coolie systems and the fascist system of forced labour, are all methods of importing living labour. The fact that the calculations of profitability used by slave-traders as early as the sixteenth century are still common is a clear indication of this.[19]

In the context of global migration the concept of the border needs to be radically re-examined. Borders are the most racialized and militarized zones on the political map. The so-called defence of the nation-state against the 'invasion' of migrants is happening in the USA and in Europe, at precisely the same time as the signing of new free-trade agreements, and the encouragement of greater flexibility and mobility of the workforce within these regions. Europe is haunted by the presence of over 12 million 'non-European Europeans'. 'Race' has become the most contested issue in American politics. Anxiety over migration and difference is part of a broader uncertainty over the form of society. Stephen Castles and Mark Miller have argued that in the last decade there have been fundamental changes in the patterns of migration.[20] The scope of migration has significantly widened. Migrants are moving from a wider spread of geographic regions across the world. As more countries are incorporated into the global migration system there has also been a greater differentiation in the types of people seeking to move. The economic resources and professional skills of migrants vary significantly and the motivation of settlement is no longer the central feature of the journey. Migrants are more and more likely to be women, who have left their homelands and families for a temporary period to work in the service and manufacturing sectors of distant countries. Filipino, Bosnian and Mexican women are moving to the Gulf, Italy and the USA to work in the informal sector of the service industries. Simultaneously, booming manufacturing plants in south-east China are filled with women recruited from the outer rural provinces.[21] The deindustrialization of the west and decentralization of production have led to the large-scale mobilization of women in low-wage jobs. Saskia Sassen has argued that the incorporation of women in the workplace has been accompanied by both a cultural distancing from their place of origin and by short-term contractualization by their employers:

> Long-term employment in export factories is highly unlikely. All the evidence points to the average tenure being around five years. After that for a number of reasons women are laid off with little possibility of being employed in another firm, given the preference for women between sixteen and twenty-five years of age. These women, laid off and westernized, have few options.[22]

The itinerization and feminization of migration is a growing trend that was overlooked in the early literature. The stereotypical image of the migrant as the 'male urban peasant' reflected the mass migrations to the industrial centres of the west in the post-war period. However, this image has little resonance in the context of globalization with its more turbulent and dispersed streams of movement. The literature on migration must now concern itself more with the relationship between gender and mobility. By focusing on male entry into industrial projects, theorists have not noticed the arrival of women through family migration schemes, and also their key role in the service industries. Saskia Sassen has argued that women have been directly affected by the processes of globalization. As production in manufacturing and electronic assembly has been exported to the Third World, young women have been increasingly incorporated in the workforce as wage-labourers. In her studies of structural changes in the workforce of global cities, Sassen has stressed that while gender is not the determining factor in the shift towards the informalization of the economy, it is impossible to consider these economic transformations in isolation from the role of migrant women.[23]

The stranger in social theory

The contradictions between restless capital and captive labour are not fresh to social theory. Given that the significance of migration was recognized by Marx, Durkheim, Weber and Simmel, this failure to develop a more subtle understanding of the exilic forces of modern society, and a more complex vocabulary for referring to the different forms of migrants, is surprising. There are numerous explicit discussions of alienation, anomie, disenchantment and estrangement in classical social theory. In the absence of a general framework which can situate the relationship between migration and modernity, it would be useful to link together these various theoretical discussions.[24]

Marx was astutely aware of the multiple levels of displacement unleashed by capitalism. Perhaps his most memorable phrase, which appeared in the *Communist Manifesto*, 'all that is solid melts into air', can still stand as a metaphor for the logic of modernity. In this poetic phrase, we can see a prescient description of the trajectory of modernity. While Marx's predictions of progress have proved to be rather hollow, the value of his most general analysis of the process of transformation has been far more enduring. His understanding of the disruptive circulation of capital and labour is still relevant and offers a powerful critique of modernity. His theory of alienation, in relation to both the extraction of surplus value from labour and the separation of 'man' from his 'species being', as well as his theory of progress from the feudal bonds between peasantry and gentry to the industrial relations between capitalists and labourers, reflects a gender-blindness and follows a modernist teleology that is now considered untenable. One of Marx's most influential concepts, which has become a central plank in the sociology of migration, was his representation of the vulnerabilities of migrant labour and the perils of industrialization in terms of the 'reserve army' thesis.[25] According to this thesis, as capital expands and contracts in an erratic manner, there is always a requirement for flexible sources of labour. This thesis draws attention to the way capital treats labour as if it were an elastic commodity, one which can be stretched or released according to the cycle of production. This flexible source of labour has been provided by migrants. Marx noted that migrants were like a reserve army that could be pulled in from the flanks to serve a strategic role. In this position they had two functions: first, to fill gaps in the labour market; and second, to keep the cost of labour down.

Durkheim was also intensely aware of the profound impact that migration had on modern society. Cohesive social values, common sets of symbolic representations, shared assumptions about the moral world were, he argued, the necessary basis for the integration of the individual into society. Abrupt changes in social structures, and sudden shifts in the rate of mobility, could thereby loosen social structures. His theorization of the shift from traditional *mechanical solidarity* to modern *organic solidarity* was underpinned by the assumption that society is always a negotiated balance between consensus and difference.[26] Traditional societies, which privileged common values over individual ideas, provided strong social links. The individual's conceptions were constantly enveloped within a broader social outlook. However, in a modern society, which Durkheim characterized as highly differentiated and a mobile social order, the stress on individualism overtakes the commitment to common social values. As people take on more complex and specialized tasks, networks of obligation and patterns of interdependence are spread across broader spatial and social structures. In the formation of such systems, Durkheim argued that the individual can experience the sense of having been released from external constraints, but that this could also entail the loss of comprehensible public norms. Suicide was the extreme case of the breakdown of social regulation. Durkheim read the rate of suicide as an index of the individual's sense of moral disconnection. He proposed the term *anomie* to address those conditions in which individuals were unable to connect their own practices with broader social values and were thus left in a state of relative normlessness.[27] In Durkheim's view, to be liberated from traditional constraints does not only provide the basis of modern freedom, but also exposes the individual to the threat of falling into an anomic state. Once disconnected from their rural-traditional societies, and not yet integrated into urban modern culture, migrants confronted the potential risks of anomie. Durkhiem stressed that new urban societies needed to develop new forms of social bonds and to place checks upon unrestrained individualism.

From Marx's economistic and Durkheim's moral perspectives, migrants were more exposed to the perils of modernity. Being separated from both their original homeland, and having few ties to their place of arrival, they were placed in an ambiguous social position. This lack of allegiance to a local labour force, and their exclusion from social networks and political institutions heightened their vulnerability. Their identity was as suspect as their tenure. They could be exploited without any protection from other political groups, just as they could switch allegiances to secure more profitable arrangements. Although migrants have historically been as willing as any other member of the working class to defend and extend the rights of labour, their loyalty to local political cultures has always been subjected to a racist 'double scrutiny'.[28]

This stereotyping of migrants as politically suspect and the intellectual ambiguity of their social identity is symptomatic of a deeper uncertainty that surrounds the relationship between migration and modernity. In some instances, the migrant experience has been evoked in positive terms. Robin Cohen's reading of Weber has led him to observe that there is a 'complex affinity' between migration and capitalism.[29] For while the outsider experience of migration can be seen in threatening terms, which may nullify all sense of meaningful existence and engulf one's perception of purposeful direction, it may also present new opportunities for self-invention. Displacement can create unexpected associations and furnish novel connections. The other side of Weber's examination of the processes of modernization through rationalization and bureaucratization which led to the 'iron cage of disenchantment', was a new spirit for self-invention and social transformation.

While the structural forms of change in everyday life were carefully mapped by the classical theorists, the actual experiences of displacement were not examined in any detail. Their attempt to understand the dynamics of complex societies were confined to the dominant institutional forms like the bureaucracy, normative structures and patterns of ownership. Hence while Marx, Durkheim and Weber charted the transformations in the spheres of economic production, institutional cohesion and bureaucratic organization, and although their critiques were firmly guided by their conceptualization of alienation, anomie and disenchantment, the complex links and ruptures between the substantive social changes and the personal experiences of displacement in modernity have been often left underexamined.

Perhaps the most astute appreciation of the complexity of displacement can be found in the writings of Georg Simmel. Throughout his work we discover a constant endeavour to represent, at both a substantive and a methodological level, a representation of the ambivalent and uneven tensions of early modernity. His classic study of money was an examination of how the dialectical process of freedom and slavery was embedded in this form of commodification and exchange. Simmel's writing is unique in that it set out to represent the inner experience of estrangement alongside the rapid torsion of the modern metropolis. He saw the stranger, and in particular the *flâneur*, as emblematic figures in modernity. Simmel's attention to the differing levels of displacement in these figures enabled him to declare that the essence of modernity as such is *psychologism*, the experiencing and interpretation of the inner world in terms of the *reactions of our inner life*, and indeed as an inner world, the dissolution of fixed contents in the fluid elements of the soul, from which all that is substantive is filtered and whose *forms are merely forms of motion.*[30]

This definition is typical of Simmel's intricate weaving of the fluid patterns that shape the forms of inner experience and social interaction. Modernity is defined by this perpetual presentation of the new as a break with the past. The shift from one state of being to another carries with it a change in historical consciousness. The more rigid social structures are substituted for fluid forms which are constituted through the connections between the 'externalities of life' and the 'ultimate decisions concerning the meaning and style of life'.[31] The external and concrete reality of social relations is thus in a state of constant interplay with inner forms whose reality is composed of multiple images which must be internalized and individualized. This pressure to experience the social as part of the inner self requires a greater degree of 'processing' of the external stimuli. Given the intensity and volume of signs that circulate in the modern metropolis, modernity becomes associated with a heightened state of nervousness and distanciation.

The interaction between the familiar and the foreign was also at the centre of Simmel's essay on the stranger.[32] This short essay can be read as one of the most insightful accounts of the subjectivity of migrants. He portrayed the identity of the stranger as someone who has come from elsewhere, whose language and practices are foreign, whose sense of attachment is partial, whose historical presence challenges the basis for social integration, and whose 'contrary' perceptions offer a different perspective from which to establish critical judgements. In Simmel's writing the stranger is not just a social type, nor is it an empirical study of a solitary figure who wanders and has no fixed relationship to place. Rather, the identity of the stranger is highlighted to illuminate the subjective experience of ambivalence. In the constant process of interacting with different types of strangers, Simmel argued that modern subjects develop social mechanisms which can facilitate both an accelerated experience of intimacy and the establishment of sharper barriers of indifference. The concentration of difference in the modern metropolis stimulated new forms of indifference towards others. Simmel defined this tension as a process of oscillation along the twin axioms of 'nearness and farness'. The figure of the stranger is also proposed as a metaphor for understanding the new modes of cultural transformation in modernity. By focusing on the 'marginal' figure of the stranger, Simmel highlights distinctive modes of perception and redefines the gravity of social relationships. Through the stranger's metaphorical mode of seeing difference in all images of similitude, and the experience of estrangement Simmel also questions the means of solidarity, the structures of community and the sense of belonging in modernity. The presumption that social bonds are defined by purity of origin, and based on an exclusive characteristic, is undermined, he argues, by the ambivalent presence of strangers. Simmel thereby claims that the most responsive visions of modernity are sustained, not by the consolidation of the unified Renaissance perspective, but through the dynamic incorporation of alternative viewpoints.

Simmel understood how the experience of modern life was constituted out of an ongoing sense of displacement. Like Baudelaire, he believed that the broad structural ruptures were most visible in the superficial and transitory fragments of everyday life. The dissolution of stable forms of experiencing the flows of time and the dilemmas over feeling attached to a place in a lasting way produced what Simmel called 'neurasthenic forms'. The culture of the metropolis is defined as 'uprooted', anonymous and overcrowded. Modern subjects struggle to see a pattern and to experience continuity within the permanent flux of the city. The collision of signs was as fleeting and as intense as the shock of strangers. The density of ephemeral signs and proximity to strangers created a peculiarly modern attitude of inner indifference. Bombarded by heightened activity and overwhelmed by urgency, people develop a blasé attitude to the world: they witness adversity and intensity without feeling pain or excitement. Interactions between people in modern societies, as opposed to traditional societies, were characterized by this prevailing sense of neurotic restlessness. The image of a modern crowd is not interpreted as a sign of social solidarity, but as connoting the paradoxical sense of being surrounded by others and yet feeling isolated. This prevailing sense of anonymity in a mass society produces a peculiar indifference to the particularity of each event and individual. Numbness and blankness become the common face with which to deal with the abrupt switching, multiple encounters and heightening of stimuli in everyday life. Simmel noted the lack of critical and emotional resources for coping with modern life: 'There is perhaps no psychological phenomenon that is so unreservedly associated with the metropolis as the blasé attitude. The blasé attitude results first from the rapidly changing and closely compressed contrasting stimulation of the nerves.'[33]

In a pessimistic extension of Simmel's idea of estrangement and the blasé attitude, Richard Sennett has argued that the distance in the modern metropolis between private and public life has become further polarized. He characterizes the dilemmas of metropolitan life through a series of oppositions: the inside is considered real whereas the outside is superficial; wholeness of being is personal; fragmentation occurs through continuous exposure to the social. These oppositions, he argues, were first articulated in Baudelaire's depiction of modern life. The bourgeoisie of late nineteenth-century Paris languish and writhe in *ennui*; they are both bored and restless: bored by the absence of the vital spark of purpose and struck by the unwinding restlessness of indecision. Baudelaire's description of the inner weariness and solitude of Parisians provides Sennett with the starting-point for his judgement of contemporary urban life:

New York should be the ideal city of exposure to the outside. It grasps the imagination because it is a city of differences par excellence, a city collecting its population from all over the world. Yet it is here that the passion of the Parisian poet – that desire for enhancement of stimulation and release from self – seems contravened . . . All the more is this true – more largely – of the races, who live segregated lives close together, and of social classes, who mix but do not socialize.[34]

Sennett's key concept for describing the modern city is the fear of 'exposure'. In Sennett's view, people confront or pass by each other at a higher rate, but the intensity of sociability is constantly diminishing. The indifference that he describes is one which emerges from the refusal to drop barriers. 'A city of difference and of fragments of life that do not connect: in such a city the obsessed are set free.'[35] He laments that, in order to survive in a modern city, one must adopt a selective focus, one cannot 'take in' the whole picture. The struggle of modern urban culture that he depicts is bound by the search for an absent form of social consciousness and the sharp presence of a unique and solitary perspective which he sees as a partial state of anaesthesia, a 'clarity that deadens'.[36] Feminist critics like Elizabeth Wilson and Doreen Massey have argued that this melancholic tone over city culture is one which specifically pertains to men. The fear of disorder and incoherence in the metropolis is linked to a deeper failure to grasp the significance of new forms of energy and vitality.[37]

The pace and form of social change have reached such unprecedented levels that the identity Simmel gave to the stranger may now require revision. Differences have compounded, and the encounters with strangers have intensified to such a degree that the distinctions that were central to Simmel's conceptualization are no longer the critical marker of difference. Simmel defined the stranger as 'the potential wanderer'. The stranger has always come from elsewhere. Strangers not only lack roots and attachments to the place they are in, but also have 'the freedom of coming and going'. Simmel gave particular stress to the qualities that a stranger can bring to a group, but these qualities gain their distinctiveness only insofar as the group is also defined as both homogeneous and settled. The stranger's identity is defined through the oscillation between being inside and outside the group. However, for this dynamic position to be established at the borders of the group, another static position is implied at its centre. It presumes that despite the complexity of the city, the settled centre comprises a homogeneous core built out of specific traditions.[38]

The relation between the local and the stranger, which in Simmel's analysis presupposed alterity and difference, may now have changed. There is no doubt that the encounter with strangers has multiplied dramatically since Simmel's time. However, as Sighard Neckel argues, in a global society which is characterized by economic interdependence, media cross-linking, spatial mobility and cultural standardization, our prior knowledge and tacit expectations of strangers have also become an active part of the social world.[39] As the stranger is no longer at the margins of social existence, the relationship to alterity has become embedded in the norms of everyday practices. Strangers are both more manifest, and knowledge of them has become more active and reflexive. This implies that a greater proximity has not necessarily entailed increasing indifference and distanciation, but rather has produced an ambivalent incorporation, or the abject elimination of the stranger from the social. The stranger is not just a subject that is selectively incorporated, or withheld from intimate social relations, but also the vilified and abused object upon which the ills of the social are concentrated.

A further consequence of the radical encounter with difference in global society is the rethinking of the boundaries between the stranger and the local. For the stranger's difference to offer a critical vantage, the local community must presuppose an identity that is characterized as unified and homogeneous. As the presence of strangers has multiplied, the contemporary experience of ambivalence has taken more jagged forms. Julia Kristeva has noted that, with the growing proximity to strangers, there has been an intensification of aggressivity against them. Her strategy, in countering this volatile reaction, is not to defend the specific qualities of strangers, but to turn the questioning towards the very categories of identity. This new level of critique has shifted the ground: the stranger is no longer defined in opposition to the settled citizen, but rather from within the parameters of belonging. To define the characteristics of strangers, Kristeva does not commence from an outline of their unique or distinctive qualities, which may or may not be interpreted as a gain for the settled community, but rather she turns to examine the degree to which we are all strangers. If identity cannot be conceived other than through the process of reflecting on what Kristeva has termed 'the strangers to ourselves', then who is not a stranger?

> The image of hatred and of the other, a foreigner is neither the romantic victim of our clannish indolence nor the intruder responsible for all the ills of the polis. Neither the apocalypse on the move nor the instant adversary to be eliminated for the sake of appeasing the group. Strangely, the foreigner lives within us: he is the hidden face of our identity, the space that wrecks our abode, the time in which understanding and affinity founder. By recognizing him within ourselves, we are spared detesting him in himself. A symptom that precisely turns 'we' into a problem, perhaps makes it impossible. The foreigner comes in when the consciousness of my difference arises, and he disappears when we all acknowledge ourselves as foreigners, unamenable to bonds and communities.[40]

Kristeva is aware that the identity of the stranger can no longer be confined to the classical image of harbinger, or the romantic notion of the outsider. The study of the stranger is no longer marginal to social investigation. Thinking about strangers is not an intellectual luxury, or an occasional option, but a necessity of everyday life. Kristeva also suggests that the representation of the stranger requires a new writing practice. Strangers exist in a diversity of forms and there can be no single typification which covers all experiences. With detailed elegance and profound historical force, Kristeva has charted the contradictory insights and extreme passions of strangers. Through her multifaceted portrait of the condition of estrangement we witness the limits of what it is to be human and revisit the conditions of the social. To avoid the pitfalls of objectification she takes the musical form of toccata and fugue as an analogous mode for sketching out the identity of the stranger, in all 'its perpetual motion through some of its variegated aspects'.[41] Strangers in all their clownish ebullience, their black silences, their irritable pushiness, their torpid solitude, their wandering longing for affiliation, their aloofness towards reality, their defensive paranoia, their celebration of the orphan's freedom, their humble sacrifice in the brutality of work, and in all their perverse pleasure, become symbols in her 'kaleidoscopic' view of culture.

This movement in and out of the different lives is a powerful celebration of the rights and creative potential of strangers, it stimulates the empathy that we feel for others, and radically extends the boundaries for defining the self, but while it suggests bridges across historical and cultural divides, it still leaves the counter-question open: who is *not* a stranger? Are we all, to a degree, strangers? Strangers are defined in every practice which involves the separation of people according to those who belong and those who are excluded from, say, the family, the clan, the group, the community, the nation. The stranger is conventionally defined in a negative fashion: always the one that is other to 'us'. For this definition to continue, however, there need to be fixed social structures which bond one group to another. In modern society, the formal distinction between strangers and locals is mostly defined in terms of citizenship. The stranger is defined as the one who does not have the same nationality. Yet modern society is increasingly generating social, cultural and commercial relations which have scant regard for national citizenship. How valid is the national identity of the stranger in this context? Where are the stable identifications against which the stranger is defined? As the boundaries between 'us' and 'them' have become more fluid has it made 'them' more vulnerable to violation?

The gender of the stranger

Marx, Durkheim and Weber, who provided the foundations of sociological thought, remained preoccupied with changes in public life and the workplace. Simmel was unique in that he sought to connect these visible forms of social change with the private and 'invisible' aspects of experience. In this respect he entered a zone that was previously marginal to social investigation and which could have led to a further critique of the public–private division. This opposition was subsequently central to feminist debates on the gender-blindness in sociology. In this respect a number of feminists have considered the example offered by Simmel and asked the question: is the stranger a gendered figure? It is important to question the gender of the stranger, for if classical theory assumed that women's experiences could be subsumed by men's, then this would reveal a significant limitation in its conceptual framework. To imply that the abstract figure of the stranger can embrace women's subjectivity could be seen as a strategy which either renders the identity of women invisible or provides a space of affinity which enables the identification of both connections and differences.

The response to the concept of the stranger by feminist critics has been contradictory. Janet Wolff has argued that the experience of women could not be compared with that of a stranger, for their presence was even more marginalized and their freedom of movement was more restricted. With the example of George Sand, a woman who wrote with a male pseudonym and who dressed in men's clothes in order to take part in Parisian nightlife, Janet Wolff demonstrates that the identity of the stranger represented a idealized position that was to be desired, rather than one reflecting the everyday experience of women. Wolff quotes from Sand to illustrate how the guise of the stranger was a form of liberation for the female author:

> So I had made for myself a *redingote-guérite* in heavy gray cloth, pants and vest to match. With a gray hat and a large woollen cravat, I was a perfect first-year student. I can't express the pleasure my boots gave me: I would have gladly slept with them, as my brother did in his young age, when he got his first pair. With those little iron-shod heels, I was solid on the pavement. I flew from one end of Paris to the other. It seemed to me that I could go around the world.[42]

In George Sand's writing, the identity of a woman was defined in terms of being static and homebound, her movement dependent on male accompaniment. This restriction stands in contrast to Simmel's concept of the stranger, where there is a freedom that comes with anonymity and mobility. When George Sand parades as a man she sees herself as the perfect stranger, she is an 'atom lost in that immense crowd'.[43] Inconspicuous as a stranger, woman finds her freedom and safety through lack of identity. From this Wolff concludes that the position of a woman in modernist literature was always as an object trapped by the regulating male gaze.

What Wolff does not address in Sand's account of the stranger's freedom through a 'lack' of identity is that this security is also supported by a plenitude in class and race privilege. Working-class men and black labourers did not enjoy the same unrestricted mobility that Sand describes. This complex interrelationship between the social divisions of race, class and gender has been the subject of investigation for the contemporary American artist Adrian Piper. The cross-hatching of racialized and sexualized boundaries over the body of the stranger was explicitly addressed in her *Mythic Being* performances conducted in the early 1970s. As a woman, who often 'passes' as white and middle-class, Piper sought to explore the changes of response to her identity when she changed her persona. For instance, when she dressed as a black man and entered the New York subway, she noted that her presence was immediately transformed from that of potential victim, to likely perpetrator of violence. As she spread her legs, while sitting on the train, it was fear that she recognized in the eyes of the other. This response was heightened through the performance of 'mugging' her white boyfriend in a public park. These experiences forced her to write.

> I am the racist's nightmare, the obscenity of miscegenation. I am a reminder that segregation is impotent; a living embodiment of sexual desire that penetrates racial barriers and reproduces itself. I am the alien interloper, the invisible spy in the perfect disguise who slipped past the barricades in an unguarded moment. I am the reality of successful infiltration that ridicules the ideal of assimilation (Funk Lessons). I represent the loathsome possibility that everyone is 'tainted' by black ancestry: If someone can look and sound like me and still be black, who is unimpeachably white.[44]

Piper, like Sand, is concerned with the sense of having crossed a social boundary, but their views of the other side of identity are very different. When Sand dressed as the perfect bourgeois she experienced freedom, but when Piper presented herself as a black man there is only the bristling sense of hostility. In Sand's case, we see how anonymity and masculinity enable mobility and autonomy, whereas in Piper's experience, the here-and-now encounter between men and women of different colour, or what she calls 'xenophobia and the indexical present', is constrained and closed by the preceding stereotypes of racial and sexual differences. Whose freedom is Wolff invoking in order to highlight the conspicuous public scrutiny and the profound domestic confinement of women? Which strangers can bypass class barriers and elude the racial stigma of otherness? Wolff's critique of the stranger suffers from the same practice of idealizing difference that she attacks in Simmel. Just as the stranger's qualities cannot be defined in opposition to the static habits of citizens, neither can women's oppression in modernity be defined against the putative freedom of the stranger.

The relationship between the stranger and the *flâneur* also requires an interrogation from their respective privileges of race and class. For the *flâneur* was an aesthete whose attention to the world was, as Baudelaire defined it, focused on all that was 'ephemeral, fugitive and contingent'. The *flâneur* loved the novelties of the industrial age, but had no need to work. He was captivated by the life of the underworld, but kept at a safe distance from prisons. He would live in arcades and cafés and never have to worry over domestic duties. The *flâneur* celebrated the life of the detached urban witness as he went 'botanizing on the asphalt'.[45]

In the literature of early modernity, the *flâneur* became a heroic figure, insofar as his whimsical fancies and disdain for all that was conventional could be interpreted as a critique of the stolid and frigid morality of the bourgeoisie. While the *flâneur* remained aloof from the ethos of industrialization, Elizabeth Wilson argues that he nevertheless embodied an aesthetic and cultural sensibility that was specific to and critical of modernity:

> In literature, the *flâneur* was represented as an archetypal occupant and observer of the public sphere in the rapidly changing and growing cities of nineteenth-century Europe. He might be seen as a mythological or allegorical figure who represented what was perhaps the most characteristic response of all to the wholly new forms of life that seemed to be developing: ambivalence.[46]

In Janet Wolff's rejection of the stranger and *flâneur* as conceptual analogues for the representation of woman's experience, considerable stress is given to their ambiguous attachment to place. She concludes that 'these heroes of modernity thus share the possibility and the prospect of lone travel, of voluntary uprooting, of anonymous arrival at a new place.'[47] Wilson is not so quick to dismiss the figure of the stranger, and in particular the *flâneur*. By focusing on the *flâneur*'s expression of a cultural sensibility, rather than the access to public spaces, she suggests that there is a perspectival affinity between the position of the *flâneur* and of women. Wilson does not overlook the differences in domesticity and mobility, between the *flâneur* and women, but she also sees a political gesture of solidarity with women *in* the *flâneur*'s cultural practice. For the really heroic task that every stranger and the *flâneur* must confront, she argues, is to rebuild an identity that has been fragmented or eviscerated by the forces of modernity. In this respect, Elizabeth Wilson goes against the grain of much feminist criticism which had condemned the *flâneur* for his voyeuristic tendencies. In the *flâneur*'s defence, she argues, that his voyeurism is not synonymous with the masculine sexuality which seeks possession through penetration. The sexual economy of the *flâneur* is not to possess but to observe, and she concludes that 'the disturbed glance of the *flâneur*' offered a challenge to bourgeois patriarchy.[48]

By forging a link between the *flâneur*'s critical gaze, and the stranger's foreign qualities and the experiences of women in modernity, Wilson is able to establish a common way of seeing change in the world. Strangers, *flâneurs* and women all embodied the fragmentary structure of urban life. The form of their life-narratives resembled a complex collage. They expressed a residual sense that something was missing from contemporary life. Certitudes were deferred and conclusions left open-ended. Their perpetual contact with 'newness' also carried with it the tinge of melancholia and nostalgia. Just as the *flâneur* presented a peculiar critique of the culture of progress and domination in modernity, the stranger's potential for 'voluntary uprooting' was checked by a series of political barriers. These contrasting readings of the relationship between gender and the mobility of the stranger highlight the difficulties of defining the agency of the migrant in modernity. There is no single experience which typifies all. Yet, in order to evaluate the differences and similarities in the experience of displacement between men and women, some level of abstraction is necessary. Wilson's intervention in the debate on the gender of the stranger and the alliance between the *flâneur* and women opened a fresh perspective on the emergence of links in critical sensibilities by different agents within modernity.

Conclusion

This debate between Wolff and Wilson highlights the need to re-examine the agency of different types of strangers, both between men and women and across racial and class divisions. Along with the need to rethink the identity of the migrant there is the complex task of understanding the relationship between modernity and migration. The dominant sociological models for explaining the causation of migration have stressed external forces. Movement occurs because there was either a force 'pushing' or 'pulling' the subject, or because of the collapse of traditional structures. These mechanistic models have usefully highlighted the structural causes; however, to understand the more complex processes of migration we need to examine the combined energy from the agency of the migrant and the spatial trajectories of movement. The mobility of signs and strangers in modernity has reached unprecedented levels. The density, velocity and multi-directionality of this mobility has baffled analysts and discredited many of the earlier models. It is now time to think of migration beyond a simple cause-and-effect paradigm and to see how it operates in a more complex and turbulent system. The way we define the identity of strangers will also impact on our view of the social. This requires not just a tolerance for certain types of strangers who can be accommodated within a predefined social space, but a more radical task of modelling a society that can include strangers without the compulsion to assimilate. The social definition of strangers is always closely linked to patterns of acceptance and rejection.

Modernity has thus far demonstrated an ambivalence towards strangers.[49] They are at the centre of its energy but outside its self-image. The narrative of the journey of modernity is unsettling: on the one hand, there is the melancholy of departure; on the other, the assumption that change will liberate us from the past. The modernist view of progress and contemporaneity implies a break with the past, which is often seen as limited and obsolete, whereas the future-present, by nature of its unknown qualities, is the space of potential and novelty. Values of positive and negative are similarly attributed dichotomously. It could be argued that the characteristic feature of modernity is the dominance of binarisms in all spheres of judgement. These binarisms are the direct result of mapping the journey of modernity in a linear mode, which is mono-directional and non-reversible. It is always assumed that what is left behind will be conveniently forgotten, that tradition is incompatible with a modern way of living, and that eventually society will develop mechanisms to eliminate waste. These visions of progress need to be revised. The journey to modernity was not always a departure from a culturally inferior but temporally anterior way of life. Modernity should not be situated at the apex of the historical hierarchy. Being modern, with all its historical claims to being part of the 'now', should not also mean being above all other forms of social and cultural organization, which can thereby be dismissed as anachronistic, out of time, pre-modern.

Part of the unhappy contradiction of the migrant sensibility is the chilling fear of having lost a certain sense of time and place. There is the impending awareness that, having left home, there is no possibility of a seamless return. Parallel to this loss is the anxious realization that having gained entrance to another space does not amount to a feeling of full acceptance. For many migrants the modernist promise of progress is often seen as a hollow victory. There is a part of the self that belongs only in another place and time, and no matter how hard one tries to recapture this identity, it never returns as a fully embodied self in the present. Germaine Greer's intervention in a debate on the politics of repatriation was a timely reminder of the bitter-sweet dreams of departure and return:

> There is an expression in English 'to make one's home' somewhere. I may be said to have made my home in England, but the English actually deny the right of the individual to make her home where she pleases. 'Do I detect an accent?' asks the optician/taxi-driver/door-to-door salesman. 'South Africa? New Zealand? Whereabouts in Australia? How long've you been here?' I too detect an accent, an accent of smug ignorance and confident superiority. . . . Just so, the migrant's adopted home is never home, but the migrant is too changed to be welcome in her old country. Only in her dreams will she see the skies of home. The ache of exile cannot be assuaged by travelling anywhere, least of all by retracing old steps looking for houses that have been bulldozed and landscapes that have disappeared under the urban sprawl and motorway. Home is one place that you can keep strangers out of; home, like the Englishman's castle, cannot be penetrated by outsiders. Because the ideology of home justifies chauvinism and racism, it is well that there is in creation no such place. . . . Failure to recognize the fact that the earthly home is a fiction has given us the anguish of Palestine. . . . The rest of us can face the fact that our earthly home is a journey away from home. Exile being the human condition, no government subsidy can provide the chariot that will carry us home.[50]

The equivocal status and ambivalent incorporation of the migrant within the nation-state reminds us of the need to rethink the conditions of belonging. The position of the migrant cannot be defined in absolute terms. Political, racial and sexual differences will never be transcended. There is no point in searching for equivalence or establishing a hierarchy among strangers, foreigners and migrants. However, the cultural affinities of the dispossessed may give us some new grounds for defining subjectivity. As Homi Bhabha noted, the migrant not only fails to slip into the allotted space, but also disrupts the mythical continuum between past and present. The awkward positioning of the migrant exposes the paradoxes and unanswered questions of modernity:

> How does one encounter the past as an anteriority that continually introduces otherness or alterity within the present? How does one then narrate the present as a form of contemporaneity that is always belated? In what historical time do such configurations of cultural difference assume forms of cultural and political authority?[51]

4

Globalization and Migration

Defining globalization

Since the 1980s the term 'globalization' has gained wide use in both popular and academic circles. It has been used, in various ways, to represent the perception of the world as an interconnected whole and the consciousness that a growing number of issues can no longer be addressed purely at a local level. Globalization has been predominantly associated with the flexible and spatially extended forms of production, the rapid mobility of capital, information and goods, the denationalizing of capital, the deterritorialization of culture, the interpenetration of local communities by global media networks, and the dispersal of socio-economic power beyond the Euro-American axis. These factors make the world seem more open and more interconnected. In the age of globalization the process of exchange and flow, it appears, is conducted on a series of smooth circuits that link distant places into a single time frame.

Yet, the social and economic relations that are characteristic of globalization can be linked to historical forms of polarization, marginalization and regulation. Globalization, it can be argued, was initiated by the expansion of world trade, the transformation of political structures and reinscription of cultural norms under colonization. From the late fifteenth century the European powers embarked on a project of exporting their own cultural practices and exploiting the resources of people across the world. Colonization laid the routes for globalization. The current discourse of new personal freedom and global interconnection masks complex forms of bondage and displacement. Despite the relative freedom of movement of capital and information, labour is subjected to increasing restrictions on entry and settlement. Border controls are now policed with the full array of military surveillance and pursuit techniques.

From the nuclear disaster in Chernobyl to the marshalling of a multinational strike force in the Gulf War, we have become aware of the complex ways in which a disturbance in one place can have implications beyond that territory. The key events which influence our everyday lives, the location of factories, the price of petrol, the content of the media, are often being defined with aims that have a global reach. However, there is little consensus over the way the local and the global have been reconfigured. On the one hand, globalization is interpreted as the formation of a total and integrated economic system, with greater level of polarization between the peripheries and more sophisticated forms of integration between the centres of power. On the other, it is seen as stimulating greater political interaction between states and promoting diversity in cultural identity.

While there is a growing awareness of the momentous changes that globalization entails, there is little consensus on the precise form that it takes. Three of the most prominent theorists who have written extensively on globalization have stressed different aspects. Roland Robertson, probably the first person to use the term, is concerned with the human experience of globalization. His work has focused on the way our consciousness of the world, and our sense of place in the world, have changed. Immanuel Wallerstein takes a more structuralist perspective and discusses globalization in terms of the economic and political integration of the world system. Ulf Hannerz draws on elements of this structuralist perspective, without privileging political economy, as he focuses on the transformation of cultural relations.[1] The sociological debates on globalization have reinvigorated two key theoretical issues: the relationship between structure and agency; and the future of the nation-state. This chapter will evaluate these debates from the perspective of global migration.

Clearly the globalizing processes do not spread evenly and in all directions simultaneously. Between the fears of an all-engulfing Americanized homogeneous culture and the hopes for postmodern heterogeneity, there are complex and often contradictory forces at play which are challenging the autonomy of nation-states. A brief list of the globalizing institutions, tendencies and forces would include: the formation of transnational bureaucracies and political institutions like the G7, World Bank, GATT and IMF; the porousness of boundaries caused by the mediatized dissemination of symbols, ideas, images, technologies and information; the pressure exerted by transnational corporations to elude local needs and rules; the restructuring of labour relations and the competition for cheaper wages; the centralization of capital investment practices in global cities; the contest between consumer culture and diasporic communities; and the formation of new political associations with multiple and overlapping networks of power that supplement the functions traditionally held by civic and national authorities. These forces and tendencies which summon the spectre of 'placeless capital' and the 'homeless subject' also have profound implications for the way we understand the dynamics of migration in modern society. At the centre of this debate is the dispute over whether the current traffic of goods, capital, symbols and people across borders involves a quantitative extension of the existing trends in the internationalization of capitalist relations, or whether we have entered a qualitatively new era called globalization.

Few critics in the debates over globalization would dispute the profound nature of change that has occurred in the past two or three decades. There can be little doubt that government policy, as the means for regulating social and economic life, has lost its ability to centralize and co-ordinate activities at either the national or the international level. The nation-state is in crisis. There now seems an irreversible trend towards cutting back social spending and welfare provision. The nature of this crisis may be revealed through the various ways in which capital is overtaking the techniques of governance as the state withers. One particular example may reveal the extent of this crisis: according to Weber the nation-state was defined as having a monopoly over the legitimate use of violence and coercion; yet, given the increasing privatization of prisons in the United States and the United Kingdom, and the superior numbers of private security guards over the regular police forces in these countries, this may spell the beginning of the end of the nation-state.

At the level of political economy, the markers of this crisis are fourfold. First, the governmental policies for the 'deregulation' of markets in the west. This did not announce the absence of all regulation of the market, but signalled the abolition of external controls on major currencies, facilitating investment in external markets and the trading of shares, equities and securities on a global scale. The demise of Keynesian social policies and the shift towards neo-liberal attitudes led to a massive programme of privatization and the withdrawal of the welfare state. The emergence of a consumer-led political culture and the contraction of the state, in its role of co-ordinating economic activity, supporting culture and academic research, was best summed up by the words of Ronald Reagan: 'government was not the solution but the problem.'[2] Second, the revolution of micro-electronics and optical fibre telecommunication, which has created a global network of trade as it has integrated the major stock markets. Third, the transfer of manufacturing and assembly production to newly industrializing countries. This has stimulated the evisceration of the inner-city areas of core industrial cities in the west as well as the bloating of newly industrializing metropolises in the Third World. Fourth, the relative stagnation of commodity trade and vast growth in the financial service sector.

The combined effect of these trends is that the bulk of global trade is now focused on speculative options, futures shares, insurance, finance and real estate, rather than in the commodity market. As the material value of the commodity decreases, and the constrictions of place for production and assembly are bypassed by capital flows, a number of critics have argued that we are witnessing the dematerialization and deterritorialization of the global economy.

Investment is less and less affected by the material cost of goods and physical distance of transportation, or by local government laws and trade union demands. The most significant costs in global trade are now increasingly concentrated in the financial services sector and the value-added 'design processes'. These new levels of research and development and design-intensity have heightened the symbolic value over the material content of commodities. Innovations and speculative ventures in financing production have also abstracted the role of the markets. Hence, the location of a factory, or the performance of labour, become secondary to the dissemination of an image and the calculation of the potential risks or gains of a commodity. We live in a time in which the promises implied by the name of a label are more significant than either the value of the material or the location of production. 'What is increasingly produced are not material objects, but signs.'[3] By extension the major players in the global economy are no longer manufacturers like Ford, but brokerage houses like Morgan Stanley. To use Lash and Urry's post-Fordist metaphor, it is the tail of financial services which is wagging the dog of industry.[4] Or, to put it in even more stark terms, borderless capital will not only lead to the demise of the nation-state as a geopolitical unit, but the new global division will divide the First and Second World in terms of service and production, and thereby entail the obsolescence of the Third World, which will function neither as a supplier of goods nor as a viable market.[5]

This grim prognosis has been borne out by the recent UN report on human development which claims that the share of world trade for the forty-eight least developed nations – representing 10 per cent of the world's population – has halved, to just 0.3 per cent, in the past twenty years, while the net wealth of ten billionaires is worth 1.5 times the combined national income of these forty-eight nations. It is also estimated that there are ninety-three countries which, by the end of 1997, are likely to have a per capita income below what it was between ten and forty years ago.[6] All the major economic indicators suggest that growth in the Third World has ceased and many countries have plunged into massive debt. With the collapse of the Soviet bloc, industrial production in places like Poland and Romania has also been reduced by 20–30 per cent. Countries like India which, since independence, have adopted protectionist national economies are now faced with the questions of sustainability and a deeper awareness of their limited powers to oppose global capital. Protectionist policies in India and Latin America were formed in a time when the international economy was still in its infancy.[7] If a nation-state opens its market to the mercantilist logic of the transnationals, then who will protect the people from the exploitative system that these oligopolies establish? But can any Third World nation-state develop a viable response to the globalizing pressures on its own? For most people in the world, globalization is not associated with greater access to commodities and communication, but with increasing deprivation and exploitation.

However, the turbulence of globalization is not confined to the Third World. Even in First World nations like Australia, the impact of globalization has also produced a disruptive and negative influence on economic and social life. Throughout the 1980s the economy was opened up to free-market forces, inflation eliminated, taxation and public spending reduced. State services were ruthlessly privatized and the manufacturing sector was decimated as it was exposed to competition with the neighbouring low-wage producers in south-east Asia. During this first wave of globalization the Labour government promoted Australia no longer in terms of a 'lucky country' blessed with boundless natural resources, but as the 'clever country' that would successfully shift the basis of its wealth to the service and information economy. They gambled with the future of the working class and by all accounts they lost. Unlike the process of expansion during industrialization, where new means of production and advances in mechanization, which displaced labour in one sector, tended to generate work in other areas, the shift to a post-industrial economy has not generated a proportionate expansion of the labour force. Manufacturing has been reduced to 25 per cent of all employment. Meanwhile the new service economy has not generated a net growth in full-time jobs for nearly a decade.[8]

Surpluses in the labour force and global competition have driven down wages, and along with the decline of the trade unions and the onset of long-term unemployment, new stresses have emerged within the structures that underpinned Australian society. Apart from an elite in the information and technology sector, the bulk of the population is experiencing a lowering of living standards. Abandoned manufacturing plants in the outer suburbs, and 'loft-living' in the inner city are reminders of how unevenly the restructuring of the economy impacts on community life. Globalization has produced both a more mobile transnational elite and an underclass trapped in new forms of dependency. Across the sprawling suburbs families and social networks are ripped apart by the new economic pressures. Women abandon their 'failing' husbands. Marginalized, isolated, frustrated and increasingly angry, men fall into a vicious cycle of abuse. Male suicide rates in Australia are now among the highest in the world. Individual insecurity, loneliness, social dislocation, long-term unemployment – these seem to be the heavy downside of globalization for the working class. In the face of all these challenges the current Liberal government of Australia remains resolute in its belief that the state best serves the nation by keeping out of the economy.

Globalization and the future of the nation-state

Globalization has exerted new pressures on the authority and autonomy of the nation-state. The integrity of the nation-state is threatened not only by the expansionist ambitions of other states and the conflict of insurrectionary forces within its territory, but also by the disruptive influence of transnational corporations. From the 1970s, as the debt of many Third World countries has exceeded their GNP, and First World governments witnessed the loosening of their grip on economic and social regulation, transnational corporations have gained in power.[9] Since the beginning of the 1990s there has been a growing trend which suggests that, of the hundred most important economic units in the world, half are transnational corporations.[10] Their economic objectives are primarily, if not solely, driven by profit maximization. Unlike government policies which are bound by territorial limitations, and which ought to balance economic priorities with social needs and cultural values, transnational corporations pursue unfettered paths in their economic activities. They are not confined to geopolitical boundaries, nor do they bow to local needs unless this in itself serves their interests. Unlike multinational corporations, which are headquartered in one country and whose senior decision-makers are also from that country, the transnational corporations have denationalized their entire operation, and their prime loyalty is to their shareholders on the global stock markets. The most disturbing effect of today's global economy has been the unprecedented shift in the distribution between capital and labour. In the United States between 1983 and 1992 the net worth of the top 1 per cent increased by 28 per cent, while real hourly wage stagnated or drifted down. This increasing polarization has pricked the conscience of even the chief economist and the staff writer of *Business Week Magazine*. As they claim,

> The market is now God: economic planning is the devil incarnate. Free market ideology has finally ridden to total victory. . . . The collapse of the Soviet Union brings to capitalism something it had always sought but never before achieved: a withering away of all the important opposition to the idea that the free market is the ideal way to organize society.[11]

The distinguishing feature of the transnational corporation is its willingness to shift operations to any place where economic opportunites can be maximized. This threat to exit and the promise of further investment have held governments to ransom. For instance, the spectacular success of George Soros and the equally spectacular failure of Norman Lamont over the crisis of the British pound illustrates how even government treasuries can no longer offer effective resistance against the impact of speculators driving down the value of national currencies. Also, in their efforts to attract inward investment, governments have been prepared to compromise on traditional labour rights and established ecological regulations. These profound changes, which have accelerated in the past decades, have provoked a vigorous debate on the future of the nation-state.

Two of the most prominent critics who refute the claim that the global economy has undermined the political authority of the nation-state are Paul Hirst and Graham Thompson.[12] In their view the totalizing claims of a new era of globalization underestimate the resilience of national institutions. While they concede that the new trends in trade and migration point to increasingly un-regulated forms of activity, they argue that this has not necessarily undermined the sovereignty of the nation-state. They stress that recent patterns of exchange and movement are an extension of economic activities that have been histori-cally conducted across discrete national boundaries. Furthermore, they claim that the primary agents of change and the dominant sites of struggle are within the nation-state. Hirst and Thompson reject the globalization model because, as they argue, this would imply that the national mechanisms of governance would have collapsed, transnational corporations no longer have home bases, and the influences of traditional political structures – both nationally and internation-ally – would decline and be overtaken by other 'multipolar' power bases. Given that these dramatic shifts have not surfaced in such an integrated form, Hirst and Thompson conclude that the nation-state continues to maintain a signifi-cant governance role in a framework of intensified internationalization.

But are the options as stark as either a borderless global system or autarchic nations? Would it be possible to conceptualize a set of movements that go in both directions simultaneously? One clear reminder of the contradictions of globalization is that despite the relative free transfer of capital and ideas, there is no nation which is encouraging mass migration. The patterns of migration in the age of globalization have become more complex and covert as policies on immigration are more selective. No nation-state has deregulated border con-trols. On the contrary, there is an increasing linkage between immigration con-trol and military defence. The counterflows to globalization can be witnessed at a number of political and cultural levels. For instance, as Great Britain inches closer to economic integration with the European Union it still insists on main-taining 'special rights' for the definition of its own immigration policies. In the last round of the GATT agreements, France led the resistance to the global hegemony of the American media industry. Other forms of counter-tendencies to globalization include the rise of ethnic nationalism in Yugoslavia and Rwanda, secessionist movements like the Lombard League in northern Italy, and the mobilization of religious fundamentalism in Afghanistan and Pakistan. These examples of political and cultural negotiation suggest a more complex pattern of globalization.

Globalization can be seen as a force which threatens the integrity of the nation-state by its sheer external pressure. Yet the history of the nation-state has always been a constant struggle to attain a sense of unity and coherence, not only against such external forces but also in relation to internal struggles. Na-tional identity has always sought to subordinate the competing sources of iden-tification that jostled within its domain and pushed against its borders. By insisting on exclusive citizenship, regulating border controls, demanding pol-itical allegiance and standardizing linguistic practice, the nation-state sought to create the 'structures of belonging'. Citizens were not just inhabitants of place but the nucleus of national sentiment. Conformity was expressed in terms of both a solidarity with the 'common good' and the historical memory of the nation's uniqueness in the world. Nation-states expect their citizens not only to abide by their laws but to also to feel pride and unity as they salute the flag. In the words of a Greek folksong, 'If my Crete is liberated so will my heart be freed.' The identification of individual with community was managed so that regional identities were relegated as particularistic, whereas the national was treated as universal. These abstract bonds were made to seem concrete through the ideological construction of identities. Other national identities which made similar claims were spoken of in terms of opposition and negation.

The nineteenth-century 'dream', that the nation-state should comprise a single culture with all the people cohabiting that space sharing a common identity, has proved to be a 'bloody nightmare'. All nation-states are products of series of invasions and settlements. Many of the historical traces of displacement and conquest may have been forgotten, but others remain as traumatic scars which serve to reinforce boundaries between different groups. Different ethnic groups with diverse cultural practices and often speaking different languages are often placed together under a common 'political roof'. The composition of this political structure may lead to its own destruction as we have recently witnessed with the collapse of the Eastern bloc. When the nation-state spans a wide range of different cultures, it is impossible to embrace and equally recognize all the cultural values. The articulation of the national culture does not aim to reflect all the constitutive cultural differences, but to produce a new culture which can structure those very differences as the condition of unity. As Stuart Hall argues, this experience of unity out of difference occurs through the ongoing 'narrative of the nation'.[13]

In the context of identity formation within the nation, both an internal hierarchy and a set of external oppositions are established. National institutions are formed like the education system. Art galleries become national treasure houses. Literary and cinematic traditions are interpreted as being expressive of a national perspective. This in turn facilitates the plausibility of the us/them form of national identity. Within the nation it is possible to subscribe to only one national identity, which is seen as fixed and rooted in the domain of the given geopolitical unit. Regional affiliations and allegiances are permissible insofar as they are already shorn of any geopolitical claims and thus not in competition with, but subordinate to and complementary with, the national identity.

Globalization, with the mass movement of labour, the mobility of elites within transnational corporations and the formation of diasporic communities that have bi-local affiliations, has created a fundamental strain on the ideals of the nation-state. Bonds can no longer be defined in terms of exclusive or singular allegiance. Historical references and linguistic practices have taken complex and diverse forms. As institutions address these questions of cultural difference the practice of socialization can no longer guarantee the embrace of a singular national identity. Individuals may feel they belong with groups whose religion, language or cultural practices are no longer bound to a particular nation. The most intimate feelings and significant relations may be stretched across a number of places. The emergent sense of community may be defined more out of common interests than territorial commitments. Where nation-states once coerced people into expressing their allegiance, they are now being compelled to face the legal and social demands of political diversity and cultural pluralism.

The debates on multiculturalism have generated considerable confusion on precisely this relationship between the cultural claims to recognition and the political rights of autonomy. Pluralist claims to recognition of the minority cultures in Canada and Australia have not been seen as a threat to the institutions and boundaries of the nation-state, as those claims are addressed only in the form of extending existing services and do not violate the existing legal-rational framework. Other nation-states like Germany have shown a reluctance to adopt the rhetoric of multiculturalism because of the romantic construction of an exclusive *Volk* in their national imaginary. While French republicanism does not confine citizenship to a specific race, it is premised on the assimilation of minority cultures. Many other European states have shown deeper resistance to adopting multicultural policies because of fear that the extension of cultural rights to minority groups will undermine their territorial integrity and political autonomy.

The singular and uniform construction of identity within the boundaries of the nation now seems to be untenable. All cultures are plural, and identity is never fixed. Whether the process of difference is acknowledged depends on other power relations. The early sociological paradigms of society which stressed the notion of an organic and integrated system have been challenged, not only in terms of the internal contests and struggles which lead to fragmentation but also, by the emphasis on the process of globalization. The threat to the unity and stability of social life is therefore to be found not just in the economic and cultural disequilibria between different classes, but in the diversity of sources of ideas of how society should be constituted and where it should be heading. These influences are no longer primarily defined by reference to specific traditions unique to the particular history of a specific place. Stuart Hall neatly defines the concept of globalization as referring 'to those processes operating on a global scale, which cut across national boundaries, integrating and connecting communities and organization in new space-time combinations, making the world in reality and in experience more interconnected.'[14] Hall is quick to remind us that the emphasis on interconnection is not unique to contemporary life, but rather that it emerges out of the historical processes and contradictory forces of modernity. Within modernity there has always been at least a dual trajectory. He argues that the drive towards national autonomy and the trend towards globalization have always operated in a conjunctural manner. This conjunction is not always oppositional. Thus resistance to one has not only been converted into collaboration, but is also a source of confirmation and validation. The exclusivity of national identity has never been as sovereign as it claims to be, just as the circulation of capital is not quite as universal as it proclaims. While the nation-state need not be seen as the most advanced form of geopolitical development, nor the most appropriate model for managing cultural difference, we still need to consider whether the alternatives offered by the age of globalization are more promising.

An important contradiction between globalization, nation-states and multiculturalism cannot be overlooked: while globalization is undermining the centrality of the nation-state, multicultural policies – which seek to address the social needs and legal rights of minorities – presuppose an institutional framework which is robust and open to extension, rather than one which is on the defensive and in recession. Multiculturalism, as a social and political ideal, did not simply emerge from the idealist Enlightenment project, nor is it simply an alibi for transnational corporate domination, but is a consequence of the historic practices of diasporic communities and the integrative dynamics of a welfare state. If globalization does not encourage new forms of settlement and severs the socio-political reach of the state, then this will dramatically limit the scope for managing the cultural differences which already jostle for space in the global cities. Will diasporic communities experience greater degrees of ghettoization, exploitation and marginalization as the regulative powers of the nation-state diminish, or will these new communities carve out a better bargaining position for themselves? Does globalization, with its rhetoric of flexibility and interdependence, stimulate more inclusive and diversified social relations, or will it continue to empower a highly mobile elite whose resources are based on symbolic global networks rather than being invested in local forms of production? What metaphors will evoke the complex and dynamic self-image of a society which is forged from the constant play with difference, rather than the conformity towards a singular and organic whole?

There is a growing fear that while the nation-state has struck a very uneasy relationship between the hegemonic and minority cultures, these historical relationships are now being sundered by globalization. The social form of the identification that linked the individual with the abstract community of the nation-state is being bypassed by globalization. However, the implosion of one sense of community has not been compensated by the coming 'global' community which offers a 'real' universalism. Paradoxically, globalization has renewed the search for 'ethnic roots'.[15] There has been both a negative reaction against the universality of the market, and the emergence of new forms of primordial identification. Concrete identifications with the nation-state are being shattered, but this has not necessarily led to a broader level of political identification. Tensions in some states have led to wars. At the social level of identification, globalization has not heightened the sense of integration but sharpened the lines of fragmentation. Under globalization the symbolic links between individuals and their imagined communities have been deterritorialized. Diasporic communities have attempted to forge new and informal networks. However, there has been no concerted project to invent new forms of belonging that could mediate between the local and the global. The contradictions between the universalizing forces of the market and the particularistic social relations that this creates are nowhere more palpable than in the global cities.

Global cities and migration

The emergence of global cities has become a focal point in studies of globalization. The phenomenal concentration of finance and technology, and the rapid means for its circulation within and between global cities, have produced some overgeneralized accounts of the possibility of flow and exchange in the modern world. Globalization has neither generated equivalent forms of movement for capital, ideas and labour, nor is the flow of labour resistant to the other globalizing tendencies and forces. The nature of this linkage is more ambiguous than most theorists have acknowledged. For instance, Malcolm Waters's Eurocentric presentation of the ideal state of globalization is unhelpful and, in one fundamental area, misinformed.[16] By defining globalization only in ideal terms and in opposition to the current 'national' structures, he overlooks the more complex and contradictory links between them. Globalization is best seen as a process rather than an end-state. His guiding theorem, which also presumes that labour markets are always localized and therefore the most resistant to globalization, needs to be corrected. This claim is made on the back of a Eurocentric calculation of mobility. While migration to, from and within Europe has been dramatically reduced since the periods of colonial expansion and the great migrations associated with industrialization, globalization has stimulated both new sources of migrants and new directions in migration.

The globalization of migration can be defined through the following features: multiplication of migratory movements; differentiation in the economic, social and cultural backgrounds of immigrants; acceleration of migration patterns; expansion in the volume of migrants; feminization of migration; deterritorialization of cultural communities; and multiple loyalties of diasporas. The combined effect of these processes will increasingly affect a greater number of locations. Migration has been and will continue to be a dynamic force in the constitution of modern societies. Economic practices of shifting labour-intensive production, and political barriers to immigration, will neither totally direct nor block the flows of migration. Globalization will lead to turbulent flows of people with patterns of movement which counter and cross economic demands and political policies. Therefore societies which previously defined themselves in terms of ethnic purity or cultural superiority will have to undergo structural adjustments to acknowledge the inevitable interactions with strangers.

I have already referred to the complex pattern of movement of people outside Europe and North America. However, it is also important to appreciate the new forms of migration that globalization has stimulated inside the First World. The uneven pulse of migration that is inherent in the process of globalization is most palpable in global cities like London, New York and Tokyo. These cities have become global control centres for banking and decision-making, and are establishing more connections with each other than with their own domestic economies.[17] Capital accumulation and financial services, which have overtaken manufacturing and production in market value, are increasingly concentrated in these centres. They are the nuclei of information control and the nodal points from which key marketing strategies, research and design, insurance and investment priorities are disseminated. This transition from industrial to information economy is what distinguishes earlier industrial cities like Manchester and Detroit from the global cities of London, New York and Tokyo. It is only in the latter that we can identify the concentration of advanced information technology, the headquarters of global corporations and international banks and the major research centres which are engaged in what Anthony King calls 'think work' on a global scale.[18] King concludes his study by stating that the stratification of London reflects both national and international inequalities. Within London the elites are 'in ambit of each other', but they do not circulate freely, nor in neatly enclosed spaces. Their territory is interspersed and bounded by other groups. While these financial elites are making decisions in response to activity that occurs outside Britain, they are also having to negotiate the social costs of the state's evisceration of welfare and employment opportunities in the inner cities. New sign systems and new ghettoes emerge side by side. The 'white flight' associated with the information economy in global cities is of a totally different nature from earlier flows that were crucial during industrialization.[19]

The process of social upheaval and urban decline that has been noted in the suburbs of Australia can be further witnessed in the evisceration of American industrial cities. The information economy and the medium-paid jobs are gravitating towards the vastly expanding sunbelt cities, while the rustbelt cities of the north slide into chaos.[20] A third of the immigrants to the USA are still heading for New York and Los Angeles despite the deterioration of these metropolises and the relocation of growth industries. Major corporations have relocated their computer centres outside the major cities. For instance, the National Association of Securities Dealers Automated Quotation of America (NASDAQ) has its data-processing centre not in New York, but in Turnbull, Connecticut.[21] Key players in these global cities are transnational corporations whose personnel are often recruited from diverse backgrounds. This diversity is of instrumental as well as symbolic value to the corporations. Personnel draw on their 'insider' cultural knowledge of a home base, while also adapting to the global priorities of the corporation. Transnational corporations demand that their workers express their loyalty to their corporate identity above their own national identities. The *lingua franca* of transnational corporations is English, but the recruitment policies are skills-based rather than ethnic. Employees are often trained to communicate with co-workers from diverse backgrounds and are required to be mobile and travel globally.[22] The formation of this transnational class is committed to a degree of homogenization among its members and to long-term processes of denationalization through the deregulation and diversification of economic production. Knowing how to speak local is part of the discourse of the new global elites. They perceive themselves as belonging to a social space whose symbolic repertoire and political sphere do not confine themself to the boundaries of a particular nation-state. At the other end of the spectrum, the low-skilled service industry that is subcontracted to these corporations also attracts migrants. These workers are the front line of the exploitation characteristic of globalization. They arrive in global cities both legally and illegally. Far from home and usually alone, these workers are trapped in exploitative working conditions. Lacking both the traditional networks of support and the formal structures of social welfare, these migrants are forced to survive in ghettoes surrounding the global cities. The success of transnational corporations may have raised the GNP of many advanced economies in the west but this has not led to improvements in wages and welfare for the majority of workers. As Saskia Sassen has noted, the wealth generated by one sector has not produced a collective prosperity.[23]

Global cities have thus been characterized as the most intensely polarized social spaces. They are cosmopolitan centres which attract both professional elites, who move within the various branches of transnational corporations, and migrants, who are manual workers in the service industry. There is a dense concentration of both financial and cultural institutions which reflect the needs and aspirations of high-income consumers, while public services in education and health are subject to severe cutbacks and privatization. As global cities are increasingly integrated with each other, they are also distancing themselves from national and domestic priorities. With the rhetoric of becoming competitive on a global scale, they have exploited the breakdown of traditional economic and political blocs, while also inadvertently exacerbating the precarious face of cultural differences. The global city has not only created greater insecurity in the workplace but has also sharpened the contact of distant cultures. For instance, transnational corporations often appropriate local symbols, employ professionals with bi-cultural affiliations as a means of developing strategies which have a global reach. Despite, or perhaps because of, such globalizing pressures the interactions between different cultural communities in global cities have not become more harmonious. Racism has taken on new forms of militancy in cities like London and Berlin, whereas in Cairo and Kabul the cultural impact of globalization is measured in terms of a threat to their traditional Muslim codes. Globalization has paradoxically stimulated new forms of exclusivism and violent forms of fundamentalism. There is no single form of globalization. It can proceed on contradictory or variable trajectories. An index to the complexity inherent in the globalizing processes of urban culture is in the linguistic range exercised in global cities: 'In 1987, 172 different languages were spoken by children in the schools of the Inner London Education Authority.'[24]

In the context of such complexity and difference there is as much to fear as there is to gain. The dynamism of globalization need not lead to a series of catastrophic cultural collisions; it may open new possibilities of interconnection and exchange. What Robin Cohen has called the 'diasporization' of communities will become a prominent feature of the global society.[25] Communities dispersed across different locations throughout the world will be able to form new levels of communication and generate new forms of identity. Cohen argues optimistically that diasporic communities have traditionally served as a bridge between the particular and the universal. Commercial links between different locations were facilitated by bi-cultural interlocutors. The dual perspective of diasporic communities also tunes their vision to 'missing' elements in the social order, and their experience of exclusion or marginalization may also heighten the call for advances in legal definitions of human rights.

As these communities maintain links with their place of origin and continue to develop new associations and affiliations in an outward trajectory, their sense of belonging and self-identity undergoes a radical transformation. The nation-state presupposed that cultural harmony was based on uniformity and singular forms of allegiance. Nation-states sought to make exclusive citizens and create unique cultural contexts. The regulation of national institutions and the standardization of language and historical narratives was crucial to such a project. Globalization has sawn away many of the branches upon which such national identities lay. The mobility and complex affiliations of people today mean that the dream of a 'pure race' or a culture bound to a given territory is no longer possible. People construct their sense of identity and communities, by defining their interests in ways that exceed the priorities of the nation-state. The challenge is to find socio-legal frameworks which can secure the rights of subjects in this increasingly cosmopolitan world.

Globalization and a sense of place

A number of social theorists have commented on the separation of the places where decisions are made and those where the consequences are experienced. We are living in a world where decisions are increasingly made elsewhere, and where power is defined in terms of access to mobility and the dissemination of knowledge. The transformation of spatial relations has been a central theme in the writing of Anthony Giddens. He has argued that one of the distinctive features of modernity is that social relations have been stretched and attenuated through the dual process of 'time-space distanciation' and 'disembedding'. In modernity our sense of time and space becomes both more abstract and more measurable. Both become quantifiable in terms of units which can be controlled and disconnected from diffuse social networks and associations. That 'could-be-anywhere' feeling and the digital display of time are banal expressions of this process of modernization.[26] With the advent of cheap transportation, the emergence of 'just-in-time' inventories, the dispersal of the links in the chain of commodity production, the utilization of electronic modes of communication rather than face-to-face forms of social relationships, we have witnessed the emergence of new practices which are mutually transforming our notions of the local and the global.

Rather than assuming that we have been dramatically elevated into a new global system or declaring the resilience of traditional structures which have historically mediated exchange relations, at this juncture it would be more appropriate to consider globalization as a complex process comprising interrelated tendencies which interact in unpredictable ways and result in uneven effects. Dicken, Peck and Tickell have mapped these tendencies and processes in a way which allows for considerable slippage and 'fuzziness': 'Globalization tendencies can be at work without this resulting in the all-encompassing end-state, the globalized economy, in which all unevenness and difference is ironed out, market forces are rampant and uncontrollable and the nation-state merely passive and supine.'[27] In the place of an idealized global system where the economy, politics and culture are systematically producing a homogeneous and total state, they have emphasized that globalization entails an integration of economic function among geographically dispersed activities; a de-privileging of national leaders and increasing influence of extra-national forces; and a complex rearticulation of cultural forms. Their mapping of globalization goes beyond the mechanistic paradigms which presuppose that the identity of a system is dependent on discrete boundaries and the integration of generic functions.

By focusing on tendencies rather than outcomes we see how social systems are reconstituted in contradictory processes and along an uneven terrain. The specific histories and locations of institutions will invariably influence the dynamic of these tendencies. Hence, the nation-state as an identifiable geopolitical unit need not disappear before we speak of globalization. Coterminously, there do not need to be universal laws allowing the unfettered mobility of labour before we can say that globalization exists. For clearly nation-states have considerable power in the regulation of exchange and movement across their borders. Yet, even the regulations for entry and exit do not exclusively reflect national political priorities but are often influenced by more diffuse cultural values and subsumed within a broader economic system. This process of diffusion and rearticulation is not a zero-sum game amongst nation-states and transnational corporations. The 'spin-off' effects from the collisions between internal and external practices, as well the unconscious shifts in the social imaginary of a global system, are producing changes in identity and culture that are beyond the parameters of the conventional sociological paradigms.[28]

The debates on globalization have affected the way we understand the relationship between migration and social change in three crucial ways. Firstly, the paths of human movement across the globe are so intricate and multi-directional that it is no longer possible to talk about international migration in terms of Eurocentric axial routes. There is a need to consider the levels of migration that occur within the boundaries of a nation as well as the complex trajectories between states. The globalization of migration defies the earlier models which presupposed a close link between migrant needs and the demands of western labour markets. Current demographic movements are not just the extension or even the inversion of previous patterns. A sense of the precarious dialectic in these global realignments is captured in Trinh T. Minh-ha's pithy formulation, 'In every first world there is a third, and in every third world a first.'

Secondly, the literature on migration which has highlighted the significance of gender and cultural identity has also provided the lever to reopen the structure–agency debates in social theory. The theoretical paradigm, which conceived the agency of the migrant purely in terms of the proletarian victim, failed to see the complex patterns of participation within the informal economy and the construction of parallel welfare structures. The specific cultural identity and differential patterns of socialization by migrants was often ignored by previous accounts that conflated the class position of migrants with the indigenous proletarians. Not only was the dynamic between industrialization and what Shanin called 'depeasantization' overlooked, but migrants who were peasants when they left their villages were considered to become proletarians automatically upon arrival at the factory in the city. This incorporation of the agency of all migrants as the 'supplement' to the proletarians failed to consider the transferral of skills, networks, values and institutions into the new urban environment, and to take account of the informal and hybrid conjunctures between the peasant and proletarian cultures.[29]

Hence migrants were less dependent on the demand of the formal economic and social structures than many analysts anticipated. As western economies continue to shift their economic activity away from industrial production, and towards the provision of services in capital management and technological research, there is an increasing participation of migrant labour in both the highly qualified and low-skilled areas of this sector. In places like London and New York migrants are not just confined to the enclosed space of urban factories, but they also circulate as the passengers and drivers of metropolitan cabs.

Thirdly, the collapse of the earlier sociological models of migration and the proliferation of surveys on international migration as well as critical engagement with diasporic communities in cultural studies has led to either a postmodern turn in the calls for new conceptual frameworks or to more empirical accounts of movement and settlement. No new sociological theory on migration has been proposed to accommodate the transformations of globalization.

Stephen Castles, one of the most coherent advocates of the earlier political-economy model of immigration has, in his most recent collaboration with Mark Miller, surveyed the growing empirical literature on international migration and presented an account which has identified a number of interrelated factors which generate and regulate the process of global migration. First, the broad causes of upheaval – ranging from economic deprivation to cultural intolerance. Second, the paths and obstacles for migration – the availability of formal and informal mechanisms that facilitate entry like historical relations which may privilege certain members from other countries. Third, the opportunity for settlement in the place of arrival, whether they are seen as temporary or permanent members. Fourth, the threats of expulsion and the programmes for citizenship in the place of arrival. Fifth, the dynamism for mutual transformation that is generated by the interaction between migrant communities and the host society.[30]

In Castles and Miller's survey of the global flows of migration, the distinction between globalization and internationalization is unresolved. It is not clear whether globalization refers to an intensification of flows across national boundaries, or involves a remapping of geopolitical and cultural relations. At the centre of this dilemma is the status of the nation-state. If we argue that the national identity of the migrant and the immigration laws of the nation are the most determining factors in the very possibilities for movement, then this would suggest that the rights of citizenship and the authority of the nation-state are not necessarily undermined by a heightened traffic across borders. The role of governance, the terms of entry, the permission for settlement are all still largely regulated on a national basis, and therefore it would appear that international pressures are being refracted through national processes.

This method of surveying migration helps to identify some of the common structures and clarifies the complex network of routes without reproducing the binarisms of earlier models. As a method for surveying, it functions differently from the models for explaining migration: rather than furnishing uniform laws it offers a broad image, combining general characteristics and specific details. However, the concept of globalization is often used as a synonym for internationalization, and it does leave open the question whether it is possible to provide a theory of global migration. An accurate map is better than a misleading model, but does this mean that the patterns of global migration are beyond theory?

The awareness that the phenomenon of migration is a dynamic feature of modernity, and that it has both intensified in volume and diversified its directions, requires a new theoretical approach. Mike Douglass has proposed a 'global-local' framework which steers a careful course between the structuralist and voluntarist models. This approach combines a world systems perspective that charts the transnational flow of economy with the recent debates on structuration and cultural context. Attention to the dimensions of space and the historical institutions which affect social behaviour thereby outlines the importance of local forces. By combining the local dimensions with the global processes it provides a more suitable framework for understanding the pressures and barriers against migration. It thereby avoids the pitfalls of deterministic models which suggest that an overarching logic of global capitalism is affecting all forms of social behaviour, and it corrects the view that intrinsically national priorities or specific cultural dispositions are determining patterns of development and levels of immigration. This framework draws from the vocabulary of other earlier models and this mixed perspective provides a more open-ended and flexible vantage point. It stresses an interplay of global process of post-Fordism (without the presumption that development proceeds according to a given model, within a regulated time frame, or towards definable goals), with local structures which are indigenous value systems. Such a decentred approach does not locate the primary force of change in external imperatives of the global economy, nor does it presuppose that societies have unique and distinct cultural paradigms which determine their own 'special development'.[31]

A fundamental weakness that is implicit in both the voluntarist push–pull model and the structuralist political-economy theory is their conceptualization of flow. Both perspectives understand the flow of human migration within a sort of 'water-pump' metaphor. Migration is seen as a system in which the flow is driven by the originating pressures of market needs, the counter-responses of individual migrants, and the regulating valves of state policies. In this mechanistic schema causation is identified in the binary terms of opportunity/prohibition, or surplus/deficit. However, such a framework is inadequate for explaining the gaps and clusters, signals and responses that operate in contemporary society.

The metaphors of flow and influence are directly related to the ideologies of cause and determination as well as expressive of broader frameworks of epochal developments or progress. Seeing migration as 'series of waves', 'links in a chain' was a way of making a pattern out of multiple individual actions. It illustrated how a migrant's decision was interwoven into the narrative of a collective. This metaphor also clearly delineated a sense of journey. It differentiated the place of departure and the place of arrival in terms of 'one-way traffic' and connoted a clear expectation of settlement: migrants were 'here to stay'. It also presumed that the greater the effort to regulate migration, the more stable will be the process of settlement and the greater the selectivity. Regulations of entry and the possibility for conferring citizenship are always determined by national governments. The conditions for determining such policies vary according to prior historical or cultural arrangements, as well as current economic and political agreements. Two contrasting modes of immigration controls can be noted in the late nineteenth-century *laissez-faire* Commonwealth arrangement which, for a limited period, allowed a relatively open passage for British subjects between the colonies and Britain, and the *Gastarbeiter* system in post-war Germany which rigidly channelled the flows of migrants for specific economic needs. The rights of citizenship and conditions for settlement often depend upon such formal political links. However, recent trends in migration are not exclusively motivated by claims for citizenship. Hence the flows of migrants cannot be traced along such formal and historical links. While the grounds for extending political rights are contracting, the flows are being generated by more complex factors. Regulation of rights does not entail the stabilization of flows in an increasingly deregulated 'new world order'. Despite the militarized practices of border controls in the USA, changing demographies and the transformation of gendered roles in domestic labour amongst middle-class American families are effectively driving the new networks for illegal migration.[32] Syndicates have been formed in South East Asia to smuggle sex workers into Japan, and 'coyotes' continue to find ways through the USA–Mexican border.

New paradigms of flow and the third identity

With the popularization of concepts like chaos theory from the post-quantum physical sciences, there has been a parallel revision of the conceptual frameworks for understanding both the process of identity formation and the mechanics of change in the social sciences and humanities. For instance, there has been a growing appreciation of the resilience of contradictory and loosely formed structures. One notable example has been Robin Cohen's attempt to clarify the blurred boundaries and opaque categories which are used to define British identity, where he borrows the mathematical process of 'fuzzy logic' which establishes a procedure via the elimination of the uncertain edges of a problem.[33] These new methodological approaches, which attempt to go beyond the limitations of earlier mechanistic models, may help to expand our understanding of cultural differences. Marxist theories of dependency and Weberian theories of modernization both tended to relegate cultural difference to a sign of underdevelopment that would be overtaken by the progressive movement of modernity. Cultural differences have proved to be both more resilient and contradictory. Difference is no longer to be seen as something that is 'out there' or 'back then', because it is already part of the 'here and now'.

Migration and telecommunication have brought differences closer together. This density produces new levels of concern. It produces challenges at both ends. In terms of migration, how will the receiving culture incorporate the 'new presence', and how will the donating culture adjust to the 'new absence'? Similarly, in terms of the interpenetration caused by the global media and economy, how does a local culture which has developed its own vernacular internalize the hegemonic symbols and practices of global culture? For on the one hand there is the assumption that the injection of the global forms will homogenize and flatten cultural production, while on the other this very injection of globalism is seen as a virus which stimulates resistance, syncretism and mutant differentiation.[34] Global culture is thus poised on the balance of uniformity and diversity.

Globalization has heightened the potential for interaction. Critics have focused on the changes in the city in order to discern whether the shifts that are being presented as features of globalism amount to a difference in degree or in kind. Firstly, there is the density of opposites that makes the global city a new form of 'contact zone'. Secondly, the acceleration which has expressed itself in two forms throughout the twentieth century; simultaneity (to be able to cross vast distances in minimal time), and instantaneity (zero delay in communication). Perhaps the urgent question shifts from 'what is modernity?' to 'which modernity?' With the claims of either the counter-modernity that aims to give voice to the descendants of slavery, the diasporic peregrination of migrants and the affirmation of a public voice for women, or the postmodernity, which rather than boasting of being the successive or transcendent phase, addresses the critical underside and the complicitous double coding of contemporary aesthetico-political practice. Both representations of modernity identify the demise of a unified and all-embracing category, as well as acknowledging the necessary plurality of conceptual claims. 'What is over is a particular kind of liberal or socialist, but essentially modernist, dream of unity and social transparency.'[35]

The postmodern turn, which stresses both the end of the grand narratives of social change and the fragmentation of the subject, is often seen as a sign of political despair. Stuart Hall, however, has interpreted this scenario as a means to establish new levels of affinity amongst those who take a critical stance towards modernity and an opportunity to learn how to speak without presuming a higher moral ground.[36] As displacement, rupture and fragmentation become the dominant motifs for articulating the prevalent forms of experience in the modern world, it becomes vital to think again about how such experiences can be communicated.[37]

The dimension of reflexivity has been a significant vector in the transformation of contemporary society; it has also played a crucial role in our understanding of the politics of representation. Reflexivity over the form of language has drawn attention to a number of relationships which are established in the act of representation. Firstly, the complicity with the institution in which the discourse is situated. Secondly, the role of narrative structure. Thirdly, the status of the 'I' of the text and the ego of the author. Fourthly, the configuration of the subject/object positions. This reflexive dimension in the politics of representation has heightened attention to the relationship between experience and the forms of knowledge.

With the economic and cultural shifts that have been described in terms of post-industrialism and postmodernism there is a need to redefine the conceptual language of migration. The structures for movement and the possibilities for settlement are more precarious and unstable. The migrant's dream of starting a 'new life' in a 'new country' now sounds strangely distant and anachronistic. There is no 'new frontier land' in which these fantasies can be staged, and the capitalist projects which stimulated these adventures are now in a state of dispersal and reversal. The semiotics of global capital are framed by concepts of 'decentralization', 'flexibility', 'out-sourcing' and 'contractualization'. The master concept is the 'circuit'. Distance is no longer a key factor on the circuit. Time has overtaken the significance of space. Hence the circulation of signs on the circuit is measured in terms of velocity. It is within the discourse of what Lash and Urry called 'disorganised capitalism'[38] that migrant labour needs to be situated. Their language for the flows in the age of globalization draws quite significantly on the terminology of computerized circuits and networks, as opposed to Marx's metaphors of industrial machines and military confrontations:

> The movement, the flows of capital, money, commodities, labour, information and images across time and space are only comprehensible if 'networks' are taken into account because it is through networks that these subjects and objects are able to gain mobility. ... Brunn and Leinbach conceive of the 'world as a map of "bridges" of communication and transport, comprising dense networks, space networks and blanks'. The issue for us in this context is what are becoming the nodal changes in this mapping in the post-organized capitalist order, that is, where and what sort of 'cobwebs' of connections on these maps are becoming denser, and which are becoming relatively sparser. Networks are made up of a few basic elements: of 'bridges' or 'links' which connect the points in a network. These bridges stand out in a lesser or greater relief from a 'backcloth' or 'support structure'. The entities that move along these links are called traffic.[39]

The transmission of information and the transportation of goods and people along the networks has, according to Canclini, necessitated a rethinking of the very foundation of social theory:

> Two conventional notions of social theory collapse in the face of these 'crossed economies meaning systems that intersect, and fragmented personalities'. One of these is that of 'community', employed both for isolated peasant populations and for expressing the abstract cohesion of a compact national state, in both cases definable by relations to a specific territory. It was assumed that the links between the members of those communities would be more intense inside than outside of their space, and that the members treat the community as the principal medium to which they adjust their actions. The second image is the one that opposes center and periphery, also an 'abstract expression of an idealized imperial system', in which the gradations of power and wealth would be distributed concentrically: most in the center and a progressive decrease as we move toward surrounding zones. The world functions less and less in this way, says Rouse: we need 'an

alternative cartography of social space' based instead on the notions of 'circuit' and 'border'.[40]

Globalization need not lead to a uniform, singular state, nor is it inevitably a system that tends towards homogenization. It may, as Robertson has argued, lead to a heightened form of relativization whereby the particularities of individual units are not flattened but are both in sharper contrast and involved in more intense dialogue with others. From this perspective globalization will accentuate both the incommensurability and the translation between cultural systems. This implies that the interaction will not be confined to the superimposition or duplication of one code over another. It also demands that cultural identity is not confined to the binarism of either particularism or universalism.

The anxieties of the nation-state in the age of globalization are evident in the debates on the future shape of Europe. Political leaders from nations across Europe are all conscious of the complexities of increasing unification, but are also mindful of the consequences of isolation and marginalization in the global economy. For all the discourse of common heritage, there has never been a point in history when there was a single European self-identity, no one has dared to suggest that there is a common race from which all Europeans originate, nor is there any consensus on where the centre of Europe lies. The narrative of Europe does not unfold as the 'nation writ large', yet the language, for and against integration, repeatedly draws on the very binarism, of either universalism or particularism, that was intrumental in the discursive legitimation of the nation-state.

The strongest voices which warn against further levels of European integration are also calls for defence of the sovereignty of the nation-state. Within this call is also an urge to retain the unique identity of each nation. From this position, it is argued that Europe can never be anything more than the abstract aggregation of discrete segments, and that neither has Europe authority over these parts, nor do the constituent parts owe their identity to the grander whole. Identity can only be secured by 'cultivating the difference-to-oneself'. One identity is thus always posed in opposition to another, and from these series of oppositions there is no grander whole which can be inferred. There is no common heritage from which the various parts are formed, nor any incontrovertible logic which draws them towards a common destiny. The historical trajectory of the nation-state is thus seen as being either exterior or alternative to that of Europe. Hence the identity of the nation-state presupposes a distanciation from the universalist claims of a common identity.

The advocates of European integration claim that, given the existing global pressures, particularism is untenable. They stress the need to project an identity on a wider plane, to realign the constituent economies, to form an exemplary cultural heritage, and redefine the boundaries of inclusion and participation. Hence there are two competitions: what will be the centre, and what will be the significant other? Increasing European integration would ultimately lead to the construction of a homogeneous cultural identity, one which could supposedly include and somehow transcend particular national identities. In this context, national identities would be destined to the fate that was once assigned to regional identities in the age of the nation-state: their particularism would become subordinate to the universalism of European identity.

This typology, which opposes particularism to universalism, always overlooks the constitutive role of one upon the other. Neither the universalist nor the particularist position ever exists in a pure form. The two positions are not mutually exclusive. The particular is constructed only in a context of generality, and the general is nothing but a specific organization and distribution of the particular: these two positions are constantly in a state of interaction. To begin to define the third position, one must therefore be conscious of the impossibility of these two other positions, and also aware of the way in which these diametrically opposed voices, which seem to lead in contrasting directions, are actually speaking from a similar position and are in fact only talking towards each other. In other words, we have to see how these positions are like two sides of the same coin. One voice is urging nationals to retreat into the exclusive and mythical image of the nation's past, and the other is pushing Europeans to embrace an unknown future. One is calling people to elevate their cultural differences to a level of non-negotiability, and the other to subordinate these differences to broader unity.

However, identity is never found by suspending the self in a mythical past, nor is it invented without a prehistory. Identity always oscillates between fixity and openness. The conflicts and transformations of globalization need not lead to either the cultural impoverishment of homogenization or a defensive retreat into 'splendid isolationism'. It may involve an extension of existing repertoires, the hybridization of identities and the creation of new modes of affiliation. Identity is always a process which is formed in what is called 'the third space', a zone that exists between the familiar and the foreign. In this 'third space', movement is multidirectional, and there is a combined sense of return and advance as identification attends to specificities of both the past and the future. The 'third space' comes between the proliferation of minor differences and the domination of the centralizing unity. Identity is neither in the interior space of already known experience, nor doomed to the exteriority of an experiment with the unknown. Cultural identity is thus never confined to the space of an enclosed segment, nor is it projected onto an open plane, but is formed through the practice of bridging both differences and similitudes between the self and the other. Bridging involves the performance of two tasks simultaneously: it requires memory and experience. To know where the self has come from is to gain a sense of belonging which enables one to risk the journey ahead.

Recent debates in cultural theory have addressed this process of exchange and differentiation, and identified the points of resistance and forms of transformation that occur as differing cultural codes interact. There is the growing appreciation that a global cultural economy does not tend towards homogenization. Translation does not always produce equivalence. The incommensurability of cultures need not imply exclusion. What a number of critics like Bhabha and Appadurai have sought to demonstrate is that the dynamics of cultural exchange cannot be captured by mechanistic models and that we are in need of more subtle conceptions of the flows, collisions, and juxtapositions across cultures. As we become enmeshed in the globalizing process it becomes all the more urgent to develop a more subtle understanding of the politics of translation and incommensurability. Guattari's observations on the limitation of mechanistic models of psychic development might offer a parallel insight into the need to develop a broader conception of the creative and heterogeneous levels of processuality in social change. 'We need to free ourselves from a solitary reference to technological machines and expand the concept of the machine so as to situate the machine's adjacence to incorporeal Universes of reference.'[41]

5

The Deterritorialization of Culture

In *Towards 2000* Raymond Williams begins his chapter on the culture of the nation with a simple domestic story:

> There was this Englishman who worked in the London office of a multinational corporation based in the United States. He drove home one evening in his Japanese car. His wife, who worked in a firm which imported German kitchen equipment, was already at home. Her small Italian car was often quicker through the traffic. After a meal which included New Zealand lamb, Californian carrots, Mexican honey, French cheese and Spanish wine, they settled down to watch a programme on their television set, which was made in Finland. The programme was a retrospective celebration of the war to recapture the Falkland Islands. As they watched it they felt very warmly patriotic, and very proud to be British.[1]

The turbulence of globalization has produced considerable dread and excitement. Social changes have already taken place which both exceed the regulatory powers and undermine the structures of the nation-state. This has also presented a conceptual challenge to the social sciences. It has drawn attention to the limitations of models which presupposed the autonomy of the nation-state, the objectivity of the detached observer, and the categorization of cultural identities according to the binary of 'us' and 'them'. The task of mapping the processes of globalization and the vocabulary for defining these changes are only beginning.

At the forefront are multidisciplinary approaches from the social sciences and humanities. No single discipline can claim globalization as its privileged object of study. Globalization raises questions which extend the boundaries and challenge the foundations of all disciplines. To grasp it in its entirety requires not only multidisciplinary and collaborative research practices but a rethinking of our metaphors and concepts for explaining change and transformation. This broader and more radical approach to understanding social change has displaced many of the positivist and functionalist models which underpinned research in the social sciences.

These mechanistic models, with their crude understandings of the dynamics of interaction, revealed the limited appreciation of the ideas on entities, energy and flow that had been developed in Newtonian physics. Just as nature was understood as a mechanical system which obeyed the mechanical laws of motion, society was also understood as an inanimate mechanism.[2] Both were viewed through the optic of the machine metaphor. Nature and society could be compared to machines because they were all systems which were made of parts that worked together to fulfil a particular purpose. It was presumed that the identity of these parts could be discerned and that their operation followed eternal laws. Patterns could therefore be determined and outcomes predicted. Unlike machines, however, nature and society have animating principles which are not predetermined by an external force. A machine can function only according to the limits of its design, use and maintenance. The limits of the natural and social order are not prefigured by such design and use principles. Structures evolve and mutate, transform and differentiate from each other in ways that no machine can. The mechanistic world-view could never address the subtle influences that were active in the process of change. It had to restrict its vision of activity to the interplay of inert matter. These mechanistic models encouraged a way of thinking about the identity of subjects and places as if they could be 'defined prior to the interactions between them'.[3] For over two generations there has been a rethinking of the models and concepts for explaining change and contemporary scientists have now challenged every aspect of the mechanistic world view: 'We are becoming more and more conscious of the fact that on all levels, from elementary particles to cosmology . . . our vision of nature is undergoing a radical change toward the multiple, the temporal and the complex.'[4]

Insights and methods developed in one field cannot automatically and uncritically be transferred to another. However, the natural and social sciences are constantly in dialogue, pursuing common questions and offering provocative answers to similar questions. There are a number of analogies that can be drawn from the chaos and complex systems theories in physics and mathematics. To explain the organizing principles in nature there has been a return to speculation over invisible influences and indeterminate processes. Of significant interest are the understandings of structures and bodies whose identity is formed through a constant process of dynamic and flexible entanglement with the outside. As scientists look more closely at the primal materials or the essence of a structure, they no longer discover single atoms which are like discrete things, but find processes with vibratory patterns of activity. This has led to a reversal in the understanding of the relationship between matter and fields. The constitution of a field is not filled by discrete pieces of matter, for matter itself was organized by the energy of gravitational fields. Here, the coherence, stability and resilience of a system is not secured by regulating the replication of identical units, nor by closing off boundaries and fortifying rigid internal structures, but rather by maintaining loose affiliations and high degrees of interlinkage.

For over a decade, James Rosenau has argued that the radical advances of modern technologies which have accelerated our scope of perception and speed of responses, the prevalence of authority crises which have undermined traditional forms of legitimacy, and the heightened analytic skills of modern agents have created new forms of social structures which are globally interdependent and in a constant state of bifurcation. More recently, he has taken the concept of turbulence from new physics to explain the complexity of these changes. Rosenau stresses that turbulence is not just a poetic comparison between the instability in world politics and stormy weather, but a conceptual tool for explaining the dynamic of transformation.[5] The changes that he claims are confronting the modern world cannot be understood merely as forms of variation in the given structures, or as fluctuation in the locus of power. Rather, it is the system as a whole which is undergoing rearrangement. Boundaries are shifting, new processes are forming, outcomes becoming more transitory as the system enters a period of prolonged disequilibrium. The dynamics of turbulence are characterized by extensive degrees of interdependence and uncertainty.

While the nation-state has not disappeared, its own norms, structures and processes cannot be defined in isolation from the global pressures. For instance, given the multidirectional flows and covert means of migration which expose the gaps between the formulation and the implementation of migration policies, there is the further need for a bi-focal approach, one which is alert to both internal priorities and external perceptions. Tightening immigration levels may appear to offer better prospects to the internal labour market, but may also harm the export opportunities upon which these markets depend. The interdependencies and the volatility of actors on the global stage are of such a density and intensity that the structures within which decisions and flows are regulated are in a constant state of oscillation. Turbulence refers to this bifurcated interplay between multicentric and state-centric systems. The interaction between the two occurs at multiple levels, and the momentum, reverberations or blockages caused by these interactions produce complex effects which Rosenau calls 'cascades'.

This perspective could serve as a valuable analogue for interpreting the processes of contemporary cultural changes. With greater flows of peoples and symbols, as well as radical transformations in work patterns, it has been presumed that cultural boundaries and formations have been radically displaced and reconfigured. It is now hard to imagine how cultural practices can be exclu-

sively rooted in one place. Cultures have fragmented and scattered. This process of change has been uneven and unpredictable, leading to unlikely cultural
formations and also threatening the basis of what seemed like time-honoured
traditions. Globalization has had profound implications for the way we understand culture. The mechanistic models which presumed that the seemingly chaotic practices of social change could be stripped down to their components and
that the order of cause and effect could be analysed in order to determine the
origins and even predict the outcome of events are no longer tenable.[6] However, there is now a fresh understanding of the relationship between the part
and the whole, order and chaos, and this has radically altered the ways we can
imagine the dynamics of culture in a globalized world.

Defining culture

The activity of culture, as suggested by the etymological links to 'gardening',
has been conventionally associated with the 'cultivation' of territory. Every
culture is supposed to come from somewhere, to have its place in the world.
While the process by which culture 'cultivates' its territory – whether determined purely by economic and political forces or operating with relative autonomy – has always been disputed in the social sciences, the 'location of culture'
has only recently been questioned. Through its exercise of symbolic representations and communicative practices, culture defines specific relations to space
and time. Aesthetic practices like literary novels or paintings are often taken to
be examples of cultural practice. They may embody the most edifying and el-
evating elements of a society's tradition, but they are, as Edward Said argues,
the articulations of a specific world-view.[7] Culture has thus been generally defined by the way groups occupied a given territory and the forms by which they
communicate their everyday social relationships. Even when these cultural texts
were interpreted as checks to temper the negative and destructive tendencies in
a social group, this in itself did not guarantee a more open-ended sense of identity. The heightened expressions of culture were often interpreted as the means
by which groups could forge fixed links to place and establish common bonds
based on exclusive and unique traits. The representation of place and the constitution of a social identity were central in the conventional theories of culture:

> Having an identity meant – above all – having a country, a city, an area: an entity
> where all that was shared by the inhabitants of a place was identical or inter-
> changeable. Those who did not share this territory, who had neither the same
> objects and symbols nor the same rituals and customs, were the others – those
> who were different.[8]

Taylor's classical definition of culture as the 'complex whole' – which included knowledge, religion, art, morality, laws and customs – provided the ba-

sis for understanding the ways in which people made sense of their world, but also established the framework for seeing other cultures as bounded totalities with discrete and specific identities.[9] Cultures were understood as being formed in particular territorial relationships with carefully established borders, separating one from another. They created systems of belief amongst their members that secured a homogeneous, coherent and continuous sense of affiliation. This interpretation encouraged a typological understanding of cultures. By stressing the boundaries, unique structures and specific beliefs that make a 'complex whole', patterns and comparisons could also be projected. The uniqueness of one culture was defined by comparing it with another. It was presumed that the observer could find 'certain forms of schematic organisation of a district or city and the social grammar that characterises the life of its inhabitants'.[10]

   This view of culture has its origin in the anthropological study of small societies. What remains problematical in the anthropological approach is the distinction that it repeats between traditional and modern formations of culture. The characteristics of traditional cultures are commonly defined as 'a given mode of life, a set of practices and beliefs characterizing a group of people',[11] whereas modern and, in particular, national cultures are defined as the normative and organizational constructions of representations which are only loosely related to a specific life-world. This distinction between local/traditional and national/modern cultures is not made to reaffirm the late nineteenth-century hierarchy, which divided up cultures in terms of dynamic and static, but only to articulate a qualitative difference in the practices of belonging and representation. It stresses that the idea of culture in the local context remains embedded within everyday practice, whereas the image of the national, first born in exile, remains an abstraction that is imposed over the lives of the people. This distinction between local and national in terms of a performative as opposed to an objectified view of culture, while misreading the performative processes in the national imaginary, does highlight the conceptual disjunctures in our frameworks for understanding culture. While rejecting the imperialist hierarchies, it repeats the anthropological melancholy over the viability of local cultures in a globalizing world, as it opposes the idea of real, embedded practices of culture *in* the social, against the hyper-real, disembedded representations of culture *over* society.

   A number of other anthropologists, who have been more concerned with migration patterns, have argued that the anthropological understanding of culture can no longer privilege a single location in order to determine the characteristics of a given cultural group. They have urged that the discipline adopt a comparative methodology which attends not only to the 'stuff' of a closed or stable cultural system, but to the ways local structures, values and practices are interlinked within a system of cross-cultural negotiation and power differentials.[12]

   The melancholic view of traditional cultures is often met with a fierce demand by members of a cultural minority to protect its integrity. In the context of multiculturalism this conflicting view of the viability of traditional cultures has produced considerable debate. While anthropology has had little part in the policy debates on multiculturalism, diasporic cultures and nationalism, some of its founding ideas on the definition of culture have been remarkably influential. As Gillian Bottomley has acknowledged, while the tension between movement and settlement has been a constitutive feature of all forms of cultural identity, the disciplinary frameworks of anthropology were developed 'in an era of the formation of ethno-nationalism, when political boundaries were being drawn around defined ethnics, many of which have become potentially lethal weapons in struggles over what are now claimed as ancient territorial rights'.[13]

The presumption that cultures are autonomous wholes persists despite the greater traffic of peoples and ideas between territories. In the policy debates of most western societies different cultures are identified by the state. They are usually defined as minority cultures and as such jostle for access to limited resources, and assert new demands for respect and tolerance. These considerations for their right to self-identity, and for the preservation of these different cultures which are proposed by both ethnic leaders and state representatives, draw on the premise that their culture is both distinctive and whole and therefore should be defended as such. The debates on multiculturalism are generally preoccupied with determining the degrees of compatibility or conflict between cultures.[14] What is obscured by this perspective are the porous boundaries between groups, the diffuse notions of identity, the deterritorialized links between members of groups, the globalizing patterns of communication and the hybrid process of cultural transformation. Homi Bhabha has further added that this perspective has failed to recognize the 'in-between space' of cultural globality. He has argued that the dynamic interactions between the local and the global occur within 'double frames' and 'in the nervous temporality of the transitional'.[15] Such flows cannot be grasped by either a critical method which presupposes a binary division between inside and outside, or a framework which determines identity and social relations in terms of pure membership.

Just as conventional methods have failed to grasp the subtlety of change at the micro level, the uneven processes of globalization have produced cultural forms with dimensions of reach that even the founding theorists could not have imagined. The classical ethnographic definitions of culture now seem inadequate to the task of explaining the current flows between diasporic and dominant cultural formations. The complexity of translation and exchange that operates at both the local and global levels has been obscured by reliance on mechanistic models of cultural regulation and domination. The key task for cultural theorists today is to develop more relational modes for thinking through the politics of cultural transformation, and to propose a discourse which challenges the stultifying binarisms that have hitherto pincered the sensibilities of the modern world:

Merely to urge students to insist on one's own identity, history, tradition, uniqueness may initially get them to name their basic requirement for democracy and for the right to an assured, decently humane existence. But we need to go on and to situate these in a geography of other identities, peoples, cultures, and then to study how, despite their differences, they have always overlapped one another, through unhierarchical influence, crossing, incorporation, recollection, deliberate forgetfulness and of course, conflict . . . the fact is, we are mixed in with one another in ways that most national systems of education have not dreamed.[16]

Between centre and periphery

While previous attempts to subordinate cultural flows as mere effects that have been caused by economic or political changes have been discredited, and while there has been a sustained problematization of the question of cultural differences in the discourses of both the nation-state and globalization, there has been no new 'overarching' theory identifying the precise alignments between social and cultural changes.[17] The interconnections between different economic and political systems, and the increased mobility of certain groups of people, have made more visible the complexity of change, the permeability of boundaries and the fluidities of identities. While our consciousness is now alert to the constant interactions between internal and external forces, however, our understanding of these dynamics is still rather crude. In the realm of cultural politics there is considerable anxiety and insecurity over the 'life forms' of different cultures. It is now necessary to pose questions over the form of diasporic culture which draws on the language of turbulence rather than, and not only in, mechanistic terms. Are diasporic cultures prone to dissipate and fall into accelerated states of entropy? Does the interaction between different cultural systems produce complex patterns that both sustain and redirect the respective trajectories of each culture? What are the feedback effects as continuous loops are established not only between the diasporic cultures and their homeland, but also via the eccentric orbits that occur simultaneously? Does the reiteration of one system in a different context imply the duplication or the perturbation of its own identity?

These new concepts and metaphors may reshape the way we define the dynamics of cultural transformation. Much of the misconception about either the autonomy or dependency of culture is fuelled by the prevailing counter-images of globalization as either a formless amoeba loosely shaped by its absorption of surrounding matter, or a restless shark which is on a perpetual and merciless path of destruction. Dissymmetries in the levels of economic and political power between different groups are routinely interpreted as determining the patterns of cultural interaction:

The West's cultural history is much interrelated. In Europe countries influenced each other more than they shuffled their borders. When the influences came from more different countries it was and still happens in terms of the West. The other way around, when other cultures take influences from the West, this is seen as an intrusion and damaging to their cultural identity.[18]

Much of the debate on the relationship between globalization and cultural production revolves around the question of whether local/non-western practices and concepts will be destroyed by the ascendant and dominant/western global forms. Contemporary culture cannot be mapped against the co-ordinates of the centre–periphery grid of political economy. This model presupposes that power is concentrated in the centre and dispersed concentrically. The direction of change is also fixated with an idealized notion of the centre, whereby advances are situated or consolidated in the centre and disseminated outwardly in a linear manner. The periphery is condemned to experience a belated modernity. The base–superstructure model which provided the twin axioms of these earlier theories of cultural development has been strongly resisted by Third World critics. For instance, Geeta Kapur has noted that the relative autonomy of indigenous cultural categories has been the focus of the debates on cultural discourse in India. This appreciation of the resilience of indigenous forms is not motivated by chauvinistic aspirations which seek to invert operative hierarchies of centre–periphery, but is a result of what she calls 'the civilizational presumptions in our cultural discourse. Deriving from a highly developed metaphysic [which] is an extensive and vastly hegemonic discourse.'[19]

Nestor Garcia Canclini's observations of cultural practices in Latin and South America have also stressed the survival of the 'traditional' and 'ancient' in the midst of the modern. In his account of cultural development and the relationship between the local and the global, which is also framed by the histories of colonialism, there is a subtle attention to the criss-crossing links between different orders, and the juxtaposition of dual or multiple perspectives. There is no suggestion that there has been linear progression out of one stage and into another, or the neat succession of one order over the other:

> In the homes of the bourgeoisie and the educated middle class in Santiago de Chile, Lima, Bogota, Mexico City and other cities, one finds multilingual libraries next to Indian crafts, cable television and satellite dishes among colonial furniture, magazines full of advice on the best investment of the week co-existing with centuries-old family and religious rituals. To be cultured, even in the modern world, is not so much to connect oneself with a repertoire of exclusively modern objects and messages but to know how to incorporate the avant-garde art and literature, as well as technological advances, into traditional patterns of social privilege and symbolic distinction.[20]

Underlying Gaulart's annotations on travelling cultures, Canclini's observation of the multitemporal heterogeneity of modern culture and Kapur's criticism of the importation of mechanistic political-economy models to explain

the dynamics of cultural transmission, there is a profound challenge to the way
we understand the concept of culture. There has been a long-standing and fundamental misconception about the identity of culture. Modernization and dependency theories tended to suggest that cultural transformation proceeded
according to a logic of either a linear progression or polar domination. This
view emphasized that traditional cultural forms would either be left behind or
extinguished by the 'fatal encounter' with modernity. However, this interaction
has not been as simple as these models suggested. The appropriation of symbolic goods has been multifaceted rather than mono-directional, and contradictory rather than consistent. As Canclini goes on to point out, it is not just literary
elites that have managed to negotiate the jagged edges between the popular, the
national and the international: 'We must take into account that the whole field
translates.'[21] This broader understanding of the translational process in cultural
activity disturbs the earlier polarities and hierarchies of progression and domination. The cultural markers between classes become more diffuse and more
complex, and the decoupling between the local and the national becomes more
pronounced as the cultural circulation caused by global migration intensifies.

If cultural transformation is activated by the infinite number of translations
at every level within a cultural system, then this suggests that there is a great
deal of uncertainty and instability in the structures of a culture. The very process of translation is a creative transformation that reorders the very languages
within which it operates. All translations are unpredictable because, like strange
attractors that shape turbulence in the physical world, their meaning and associations are formed in a field that is not predetermined by a fixed set of co-
ordinates but shaped by signs which themselves are mobile and bifurcate through
their own operational stretching and folding. Therefore the viability and resilience of a cultural system depends on the particularities in the patterns of interaction.

Globalization has heightened the contact points between different cultural
systems. There is the fear that the global empowerment of a specific order will
lead to the homogenization of all cultural systems. Before outright homogen-
izations can triumph, however, there is the infinity of practices and negotiations
within which cultural creativity, political expediency, spatial distribution and
economic necessity are mutually entangled. As Foucault pointed out, freedom
at one level is understandable only in relation to its other. Any effect which is
dependent upon the feedback of its neighbours will ultimately generate new
levels of complexity and bifurcation. The continual reabsorption or enfolding
of the past in the present, the foreign in the familiar, the self in the other, has a
rolling, hybridizing effect. Nevertheless, it is vital to appreciate the ambivalence associated with these turbulent patterns. Uncertainty and instability are
experienced in two ways. Within every act of translation there is the confrontation with the abyss of meaning. The non-correspondence between terms, the
missing information that would enable a difference to produce an equivalence,

heightens the creative sense of alienation in language. Coupled to this is the further uncertainty of not knowing where these new conjunctions lead.

From contamination to transformation

The fear that culture is endangered by contact with modernity partly comes from the nostalgic view that genuine cultures are pre-modern. There is a certain anthropological melancholy that constructs cultures like fragile species that need delicate protection, or suggests that their solemn rituals demand hushed reverence. This 'salvation paradigm' often remains oblivious of its own contradictory logic: if a culture is defined as the mechanism for constructing meaning in the world, why does it need to be sheltered from the very forces that it seeks to explain? These conflicting images of culture are linked to the contradictory understandings of culture as being, on the one hand, the dynamic process by which we make sense of everyday life and, on the other, as those fixed and specific rules which precede the current changes and guide the practices of living in the world.

Stuart Hall's pithy definition of culture as the 'dialectic between conditions and consciousness' and Pierre Bourdieu's theory of 'habitus' help us move out of the territorialized paradigm. Culture is not a fixed script which actors are bound to follow. The degree to which culture is an open-ended system relates to its own principles of interaction and reproduction. Its tendency towards continuity does not presuppose uniformity and coherence, but is conceived in terms of an oscillation between the actions of agents and the dynamic patterns of everyday life. The concept of habitus draws attention to this cultural dynamic of transformation. Habitual structures affect the lives of individuals but, in turn, the way agents inhabit these structures in their everyday life, affects the contours and trajectory of these structures. This can be clearly seen in the rituals for giving hospitality to strangers. These are mechanisms by which the foreign is made familiar, the outside is brought inside, without the absolute demand of assimilation. Bourdieu's attention to the interaction between structure and agency has reasserted the power dynamics in culture. Thus the idea of habitus does not privilege either the structures of society or the agency of the individual. It suggests that culture is not simply in the objective conditions of a society, or purely in the subjective consciousness of the individual, but is, rather, the constantly mobile and transformative exchange between the two.

This anxiety about the fate of culture in an age of globalization has produced much discussion about the destruction or resilience of specific cultural forms, but very little reflection on the mechanisms of cultural survival. Just as we need to examine the various forms of cultural exchange and domination, we must also consider the means by which different cultures interact with each other. A central question that will increasingly dominate this process is: how do we translate cultural differences? For thinking about, and judging between, different cultural viewpoints and practices presupposes the ability to translate across them. It is important to stress that cultural transformation is not all one-way. Stuart Hall has suggested that the models that social scientists developed to explain the integrative and crushing powers of globalization have emphasized the drive towards commodification but ignored the specific contexts within which it operates:

> As a consequence, we have lost sight of one of the most profound insights in Marx's *Capital* which is that capitalism only advances, as it were, in contradictory terrain. It is the contradictions which it has to overcome that produce its own forms of expansion. And that until one can see the nature of that contradictory terrain and precisely how particularity is engaged and woven in, and how it presents its resistances, and how it is partly overcome, and how those overcomings then appear again, we will not understand it. That is much closer to how we ought to think about the so-called 'logic of capital' in the advance of globalization itself.[22]

Janet Wolff has been even more direct in her criticism of the models proposed in the social sciences for understanding the processes of globalization and cultural formation. She attacked the social sciences for their perpetuation of an undifferentiated notion of culture, for their refusal to examine the discursive constitution of axiomatic concepts, for their inability to develop a materialist theory *of* culture rather than the extension of a materialist theory *to* culture, for the lack of awareness that ideologies operate through gender differences, and, finally, for their failure to follow current advances in the understanding of social process and representation that have already occurred elsewhere in the humanities.[23]

From this perspective the relationship between local cultural production and the 'advance of globalization' is not confined to defensive retreat into isolationism, where all contact with the other is warded off, or to an ethnocidal imposition of one culture's hegemony upon all others. Between these two unsustainable extremes lie a number of synthetic, reconciliatory and critical alternatives. And it is over the processes within this broad spectrum of cultural incorporation, appropriation and alternation that there is now a more lively debate about the way meanings in one culture shift, as they are reconstituted through interaction with other cultures.

The doubling of cultures

The idea that there can be a neat synthesis or equivalent translations between different cultures has been rejected in favour of views that stress the discrepancies, incommensurabilities and surpluses between cultures. This attention to the slippage and non-correspondence between cultural codes does not suggest that the process of exchange is undermined by difference, but rather that the remainder of a difference stimulates a reach towards unexpected horizons. The constitutive dissonances and residual gaps of silence between different cultures do not remain as the intransigent signs of cross-cultural impasses, but announce the compulsion for naming what has been referred to as the 'third space'. This perspective clearly addresses the disruptive flows of globalization, but it does not fall into the defensive mode of cultural chauvinists, nor adopt the redemptive tone of the salvation paradigm. Rather, it tracks the dynamism within displacement and emphasizes the agency within specific practices of ironic appropriation and critical incorporation. It stresses that cultural categories and forms, when inserted into different contexts, tend to take on contrary meanings and values. This 'double consciousness' of the gaps and excesses between intended and received meanings has the potential to expose the oppressive cultural hierarchies that are generally associated with globalization. The strategy for living with difference can thus vary from deliberate acts of sabotage to subtle forms of amendment.

A considerable body of writing in cultural studies and sociology has argued that the tendency towards globalization has not resulted in the homogenization of all peripheral cultures, or conversely the Americanization of global culture.[24] The indigenization of global culture has been represented within frameworks which stress the agency and reflexive practices of incorporation. The representations have also spawned an important range of critical terms like disruptive mimicry (Bhabha), critical appropriation (Gilroy), catachrestic naming (Spivak) and dynamic translation (Lotman). The fear that globalization would flatten differences has been replaced by a perspective which is more attuned to the ambivalence and contradictions that either spark from the contact between different cultures or unfold in the dynamics of incorporation. Celeste Olalquiaga's dazzling study of the incorporation of kitsch within traditional religious iconography in Latin America gives insight into the complex lives of contemporary cultures:

It can be said that each degree of religious imagery satisfies the desire for intensity in a different way: in the first degree through an osmotic process resulting from the collection and possession of objects still infused with use value; in the second degree by the consumption of the commodified nostalgia; and in the third degree by cannibalizing both the first and second degrees and recycling them into a hybrid product that allows for a simulation of the lost experience. Even though they're produced at different moments, these three degrees cohabit the same contemporary space. Their synchronicity accentuates the erasure of cultural boundaries already present in third-degree kitsch, throwing together and mixing different types of production and perception. This reflects the situation of the urban cosmopolis, where myriad cultures live side by side, producing the postmodern pastiche. Such an anarchic condition destabilizes traditional hegemony, forcing it to negotiate with those cultural discourses it once could oppress. The ability of cultural imagery to travel and adapt itself to new requirements and desires can no longer be mourned as a loss of cultural specificity in the name of exhausted notions of personal or collective identities. Instead, it must be welcomed as a sign of opening to and enjoyment of all that traditional cultures worked so hard at leaving out.[25]

Containing cultures

One difficulty of trying to map these forms of cultural exchange is that of defining global culture. Is there a single global culture? Does a global culture share the same features as a national culture? Anthony Smith, for instance, has struggled to define global culture because of the absence of the crucial structures that confer a sense of belonging, namely the role of memory, lineage, landscape, history and language.[26] It is through social institutions and collective practices that national cultures captured the imaginations of their citizens and generated such intense notions of loyalty that they were prepared to die for the sanctity of this idea.

Benedict Anderson has given us a convincing account of how the formation of nationalism was linked to specific historical developments and the generation of unique media practices.[27] Nationalism succeeded in constructing an image of unity amongst diverse and dispersed people because it relied on the formation of a distinct reading public. The daily task of sharing common news of the world helped define a sense of a unique people in a given territory. This geopolitical unit was never timeless, it was to a large extent a nineteenth-century invention. Through the enlisting of mythological references, the rewriting of history and no small dose of messianic conviction, the narrative of the nation was imbued with eternal if not salvific dimensions. The story of the nation has often been figured as a titanic struggle against evil aliens, with the actors seeing themselves as bearers of divine qualities. It is within the crucible of past heroic battles that the identity of the nation is forged. Most nations, irrespective of their location, tend to see themselves as the centre of the world. Given the intensifying pressures of globalization, however, will the narrative of the nation survive? Will the myth of a pure folk and a common stock endure through the traffic of modern migrations? Can the idea of a unified nation gloss over mounting social divisions? Will the new transversal social movements organizing themselves under the headings of gender or ecology feel bound to the structures of the nation?[28] Can the story of national origin continue to forget its own incontrovertible hybridity?[29] For how long will all the languages within a nation yield to one 'mother tongue'?

Despite the limitations in the discourse of the nation, there is no global culture which has developed such deep structures of belonging. But does that imply that there is no culture implicit in the process of globalization? Or that our imagination of cultural interaction is confined to the exchanges between national cultures? This tension between the status of cultural difference within the nation and the pressures of globalization is evident in the redefinition of the role of diasporized cultures. Even when the self-legitimating discourses of nation-states have adopted multicultural narratives with positive references to the diverse origins of its members, this representation of difference is projected only to confirm the greater image of the national culture. Instead of configuring the nation state through a self-image which prescribes a singular ideal, it now reconfigures these symbolic boundaries into the form of a mosaic, whereby it is through the combination of fragments into a single field that unity is found. The image of diversity that is promoted in the multicultural rhetoric is rarely presented as a threat to the boundaries, for it is premised on the assumption of cultural complementarity. It does not seek to displace, but only to multiply the foundations of the nation-state. However, the extent to which nations will find stability in the new global configurations will depend on our ability to translate the culture of one for the benefit of others and for the purposes of dialogue. But where will the cross-cultural communication be situated? Will this desire for communication necessarily lead to a universalist plateau upon which all cultures can be placed evenly and speak openly? There is little in the appropriation of concepts like multiculturalism by the nation-state that suggests a greater appreciation of the dynamic flux mobilized in all cultural identities. Rather, the promotion of essentialist and fixed views of culture within a multicultural framework has, according to Gillian Bottomley, been facilitated by the conflation between ethnicity and culture in order to overlook the 'relations of power within which ethnic boundaries are being drawn'.[30]

Circuits as spaces for community

The heightened movement of peoples, symbols and practices has not only undermined the structures that attempted to confer a sense of homogeneity in the social, as it embedded the identity of subjects within given geopolitical units and linear narratives of history, but has also problematized the degree to which migrants have made an exclusive identification with their place of work and living. The increasing polarization of migrant communities and itinerization and illegality of movement have cut against the conventional practices of settlement and adaptation. As rights of movement have become more restrictive, passages across borders more criminalized and possibilities more precarious, the spaces of diasporic communities have undergone transformation. The idea of permanent resettlement has become more remote. The classical migrant trajectories which were, for the most part, mapped in linear and unidirectional terms no longer correlate with the turbulent patterns of global migration. New patterns have emerged which highlight the provisionality of settlement.

From the wealthy 'astronaut' Asian entrepreneurs who maintain an active presence in a number of locations across the Pacific, to the 'illegals' who criss-cross the Rio Grande in search of seasonal work, migrants are increasingly adopting strategies which realign the relationship between their cultural identity and their sense of belonging. As Phillip Mar's study of Hong Kong migrants to Sydney has revealed, this has not always produced dysfunctional social relations. 'Such strategies belie conceptions of migrant cultures as beleaguered communities in a strange land whose cultural development is somehow "frozen" at the moment of migration.'[31] Mike Douglass has also noted that for the Korean migrants with high incomes, who 'commute' between the USA and Korea, there has been considerable cultural transformation at both ends of their journeying:

> Their situation cannot be captured by conventional concepts of permanent migrants, return migrants or sojourners. They are, for the most part, members of two or more societies and often move freely among them. They thus represent more than just migrant labour, they sustain ties to their home societies and their families tend to remain functional across national boundaries.[32]

The multiple displacement effects associated with globalization have had a radical impact on the way communities are 'grounded'. Communities are conventionally understood as being bound to specific places. Their identity and cohesion come from relationships that are patterned within a given territory. The strength of community, it is assumed, is dependent on the density and intensity of these relationships. Hence, when people 'move out' it is thought that they have left that community or, at best, that their active presence will be transformed into the more passive role of those who just keep 'in touch'. Membership of a community is thereby seen in terms of proximity and contact with the centre of that space. The further away from the centre one is situated, the looser, more irregular, less connected one feels. The further towards the periphery one gets, the more one is regarded as a stranger. However, this concentric and territorial construction of community has been challenged by the technological advances in communication and the multidirectional migrations of globalization.

The incessant flows of capital and symbolic forms across borders, and the routinized forms of dialogue by means of telephone or other media, have all altered our relationship to space. The ability to have a determining influence in a community is no longer dependent on having an ongoing presence in that space. Clearly these technological innovations have paved the way for transnational corporations to realign their control centres and extend their powers into the most remote corners of the planet. Yet the processes of global migration have also generated new cultural developments.[33]

Migration always affects the social and spatial relations of community. In the past social scientists tended to confine this process of transformation to an 'adjustment problem'. Movement from one place to another was seen as a negotiation of one discrete culture with another. Measuring these negotiations became an exercise in tracking the success or failure of different communities in assimilating with each other, or of one community in adapting to the needs of the new locale. This bi-polar framework, with its emphasis on a unidirectional transition from one state to another, overlooked the more complex movements between and within different zones. More recent studies of migrant communities reveal spatial arrangements which are multidirectional, and social relations which maintain involvement with numerous places. Roger Rouse's study of Mexican migrants in California illustrates this process of deterritorialization.[34] The everyday life of these migrants is one of profound rupture and transition. Yet within these dislocations he traces the dynamism of intercultural and economic movements that connect and redefine both the migrant community in Silicon Valley and the rural Mexican town of Aguililla from which these migrants have come. Rouse stresses that these two communities can no longer be seen as separate entities. The frequency of 'return' visits, the economic dependencies and the symbolic transfers are of such intensity that their culture has been deterritorialized:

> Today, Aguilillans find that their most important kin and friends are as likely to be living hundreds or thousand miles away as immediately around them. More significantly, they are often able to maintain these spatially extended relations as actively and effectively as ties that link them to their neighbours.[35]

Through this heightened form of transnational circulation and interaction, Rouse argues, they are better understood as forming a 'single community spread in a variety of places'. What becomes determinate in defining this new sense of community is not a specific locus in which relations are *principally* grounded but the process of being in a circuit. What characterizes this community is a simultaneous engagement with different social practices rather than gradual adaptation of one to another. This provides an interesting comparison with Mar's observation that for Hong Kong migrants in Sydney, 'settling in this context may entail disposing oneself comfortably to arrangements involving moving between places.'[36]

Defining deterritorialization

The deterritorialization of culture refers to the ways in which people now feel they belong to various communities despite the fact that they do not share a common territory with all the other members. It also refers to the way that a national or even a regional culture can no longer be conceived as reflecting a coherent and distinct identity. This attention to the way communities are connected, despite being spread across considerable distances, and redefined through exchange across multiple borders, has challenged the classical ethnographic assumptions that cultures could be mapped into autonomous and bounded spaces. The authenticity of a cultural formation is no longer singularly linked to its physical proximity to a given cultural centre. This perspective would reject the centre–periphery model which concentrates power and resources in one location and then distributes them concentrically with diminishing effect. Rouse proposes that the reconfigurations of influence and capital in the global order require an 'alternate cartography of social space' based more on the notions of the 'circuit' and 'border'.

Deterritorialization is also the key concept for Arjun Appadurai's representation of cultural formations in modernity. Appadurai gives greater stress to the instability and volatility in political expressions and cultural affiliations that emerge from the process of deterritorialization. Diasporic communities have not always championed new and more inclusive modes of cultural understanding. They have also forged intense attachments to fundamentalist beliefs and offered financial backing to chauvinist campaigns in their homelands. When identity is at the cusp of transformation there is also a tendency to retreat into, or even to fabricate, hostile narratives which bolster boundaries and exclude any identification with the other. The contradiction between the Greek, Jewish and Hindu diasporas for, on the one hand, the preservation of their cultural rights in their adopted places of residence, and, on the other, their support for intolerant and exclusivist policies in their homeland, deserves closer critical scrutiny. The Bosnian war provided the most stark arena for the battle between fundamentalism and cosmopolitanism.[37] The political struggle to reterritorialize the different communities cut against the grain of centuries of cultural intermingling and numerous mixed marriages. Yet the violent complicities between nation, religion and land seemed to override any counter-histories of transcultural unity and coexistence.[38]

On the other hand, the process of deterritorialization has created new cultural links that have transformed practices at both ends. Diasporic communities, for example, provide additional markets for Greek film companies and the Hindi music industry. The establishment of a Greek-Australian film festival and the development of Bhangra music in Britain have given new inflections to traditional forms, as well as generating new hybrid representations, of cultural identity. Bhangra, for instance, has a complex history, and not all of its current exponents trace its heritage back to rural Punjabi harvest dance music. Bhangra is a crossover music, which has as much influence from the sampling techniques of rap and urban punk jungle sounds as from traditional and ecstatic forms of Qawwali. It has no clear-cut form or resolution, as its development constantly oscillates between a UK metropolitan, diasporic sound and the reactivation of traditional music in India and Pakistan.[39] The circuit that feeds these musical forms often bypasses the metropolitan and commercial music networks.

Despite these complex routes of influence and distribution, audiences are not necessarily confined to ethno-specific groups. The cultural dynamic of deterritorialization has decoupled previous links between space, stability and reproduction; it has situated the notion of community in multiple locations; it has split loyalties and fractured the practices that secure understanding and knowledge within the family and social unit. This complex set of relationships has created more ambivalent images of homeland and put greater stress on the need for re-imagining the possibilities of belonging.

The concept of deterritorialization was first used by Deleuze and Guattari to locate the moment of alienation in language. Referring to Kafka's unhomely relationship to German literature, Deleuze and Guattari stress that his radical practice of defamiliarizing the everyday and his distanciation from the conventions of the dominant language facilitate a creative vision even as they heighten the experience of exile. By refusing to give up the proper meaning of terms, or by undermining the certitudes of belonging, Kafka articulates a mode of becoming which is open, fluid and nomadic. His use of language serves 'to express another potential community, to force the means for another consciousness and another sensibility'.[40] For Deleuze and Guattari deterritorialization is most evident in what they called 'minor literature'. The term 'minor' does not relate to status but rather towards its critical position in relation to canonical writing and its subversive use of the dominant language. In minor literature the code of representation is deterritorialized as identities and meanings are decoupled from their conventional positions to produce an exilic effect in language. While artists and writers like the former members of the Border Arts Workshop embraced the concept of deterritorialization in order to highlight their 'borderized' cultural practice,[41] cultural critics have developed a more cautious approach in its application in the cultural politics of the diaspora.[42]

In a feminist extension of Deleuze and Guattari's scheme of thought Rosi Braidotti has stressed that the image of deterritorialization refers to 'a critical consciousness that resists settling into socially coded modes of thought and behaviour'.[43] It is the subversion of conventions and resistance to all claims of authenticity rather than the physical act of movement which is the critical feature of this subjectivity. Flow from one set of experiences to another and the rerouting of associations and naming practices are highlighted to undo the centrality of a mother tongue and sovereign self, and thereby heighten the intensive interconnectedness and ethical relationships which come with polylingual practices. However, as Caren Kaplan pointed out, the extension that Deleuze and Guattari make, from the radical edges of modernist literature to the cultural politics of immigrant communities, tends to overlook the fields of power relations in which displacement is constituted, and underestimates the necessary resources for the production of narratives that reterritorialize the subject.[44]

In their final collaboration Deleuze and Guattari returned to the concept of deterritorialization to confront its utopian associations and expand upon the complex relationship between thought and territory. 'Thinking is neither a line drawn between subject and object nor a revolving of one around the other. Rather, thinking takes place in the relationship of territory and the earth.'[45] Despite the critical relationship between the concept of utopia and philosophy, Deleuze and Guattari rejected its linkage with deterritorialization. In their view the common usage of the concept of utopia has been 'mutilated' by its associations with a fabled alternative or an idealized transcendence. By questioning the relationship between the philosopher and his or her homeland, they moved between the spiritual and the physical sense of exile. Deterritorialization, they claim, is not a form of romantic detachment or cosmopolitan rootlessness. The homeland of philosophy is always unknown, lost or forgotten, leaving the philosopher in a deterritorialized state, and it is through thought that a reterritorialization is regained. They stress that the prior states of the homeland and deterritorialization are not reducible to an imaginary origin or a transitional period by this process of reterritorialization. Reterritorialization is never complete or final, but a constant oscillation between the other states. In the exilic search for home, they cannot even determine which comes first. For the very act of seeking a territory implies a prior deterritorialization and its own reterritorialization in the realm of myth and dream, or land and commodity, with each movement occurring not in a linear sequence but within a knotted entanglement. Furthermore, within each movement there may be counter-movements. Deterritorialization may also envelop a negative movement that takes a chauvinistic turn towards the homeland rather than the positive view which seeks to unhinge itself from notions of exclusivity and purity. Similarly, within the attractive concepts of hybridity and semantic heterogeneity there may be the repulsive dogma that seeks to cut itself out of the field of difference. Attractive and repulsive concepts, negative and positive movements are all folded within one another and form the complex planes which either connect or bifurcate. These processes, Deleuze and Guattari argue, are so inextricably mixed that they can only be diagnosed through the psycho-social types like the exile, the stranger, the migrant.

Critical modalities and mobile subjectivities

The concept of deterritorialization has been a useful mode of understanding the fissures within language and cultural identity. It suggests more than just a kind of intellectual mobility but refers to a critical sensibility of innovation and improvization. Through the process of extending forms as they are translated into different contexts or transforming concepts through elaboration with new materials, the deterritorialized subject both develops a more dynamic relationship between past and present, and offers new interpretations of the flows in the world. Edward Said is ever vigilant over the differences between an intellectual and a refugee, and yet he remains convinced that, from Adorno's cogitations on loss and freedom to Shariati's dialectics of motion and struggle, the migrant intellectual is capable of at 'first distilling then articulating the predicaments that disfigure modernity'.[46] Said's faith in the migrant intellectual is not premised on a romantic disposition that correlates creativity with adversity, but is linked to his deeper claims for promoting a relational rather than fixed consciousness. It is the ability to relate the political struggles for liberation with the experiential consequences of displacement that energizes Said's interpretation of culture. Repeatedly he stresses that it is those who fight against the opposition between the fixed and the homeless, the centre and the periphery, that will open a new consciousness for our age. Yet it is crucial that this modality should also be located in the specific contexts of its own displacement and be aware of the limitations of an oppositional discourse. As Appadurai notes, the complex task of producing a sense of locality within the contradictory interactions of national political formation and global electronic mediations has meant that the new language for articulating the movements and aspirations of diasporic communities has been trapped by self-defeating logic:

No idiom has yet emerged to capture the collective interests of many groups in translocal solidarities, cross-border mobilizations, and postnational identities. Such interests are many and vocal, but they are still entrapped in the linguistic imaginary of the territorial state. The incapacity of many deterritorialized groups to think their way out of the imaginary of the nation-state is itself the cause of much global violence because many movements of emancipation and identity are forced, in their struggles against existing nation-states, to embrace the very imaginary they seek to escape. Postnational or nonnational movements are forced by the very logic of actually existing nation-states to become antinational or antistate and thus to inspire the very state power that forces them to respond in the language of counternationalism. This vicious circle can only be escaped when a language is found to capture complex, nonterritorial, postnational forms of allegiance.[47]

Alongside the motion associated with mass migration, Appadurai argues that the media have initiated new global cultural processes. Originally, as Benedict Anderson noted, the press played the key role in presenting the 'imagined community' of the nation as the space in which a sense of belonging could be grounded. Appadurai is not as explicit in his identification of the precise media which are conferring the complex and multiple senses of belonging in what he calls the 'postnational political world'. However, he is clear that the media constitute a wider field and that the concept of the imaginary and the workings of the imagination have a more central role in the formation of these new social and cultural practices. The imagination, he argues, is no longer to be understood as mere illusion, as opposed to real work, nor as idle escapism or elitist contemplation, but as an 'organized field of social practice, a form of work (in the sense of both labour and of culturally organized practice) and a form of negotiation between sites of agency (individuals) and globally defined fields of possibility.'[48]

Imagination has become central to all forms of social practice. Even the most intimate personal relationships routinely involve negotiation across vast distances and the juxtaposition of unrelated concepts. If you have not been forced to move far, it is quite likely that your neighbours have come from a distant location, or someone else that is close to you will move to a foreign place. The work of the imagination as well as the dynamics of migration are both constitutive features of modernity. From the telecasting of global events like the Olympic Games to the establishment of ethno-specific radio stations by diasporic communities, the dissemination of information and the representation of events are stretching the notions of collective participation and redefining the resources for self-definition.

To enable a mapping that links the disjunctive processes of globalization to the new relationships to space, Appadurai has proposed five key terms; ethnoscapes, mediascapes, technoscapes, finanscapes and ideoscapes. Each of these terms is defined by the tensions of mobility and stability and the social practices that oscillate between imaginary and material divisions. In Appadurai's theory of modernity motion is ongoing, either at the level of physical displacement or in the imaging of otherness, and as he notes, the pathways of this geographic and conceptual motion are often in contradiction with each other. There has always been a gap between how far people want to go, and where they can enter. But the relationship between the imaginings of other spaces and the physical possibilities of participating in these worlds has never been so polarized.

Appadurai explores this tension through Pico Iyer's account of the adoption of American popular culture within Filipino society. One would assume that the genre of 'country and western music' would not exactly speak to the hearts and minds of young Filipinos, and if it were successful, this would be merely evidence of cunning marketing and the last cultural residue of dependency in a former colony. Appadurai argues, however, that Filipino identification with this music cannot be explained away as evidence of the weakness of the indigenous culture or in terms of a passive yearning for the dominant culture's lifestyle. He stresses that while the adoption of this music goes against the grain of material differences, it is also an act which 'plays havoc with the hegemony of Euro-chronology'.

How does this practice break out of the vicious cycle that confines the servant to merely repeating the master's voice? Firstly, Appadurai points out that this identification with American country and western music does not express a yearning to return to a folkloric past, but rather is a means of making some claim to be part of a modern present. The music is clearly nostalgic in America, but for Filipinos who do not have those memories, this nostalgic modality is just a way of being in the present. The competence with which Filipinos can reproduce this music suggests that memory is not the crucial factor in their identification. This difference will generate a set of practices and responses which do not neatly correspond to those in America, where the nostalgia for a lost idyll is the central feature of the music. Hence the Filipinos, by short-circuiting the relationship between past and present in popular culture, are creating what Appadurai calls 'non-isomorphic paths in the global flows'.

Appadurai goes on to propose a four-tiered model which will counter the simple equation between globalization and homogenization. Firstly, the flow of capital and industrial infrastructure will not necessarily be facilitated by the dissemination of knowledge. Secondly, the development of ethnic politics will not be contained within the prevailing political structures or accord with the historical narratives of the nation. Thirdly, production fetishism, that is, the idiom of embedding production within a local context, will demand attention to cultural specificity. Fourthly, as choice is elevated as the highest social goal, the fetishism of the consumer will impact on the construction of agency.

From this model we become not only conscious of the deep connections between political, economic, historic and symbolic orders but also aware that, despite the contradictions between these levels, cultural flows continue. This presents us with a perplexing sense of what culture is and how it can be mapped. Appadurai suggests that, in order to pursue these cultural configurations, we need to move away from earlier paradigms of culture which stressed highly localized, boundary-oriented and holistic units, and proposes that contemporary cultural forms are better understood by drawing on the vocabulary of new physics. Hence his view of the culture that is produced by deterritorialised communities, where the reference points for the generations within a single family will vary not only in temporal order but also in spatial location.

Migrant communities no longer define themselves in terms of a singular vectorial link to the place of origin. Not only has the dream of returning to the native land been deferred, but also the sense of being centred in one place, where personal meaning can find an ordered relationship with social structures, has been displaced. How can traditions mutate in order to be meaningful across generations which are separated not only in the temporal perspective but also by vastly different relationships to place?

6

The Limits of Cultural Translation

How many people live today in a language that is not their own?

G. Deleuze and F. Guattari, *Kafka: Towards a Minor Literature*

Much discussion of the concept of culture has so far been confined to how it has been affected by the global changes of mass migration, economic transformation and the new technologies for communication. However, the deterritorialization of culture requires us to rethink not only the significance of place but also the process by which cultural change occurs. The displacement of peoples and the greater interpenetration of information and values has led to rapid and profound levels of cultural change. At the forefront of these changes is the dissemination of the icons of western capitalism. The omnipresence of McDonalds and MTV, Nike and Coke have stimulated fears of global consumerism being the form of a new cultural homogenization. Cultures, which were once seen to be meaningful because they were presumed to be discrete, stable, coherent and unique are now increasingly seen as interconnected, dynamic, fragmented and amorphous. If the shape of culture shifts towards flux rather than stability, how does this affect our way of understanding cultural practice?

Cultures were considered significant insofar as they could enable people to gain a clear image of themselves and present a distinctive world-view. Identity is the process of making sense of oneself, and the system by which this is communicated and shared is culture. These images and perspectives were said to have been formed over a considerable period of time and to be unique to a given place. It was thus imperative for a culture to be 'master' over its own history and geography. The survival of culture may have been threatened by invaders who occupied its territory, but a people could always claim that the culture lived through the 'spirit' of a people as they struggled for their return to their mythical homeland. Adherents to a particular culture not only saw it as their duty to preserve their specific practices and symbols but also felt bonded to each other. Culture was thus seen as embedded in a given place, continuous over a long stretch of time and exclusive to a particular group. With the radical transformations that colonialism introduced, and most recently accentuated by globalization, such views of culture have been brought to a crisis.

Globalization has not rendered culture an obsolete concept. People still form groups, and they require symbols and systems with which to communicate. The meanings which are generated and shared by this process of communication are, as before, an expression of culture. Communities are formed out of these interactions. Even in the extremes of colonization or the most turbulent phases of globalization, there is the enduring tendency to form what Stuart Hall calls 'systems of shared meaning'.[1] The transformations brought about by globalization may further dismantle traditional structures for shaping cultural systems, disempower key agents, discard earlier forms of knowledge, or even reinscribe the narratives of solidarity and unity, but globalization must also present new cultural symbols and practices through which individuals will understand their position in the world. Globalization may present us with a more oppressive and restrictive form of culture but the new manifestation should not be confused with the death of culture.

To understand the means by which identities are shaped in contemporary society, we must recognize the ways in which globalization has shifted the boundaries and transformed the media of culture. Different cultures may struggle for ascendancy and domination over each other. Rival interpretations and competing norms may emerge or recede. We have come to appreciate that cultures do not need to be rooted in a given place, that fragments of culture can survive in multiple places, that cultural meanings may leap across generations and transform themselves across the gaps of time. Yet this appreciation of the 'diasporization' of culture has been remarkably undertheorized. Tradition and modernity appear to be caught in a duel to the death over the identity of culture. The demand is for either the total preservation of the 'old' body or the birth of an absolute 'new' culture. What is obscured by this adversarial model of cultural struggle is the resilience of the old in the form of the new, the unconscious repetition of previous habits in current practices, the subtle transpiration of traditional values in contemporary norms. In short, cultural supremacy is defined in absolute terms. Cultural commentators have often missed the more subtle forms of interdependency between old and new because of a preoccupation with measuring the impact rather than understanding the processes of cross-cultural exchange.

Since Edward Said's influential study of orientalism, the uneven patterns of exchange between different cultures have been well documented.[2] Much attention has been focused on the way colonialism invaded established traditions, introduced new relationships of dependency and created new hierarchies. The patterns of influence were considered unidirectional – emanating from the imperial centre and dispersed outwardly across the peripheries of the colonies. The new cultural patterns of globalization differ from colonialism: rather than appearing as a centre–periphery binarism, they resemble a multidirectional circuit board. Again, traditional communities and established customary ways of life are being realigned and displaced according to priorities and desires which are defined elsewhere. Meanwhile, the metropolitan hierarchies have been significantly reconfigured.

The main purpose of this chapter is not to trace what Doreen Massey calls the uneven 'geography of power',[3] but rather to investigate the processes by which cultural differences are internalized and understood. For the concept of culture to continue to be useful we must recognize the process by which communication occurs across boundaries. This chapter will also relate contemporary practices in the visual arts with the debates on culture. The aim is not to use art merely to illustrate abstract theoretical points, but to examine the way the nature of art is already entangled in the dynamics of cultural translation. In this chapter I will not attempt to establish the unacknowledged significance of the exilic sensibility in modernity, rather I will focus on the concept of translation as a metaphor for understanding how the foreign and the familiar are interrelated in every form of cultural production. The theoretical discussion on cross-cultural exchange and the commentary on the work of Yinka Shonibare and Jimmie Durham will thereby aim to illuminate the conceptual as well as the experiential role of exile in contemporary culture.

Syncretism and the signs of difference

Although mainstream art criticism has shown a reluctance to address the question of cultural difference in Euro-American art, it has enthusiastically greeted the ethnographies of 'otherness' in the art practices of non-Euro-American artists. This ambivalence to the domain of culture is symptomatic of a deep-seated belief that western artists must always transcend their particular context and be representative of a universal perspective. The same status of universality is not extended globally. For instance, Rasheed Araeen, who has worked exclusively with the grammar of modernism and championed internationalist perspectives in art discourse, has lived in London for over thirty years but is still referred to as a 'Pakistani artist' by critics.

Yet when the German artist Lothar Baumgarten quotes from the Cherokee language, or references his experiences in the Amazon, mainstream critics do not dismiss this as quasi-anthropological forays, nor do they question the elasticity of his ethnicity. Reflecting on his own motivations, Baumgarten has claimed: 'The spiritual and intuitive force that drives me is rooted in dissatisfaction . . . the dream of creating the world all over again within oneself. . . . Though trapped in my Western thought patterns, I have always been interested in the "Other", the societies without a state.'[4] Such a confession is never interpreted as pure regression but as a legitimate strategy in the search for lost origins. Such 'noble' expressions of nostalgia and the hope that the west's own past can be found in the 'savage' present of the 'other' presuppose that cultural development follows a universal, linear time scale. The west can look back at the 'other', because it already believes that the state of modernity is the benchmark in its own myth of human progress, that it has advanced ahead of both the 'other' and its own roots. The 'other' lives in its own present but this is also the past of the west. For the 'other' to come to the west and seek to comment on the present of modernity would require a historical leap over its own belatedness. The western artist can step back into the time of the 'other', but the reverse is not sanctioned: the leap forward is seen as a form of modern-day hubris. The 'other' can only speak with authority about its own past, while the western artist is imbued with the melancholy privilege of living in the present. It is this burden of dissatisfaction with modernity which spurs the search for its own innocent origins in the 'other'.

This binarism of the west and its 'other' is indicative of the implicit hierarchies and the prescribed directions of influence in contemporary art. The mainstream discourse still presumes that authentic – genuinely global – developments in modernism can only occur in the context of its own metropolitan culture. There is little recognition of the possibility that as modernity has been dispersed across the globe, parallel or even revolutionary expressions of modernism have been articulated in non-metropolitan cultures. If the sign of difference in origin were no longer discredited, then our conceptual frameworks for cultural translation might be expanded through an understanding of the relationship between different practices in art. Cultural exchange is a precondition of art, and therefore attention to its processes can not just register the transcendental signs of value or taste, but issue an inventory of the dynamics of change. Yet, as Jean Fisher warned, this forward-looking orientation is not without its own traps and limitations:

> The dilemma remains how to express one's worldview, with all the multiple cultural inflections that inform it, without betraying either one's historical or geographic specificity or art, and without being caught in the web of signs that are all too consumable as exotic commodity. Perhaps one needs to think of cultural expression not on the level of signs but in terms of concept and deep structure: to consider both the work's internal movement and what governs the aesthetic choices an artist might make about materials and process, and the material relation the work has with the viewer.[5]

The question I wish to ask is not so much about *where* culture is located, or *what* is happening to culture, but *how* different cultures interact. This will require me to focus more directly on the processes of exchange and translation. The discussion of the limits of translation, and the resistance to exchange, is not undertaken with a view to arguing either the dysfunctionality or the impossibility of cultural interaction, but as a challenge to our very understanding of culture.

The concept of translation has been largely overlooked in the sociological and anthropological literature on culture. With the exception of the anthropological discussion on syncretism the conceptual frameworks which have sought to address the cultural dynamics of exchange have remained on the fringes of the social sciences. Yet even this discussion on syncretism is of limited use as it has been confined largely to the synthesis of distinctive religious practices.

Syncretism has an ambivalent status in anthropological debates on cultural exchange. It is often used pejoratively to suggest the dilution or corruption of indigenous religious systems through the proselytizing order of Christianity.[6] According to the *Oxford English Dictionary,* one of the accepted meanings of syncretism is as a derogatory term for the 'inconsistency of accepting incompatible principles or beliefs'. The more pragmatically minded missionaries discovered that the road to conversion was not cut open by the absolute abandonment of earlier beliefs, but paved by the mixture and absorption of indigenous rituals and beliefs within Christian structures. Contamination can occur both ways. Missionaries began to tolerate, sometimes even participate in, practices which the dogma of the Church deemed pagan. Traditional spirits and animistic beliefs which were worshipped alongside and through the figure of Christ represented, to some critics, the failure for one system fully to assimilate the other according to its own rules and hierarchy. This reconfiguring of the expressions of spirituality was also interpreted as an indicator of the resilience of traditional cultures after their contact with the 'repressive' or 'modernizing' forces of the West.

These views of syncretism which tended to accept the colonizer's superiority did little to break the paradigm of purity/contamination in which the debates on cultural translation tend to be trapped. One notable exception is the work of Bequer and Gatti, who have attempted to repoliticize the concept of syncretism, by not only retracing the word's etymology – Plutarch first used it to refer to the tactical union of communities of ancient Crete in the face of a common enemy – but also by problematizing its historical deployment. Their reinscription of the concept of syncretism is presented in conjunction with a critique of the filmic representation of 'vogueing'. This dance fad, they argue, became a subcultural practice by which poor, young black and Hispanic gays could, in the space of a club, adopt various glamour poses as a symbolic challenge to each other and in general, strut out against the status system. 'Real' poses from the magazine *Vogue* were exaggerated, inverted and fused with movements from break-dancing or, in more overt ways of referencing cultural difference, with Egyptian hieroglyphics. There was no effort to mimic the established norms or to present a neat synthesis into a new and unique third form.

The energy of vogueing, like syncretism, they argue, challenges the transcendental stability of concepts like identity and difference. When other signs are adopted there is no attempt to resolve or elevate them into a higher order. Rather, syncretic dynamics are defined in terms of a constantly mobile relation between different signs. By being conjoined or juxtaposed, these new relations operate like a language. These affiliations between difference and similitude are not absolute, but shift according to both context and performance. The tendency within this combinatory logic is not towards an uncritical adoption but towards a rearticulation of symbols that both reaffirm a suppressed heritage and offer a challenge to the hegemony of the dominant culture. While this representation of vogueing as a syncretic articulation refuses to repeat the essentialist binarisms of identity by proposing a radically heterogeneous concept of agency, it leaves open a number of questions about the politics of transculturation. Through the work of Becquer and Gatti, syncretism becomes a metaphor for a more open-ended understanding of cultural practice. However, all this amounts to little more than a shift away from laments about degradation to celebration of a more tolerant mode of resistance and renewal. The processes by which this mixture comes into being still remain undertheorized.

Translation as a model for meaning

Language is not only one of the strongest and most resilient media for shaping cultural systems but can also serve as a model for understanding how meanings are produced and transmitted within culture. Since the pioneering work of Whorf and Sapir we have been aware of the ways in which people who share a language also develop common ways of seeing the world.[7] Whorf used the example of Hopi Indians to demonstrate how even fundamental experiences like the passing of time are understood and communicated in ways which are specific to their respective language. This experience of time and the specific value that is given to it is shared by all those who use that language. The way they see and the manner in which they speak about the world are deeply related. It is for this reason that communities become passionately attached to their language and then defend it so fiercely. Many struggles for national independence have been mobilized by the call for the right to maintain one's native language, and by the desire to be released from the yoke of the oppressor's language.

Cultures make sense of the world predominantly through the system of meanings that operate in language. These meanings are not fixed or singular. Meanings both shift and transform within a given language, and differ between languages. Not even a basic concept like time is identical in all languages. To understand how meaning is secured across these differences, we need not only to consider how culture works like a language, but to expand the conceptual reach of the trope of translation to incorporate the processes of transculturation and hybridization. We need to investigate the means by which people, with different cultural histories and practices, can form patterns of communication and establish lines of contact across their differences.

Mary Louise Pratt has argued that the space of colonial encounters bristles with the contradictions and conflicts of uneven exchange, and that these 'contact zones' ignite radical and new forms of co-presence between subjects who were previously strangers.[8] It is during these delicate and volatile moments in the 'contact zone' that transculturation occurs. Colonized people, forcibly brought into contact with colonial regimes, and with new systems for social organization, were compelled both to internalize the dominant order, and to invent new strategies for cultural survival. As most studies of colonialism have tended either to condemn or to celebrate the perspective of the colonizer, little attention has been paid to the actual strategies of survival and adaptation by the colonized.[9] For while the colonized had little control over the dominant culture, they were not always willing to reproduce, in either a pure or wholesale manner, a world-view that was alien to them.

The complex and profoundly asymmetrical negotiations that were conducted in these 'contact zones' are testament to how cultures are transformed, but not determined, by power relations. They also reveal the subtle mechanisms for resistance and cultural survival that are exercised by subjugated and marginalized people. The concept of syncretism can be radically expanded if it is applied to the broader practices of transculturation. Here we can witness that it is in every aspect of communication, and not just in religious adoption, that there is a process of critical appropriation. The subversive potential of transculturation is particularly apparent in Jean Rouch's film *Les Maîtres Fous* (1953–4),[10] filmed in the Gold Coast three years before independence. Rouch follows a gang of migrants from the villages of Niger – roadworkers, shopkeepers and petty criminals – as they leave the city of Accra and take a trail into the jungle. Upon arriving in a remote clearing, they immediately begin to whip themselves into a writhing frenzy and perform mouth-foaming rituals of sacrifice and loyalty. These men, we eventually realize, have created a performance which both mocks and mimics the inauguration ceremonies of the Governor-General. The language with which they communicate is a creole that includes both the colonizer's language and their own various languages. The symbolic sacrifice of a rooster, and their visual performance of dressing and undressing, jest at the starched and plumed uniforms of their colonial masters. This ceremony is a hybrid cultural form that seeks to reverse the social relations of colonialism. The relationship between the ruler and the ruled, guards and subjects, is played out in a series of bizarre forms, in which licence is given to the expression of thoughts and actions unimaginable in the 'proper' context of colonialism.

Through the example of this film, we can see the consequence of different cultures interacting within the 'contact zone'. The effects of this interaction can be referred to as transculturation, creolization or hybridization. We have noted that the patterns of influence under colonialism were dominated by metropolitan cultural values, and that under globalization, these patterns have been significantly dispersed and decentred. In the era of globalization the 'contact zone' has become more jagged. When more people are displaced than ever before, and information networks are moving with greater speeds, then the spatial points of contact between different cultures become more dispersed and fragmented, and their duration more contracted and irregular. To examine these processes we need to return to the concept of translation.

To apply the translation models, however, requires that we wrestle against many of the presumptions that confine translation to the mere communication of meaning from one language to another. The potential for understanding the dynamics of translation is caught between conflicting theories of language. On the one hand, there is the view that the deepest secrets and most intimate expressions in one language can never be communicated in another. On the other, there is the assumption of the existence of universal ideas, which implies that there are corresponding meanings between different languages, and that equivalent transferrals from one to another are possible. The latter view stresses that the relationship between the form and content of a word is arbitrary, that the content of a word can be separated from the specific form it takes in a given language, and then transferred to different languages. This approach also presumes that words in other languages will carry foreign concepts, or that an equivalent concept exists in the other language. Either way, the act of transferral is not seen as disrupting or transforming the content. The translation, if executed properly, is seen as either retaining or mirroring back the original meaning.

This was the view adopted by numerous Christian missionaries as they proceeded to transmit 'God's words'. Their translations of the Bible into other languages were considered to be unproblematical, because they believed that there was only one universal truth that could be equally represented in different languages and not transformed or disrupted by the processes of translation. But, as Birgit Meyer has argued, it was not so much a matter of the missionaries *giving* the word as the converts *making* it. In her analysis of the syncretic practices between Christianity and the Ewe she shows that the process of communication is always polysemic and that 'as a result of translation terms are transformed; they no longer mean what they meant in *either* the source *or* the target language.'[11] This does not imply that because there is no equivalence or pristine transferral, translation is impossible. Indeed all translators perceive the incommensurability or the intransigence of languages:

> But despite this, in practice, translations are still made. Rather than stating their theoretical impossibility, one should wonder what actually happens when meanings practically cross linguistic boundaries. Mutual intelligibility between two languages is neither a given nor an impossibility, but something to be constituted

by intersubjective dialogue across cultural boundaries. Translation, then, can be understood as interpreting and transforming the original statement, and thereby creating something of a new statement.[12]

This transformative view of language goes against the grain of the traditional conceptual balance between 'fidelity' and 'freedom' that underpins most discussions on translation. The conventional role of the translator is to reproduce a text in another language while remaining faithful to the meaning of the original. Such a contract can never be fulfilled in total, for one side always remains in conflict with the other. Nor can the translator assume freedom without sacrificing fidelity to the text. Words in themselves are always in a state of flux. Their meanings change over time, both as they evolve within their own context, and as they are moved to other places and reinterpreted. In Plato's view, there is no objective relationship between a word and its meaning, and therefore translation can only lengthen the shadowy spaces of language.

The irreconcilable tensions between fidelity and freedom have been most acutely observed in the translation of poetry. Schopenhauer declared: 'Poems cannot be translated, they can only be rewritten, which is always an ambiguous undertaking.'[13] Translation is seemingly caught between two impossibilities: that of isolating the essence in the original and that of determining an equivalence in the other language. Thus translations can never communicate the exact meanings of a text. However, this limitation does not grant the translator the licence to recreate the text through the act of translation. To assume such a freedom would imply that meaning in one language is beyond communication, and that ultimately all meanings would remain closed and resistant to any transferral. Hence, translation would not be the process of connecting together the relationship between languages but a substitution for an otherwise impenetrable silence.

While acknowledging that in all languages there are words which are so intricately woven into their context that any attempt to transfer them would rupture the crystalline configuration which holds their meaning in place, Walter Benjamin argued against the view that the translator must either seek to reproduce the exact meaning or be condemned to silence. The task of the translator is, he argues, one which consists in 'finding that intended effect upon the language into which he is translating which produces in it the echo of the original'.[14] This echo does not come about by the translator's assuming the authorial role of initiation and assemblage of the text, but through a structural approximation of its orientation.[15] From this perspective Benjamin clearly situates the modality of translation as being midway between poetry and doctrine. Benjamin, however, offers two metaphors to express a more ambiguous line between creative independence and rigorous derivation.[16] The former suggests that blind fidelity to the original impedes the rendering of sense, while the latter stresses that translation can only succeed when the boundaries of both languages are stretched to the point of touching:

Fragments of a vessel which are to be glued together must match one another in the smallest details, although they need not be like one another. In the same way a translation, instead of resembling the meaning of the original, must lovingly and in detail incorporate the original's mode of signification, thus making both the original and the translation recognizable as fragments of a greater language, just as fragments are part of a vessel. For this very reason translation must in large measure refrain from wanting to communicate something. . . .

. . . Just as a tangent touches a circle lightly at but one point, with this touch rather than with the point setting the law according to which it is to continue on its straight path to infinity, a translation touches the original lightly and only at the infinitely small point of the sense, thereupon pursuing its own course according to the laws of fidelity in the freedom of linguistic flux.[17]

Translation as a metaphor for the very process of communication – emerging out of fragments, approaching the totality of the other, confronting the foreignness of languages but also regenerating the basis for reciprocity and extending the boundaries for mutual understanding – can also provide an entrance into the mechanisms through which dialogue and negotiation between cultures is possible. To think of translation neither as the appropriation of a foreign culture according to the rules of one's own culture (where the original is treated as an inferior source that needs correction), nor as a reproduction which totally reflects the world-view of the other (where the translation aims to be identical with the original), but rather as a dynamic interaction within which conceptual boundaries are expanded and residual differences respected, may allow for a more radical understanding of the multiple levels and diverse routes of cultural exchange in modern society.

The politics of translation

A transformative theory of translation does, however, open up a new set of questions. On what basis do we decide between different translations of the same text? Are all translations equal? If we take the perspective that translation is the condition of all thinking, then we are forced to consider such questions beyond the boundaries of semiotics. Translation occurs in all forms of cultural practice and is implicit in every act of judgement. In everyday life we assume that our responses imply some sort of standard which reflects a set of firm beliefs, and against which actions are judged, values defined. Yet when we are called to define this standard, it appears rather elusive, fragmentary and incoherent. This *gap* between judgements based on implicit beliefs or intuitive responses and those which are applications of codified laws or moral maps exposes us to one of the most complex tensions in modernity. As change becomes the predominant feature of social life, it is inevitable that the certitudes underpinning cultural judgement are also fractured.

Clearly, there are instrumental rules and conventions which guide our everyday actions. That is not what is at stake. The problem is not confined either to keeping within the legal boundaries of propriety or discerning the likely consequence of either pleasure or pain. A deep discomfort arises when we question the moral foundations on which rules that govern daily life rest. Is there some integrated theory which binds them all together, or is judgement just a patchwork of necessity and compromise? In philosophical discourse the practices of translation are acknowledged as an integral part of framing judgement. However, the specificity or generality of the translational process is in itself subsumed within a broader consideration of relationship in the relationship between language and reality. This discussion is formulated from either a universalist or a relativist perspective. The unresolved argument between relativism and universalism has been reactivated by recent philosophical debates over identity politics.

Jean-François Lyotard's concept of the *differend* addresses the dilemmas that spring from the shortcomings of both the universalist and relativist perspectives in modernity. Lyotard defines the *differend* as 'a case of conflict between (at least) two parties that cannot be equitably resolved for lack of a rule of judgement applicable to both arguments'.[18] In this situation the legitimacy of one argument does not imply the illegitimacy of the other. This form of conflict may involve rival claims over an object. If the rule of judgement over this object is applied equally and uniformly to both parties, Lyotard argues that this may still do harm to one. Such conflicts are not resolved by a discourse that can only adhere to one set of rules for defining the rights to that object. A *differend* emerges when the rules for judging between the rival claims are not equally placed for grasping the specific genres within which the points of contestation are claimed. In fact, the very practice of seeking resolution only compounds the conflict. This is not an isolated or marginal feature of modern life. For despite the intensity and multiplicities of cultural interactions, Lyotard notes that a 'universal rule of judgement between heterogeneous genres is lacking in general'.[19]

The violent aftermath of colonialism provides countless examples to which Lyotard's concept of the *differend* can be applied. For instance, a mining company surveys a territory and concludes that the land is both uninhabited and rich in minerals. The company then applies to a government agency for the right to exploit these resources. An aboriginal community protests, claiming that the land is actually inhabited by sacred spirits, and asserting their ancestral duty to protect it. Here is a conflict in which at least one party fails to recognize the legitimate claims of the other. How will both parties go before a neutral tribunal that will decide between these competing claims? And if the law is already disposed to measure the inhabitance of land in terms of dwellings and active utilization, are spiritual claims to be dismissed by the tribunal on the ground that they are intangible and irrational? If the aboriginal community is then forced to defend its claim in terms of its prior right to exploit the resources of this land, will they forfeit their rights of spiritual attachment?

Here the aboriginal community and the mining company are faced with an impasse: there is no common language in which both cases can be simultaneously posed and comprehended. The spiritual cannot be translated into the language of a tribunal which decides land rights in terms of material 'development'. If the aboriginal community adopts the language of this tribunal, their case vanishes. They remain silenced and defeated. They are faced with the *differend* of having lost their land and not having a neutral tribunal which can hear their case. The defining feature of their *differend* is that their case cannot be proved, they feel the double pain of loss – of their land and of their voice – for their case demands to be heard, but it remains mute before a tribunal which cannot translate their words. Yet this practice of silencing is not a negation of the translational process. It may become another sign, a negative space, supporting another line of contestation.

Similar dilemmas can be observed in the field of contemporary art. How will the discourse of contemporary art, which is predominantly Eurocentric and presupposes a break with the past, address non-Euro-American art practices that display a complex negotiation between tradition and modernity?[20] Given that there is genuine interest, an active market and institutionalized networks that circulate art objects from all over the world and constantly create hierarchies of significance, what frameworks are available for judging between artworks from different cultures? Can practices which were previously categorized as the 'other' suddenly emerge within the parameters of modernity's self-identity? Take for example the celebrated juxtaposition in the Pompidou Centre between Richard Long's *Mud Circle* (1989) and the Yuendumu community's ceremonial ground painting *Installation* (1989). What connections can be forged between works which were previously considered as polar opposites? In both Richard Long's wall painting and the Yuendumu ground painting we can observe superficial geometric parallels in the use of concentric patterns. Both works also invoke a relationship between the natural and the supernatural. However, the positioning of both practices within the fields of formalism and spirituality is so radically different that one must question the validity of the curatorial claim that such juxtapositions will offer a starting-point for a new dialogue in art and culture.

Redefining the margin

The problems of translating cultural practices previously excluded from the context of modernism into the institutional boundaries of the contemporary can no longer be resolved by repeating earlier strategies that effectively relegated these works to the margins, labelling them 'ethnic art' or 'neo-primitivism'. It has been posed in various forms by almost all the major metropolitan art galleries. The two most scrutinized exhibitions were 'Magiciennes de la terre' in Paris

(1989) and the Whitney Biennial in New York (1992).[21] At the centre of these critiques is a re-examination of the romantic idea that creativity lies at the margins of social existence. This view has gained greater purchase as the position of the margin has both expanded and become more jagged.

Responding to a conference called 'Identity: Postmodernism and the Real Me', the black British cultural theorist Stuart Hall commented: 'Now that in the postmodern age you all feel so dispersed, I become centred. What I have thought of as dispersed and fragmented comes, paradoxically, to be the representative modern experience.'[22] The irony in Hall's voice is seldom noted. All too often, such comments are interpreted as signs of cultural equality. Further evidence of the greater appreciation of margin, if not a broader claim that cultural differences are translatable, is the awarding of the highest literary prizes in Britain to writers from the former colonies of Australia, Jamaica, Nigeria and India. Yet these awards have done little to stimulate a deeper understanding of the complex links between an exilic consciousness and the cultural representations of modernity.[23] Hal Foster has outlined three factors which help explain why the ambivalent social position of the artist from the margin is interpreted as giving rise to a heightened critical perspective:

> First, there is the assumption that the site of artistic transformation is the site of political transformation, and, more, that this site is always located *elsewhere*, in the field of the other. . . . Second, there is the assumption that this other is always *outside*, and, more, that this alterity is the primary point of subversion of dominant culture. Third, there is the assumption that if the invoked artist is not perceived as socially and/or culturally other, he or she has but *limited* access to this transformative alterity, and, more, that if he or she is perceived as other, he or she has automatic access to it.[24]

The argument about the need to expand the cultural boundaries of art seems to have been interwoven with a fetishization of the alterity of the artist from the margin. Considerable attention has been given to the powers of the individual artist, in particular those artists who have come from such a space and can translate back, in potent forms, the relationship between centre and periphery. However, the means for defining inclusion and the creation of a framework for understanding the significance of cultural differences have not been so forthcoming. This dilemma was most evident in the curatorial practices that sought to construct a new cultural order by assembling works from cultures about which the curators had only limited knowledge. The failure to question this process, Gerardo Mosquera contends,

> implies an acceptance of the curator's capacity to make transcultural judgements and from here the belief in the universality of art. To deny it would imply an anagnorisis: acknowledging that a selection is made from local criteria (from a particular institution, culture and aesthetic) leaving behind any globalising discourse.[25]

Further questions follow from this perspective. Can contemporary art be defined from a universal standard? Does the proliferation of multiple cultural practices and perspectives presuppose the legitimacy of all? If the critical discourse of contemporary art engages with artworks from other cultures, will it also embrace other histories of practice, introduce new conceptual schemes for interpretation and appreciation? In short, how will the foreign suddenly be made familiar? Will the *differend* between different cultural practices alert us to the silencing that occurs by the very rules of representation in the discourse of art? Or will that which remains untranslatable summon a critique of the very language of art and culture?

Interweaving and retranslation

This dilemma is not confined to contemporary art. It is implicated in almost all the spheres of representing cultural identity in modernity. Under the political machinations of multiculturalism the most prominent forms of representing identity are the loud and resolute calls for distinctiveness and purity. This strategy is contradictory, for it tends to draw clear boundaries and insist on the uniqueness of distinct 'ethnic' communities, while demanding that the mainstream culture dismantle its boundaries and debunk its own claims to superiority.

After two decades of official multiculturalism, in places like Australia and Britain, some gains have been made in terms of defining the substantive needs and boundaries of minority cultures, but there has been little advance in understanding culture as a relational practice that exceeds national priorities. Multiculturalism has been successful in combating exclusivist and racist conceptions of nationalism; it has broadened the discourse of inclusion and social cohesion by pointing to the diverse constituents of the modern nation, and also stressing that certain forms of cross-cultural exchange offer a positive contribution to society. Calls for national purity have been replaced by the celebrations of diversity. However, these forms of exchange and celebration have often been confined to culinary and folkloric practices which do not challenge the hegemony of the dominant culture. Jimmie Durham expressed this limitation succinctly when he declared that

> Multiculturalism might be considered a viable strategy if anyone out there, including a soon-to-be-realised Europe, had any culture. But I expect not even then. Instead we would end up with something like an international 'sale of work', a 'garage sale' of trading units.[26]

The viability of multiculturalism depends on the reterritorialization of culture. As long as the concept of culture is pinned to an exclusive place, the relational potential cultural exchange is easily overtaken by nationalist and commercial priorities. Monoculturalism has been discredited because of its constrictive definition of the national culture. However, the pledges of multiculturalism may enable the nation-state to redefine the terms of entry without having to change the social hierarchies or dominant codes of power.

John Lechte and Gill Bottomley have argued that a multicultural experience can expand the symbolic and imaginary practices for representing our knowledge of the world. For this to occur, they maintain, we need to arrive at a broader understanding of subjectivity and go beyond the policy dictates of culture. Their definition of the multicultural experience is premised neither on the salvation of the uniqueness of the minority culture, nor on presupposing an oppositional confrontation with the dominant culture. The multicultural is significant in their terms not just for the articulation of other world-views but also for the renegotiation of our ways of seeing the world. The potential for this more relational optic in cultural experience emerges from the oscillation between 'the "semiotic" as the material, drive component of language, manifest in the rhythm and song of poetry, and the "symbolic" as the conceptual and representational component of language.'[27] This distinction, which draws on Kristeva's theory of language, stresses the gap between the formative drives which bring forth new ways of thinking of the world and the already formed conceptions of the world within the dominant language. The migrant, by virtue of being dislocated from his or her context of origin in which certain conceptions of the world were secured, and being slightly adjacent to the given views in the new context, feels the gap between the 'semiotic' and the 'symbolic' all the more palpably. It is this process of translating the previously known together with the unknown into something that is knowable that creates a slippage between naming and associations, and engenders new meanings. This dynamic relation between experience and representation distinguishes the migrant's coming into language again, and validates the transformative claims that the critical discourse associates with this practice.

This bridging role between the 'drive' and the 'concept' that the multicultural experience can offer presupposes that the dominant discursive practices have both severed and prohibited the vital connection between experience and representation. Thus the potency of the migrant's perspective lies in reactivating a process that is essential for cultural renewal. Lechte and Bottomley have defined this process through two key terms: 'interweaving' and 'retranslation'. Interweaving refers to a constant interaction between different cultural practices that leads to mutual transformation. This implies that cultures never exist in a pure state but are constituted in and through negotiation with other cultural practices. Retranslation is the process by which 'foreign' elements are introduced into a culture. What distinguishes this model from conventional anthropological discussions on syncretism is that this form of cultural exchange does not presuppose an original which the process can refer back to, nor does it impose fixed terms of meaning. Retranslation is part of the ongoing practice of interpretation, and central to the very construction of culture.

An example of this process of interweaving and retranslating can be found in the artwork of Yinka Shonibare. Shonibare was born in London of Nigerian parents, grew up in Lagos and later returned to England for his education, where he now practises as a visual artist. As a child he was exposed to a wide variety of cultural influences: he recalls the pleasure of watching programmes like 'Skippy the Bush Kangaroo' and listening to Fela Kuti. He claims that switching from one cultural practice to another was considered part of the 'normal' process of growing up: 'The idea of some kind of fixed identity, of belonging to an authentic culture, is quite foreign to my experience.'[28]

As a student of painting, he endeavoured to explore the complexities of cultural identity. Yet the shocking response of his art teachers in London was that he must pursue more authentic forms of his native culture. Despite these rebukes, he continued to make work which problematized the questions of authenticity. For instance, in *Double Dutch* (1994), he began a series of paintings which revealed the complex 'genealogies' of African fabrics. These paintings, displayed against a shocking pink wall, consisted of flowing organic patterns that spread across the fronts and sides of fifty panels. In each case, the traditional canvas had been replaced with African fabric. An overlay of thick, bright-coloured paint both echoed the underlying patterns of batik and competed with the minimalist codes of colour-field painting. These dazzling paintings, with the paint extending around the thick frame, collectively shimmer like a Gaudi mosaic. Spermatoid and egg-like shapes hover across the wall, along with the more conventional floral patterns and dot configurations. When one pauses to acknowledge the grid in which they are hung, the referencing to abstract formations is lost under the pressure of a hilarious display of colour and subject. This irreverent strategy was repeated in *Feather Pink* (1997) and *Deep Blue* (1997). These two series of paintings, each consisting of twenty-five panels, once again utilized African fabrics as the surface upon which thick dollops of impasto paint were let loose to seduce. Kobena Mercer explains this link between postcolonial irony and modernist authenticity:

> By playing with the metonymic link between the origins of the cloth, and his own origins amongst a transnational generation of hyphenated hybrids, he disinters modernism's tired equations in which the high serious gesture culminating in Clement Greenberg's doctrine of formalist purity required a subordinate set of negatives: if colour-field = abstract = heroic, then fabric = decorative = frivolous. Shonibare's strategy is about representation, but it is not figurative. It is about abstraction, but it is not expressive. It is about what he calls, 'purloined seduction or pretend authenticity', in which the polarities of masculine, Western high art and feminine, non-Western craft are sent packing by means of his elegantly simple substitutive ploy.[29]

Shonibare's research on textiles uncovered various colonial links. He learned that the batik design of African fabrics actually originated in Indonesia. Batik was introduced to Europe by the Dutch and then mass-produced in Manchester, and from there exported to Africa. In Africa, both the material and the design would be transformed by local industries catering to everyday needs and special events. To commemorate, say, a state visit, special fabrics featuring the portrait of the visiting president or king would be commissioned. This design would then be printed in Manchester and distributed in Africa. Shonibare purchased his fabrics from the Brixton market in London after they had been imported 'back' and sold as 'authentic' African fabric. The journey of these fabrics becomes a metaphor for the interweaving of cultural identities in post-colonialism. As Kobena Mercer noted, Shonibare's practice retranslates the ground of abstraction in art history as well as commenting slyly on the production of materials which were 'made in Europe and yet made to mean Africa'.[30]

Alongside his painting Shonibare has used African textiles to restage a number of the icons of colonialism and the ruling class. On the invitation card to the exhibition *Double Dutch* (1994), Shonibare presented a photograph of himself dressed in the full regalia of an eighteenth-century aristocrat. *How Does a Girl Like You, Get to be a Girl Like You?* (1995) was an installation of three women's costumes identifiable as high Victorian, but made of cotton printed by wax-resistant technique with African designs. Positioned on a plinth, these costumes with their multiple layers which normally drag along polished surfaces, cetainly raised a number of eyebrows when they were shown in the *Africa 95* exhibition at the Barbican Centre, London. *Victorian Philanthropist's Parlour* (1996) also transposed African designs and images of black British football players across the wallpaper, upholstery and rugs of a stereotypically English interior. Similarly, *Dressing Down* (1997), and *Cha Cha Cha* (1997), subverted the Victorian crinoline dress and dancer's shoes with tantalizing suggestions of sexual freedom. Shonibare's practice has consistently reworked the cultural icons of contemporary Britain. He has sought to demonstrate not only the hybridity that exists in his place of origin but also to 'ethnicize' the institutions that symbolized the centre of empire.

Translation as reactivation

This example of the cultural practice of retranslation takes us closer to Benjamin's understanding of the relationship between an original and a reproduction. The distinction between the two states is not one of purity and contamination. By means of reproduction the original object is alienated from its context. It is separated from its domain and dispersed into a number of others. Without any of the conventional laments, Benjamin declares that this process of reproduction is a reactivation of the 'object reproduced'.[31] It is not a matter of seeing the fullness of an object's meaning only in its original context and dismissing the reproduction of the object in a foreign setting as either the negation or dilution of meaning. Rather, reproduction and relocation demand a radical form of trans-formation. While the 'aura' of a work, its specific presence in time and space, withers with reproduction, the detachment of an object from its specific traditions by the techniques of reproduction opens up the way for new relations that can occur in the context of the beholder and multiple forms of perceptions. As images of an object circulate within the domain of the social, new interpretations can also disperse and multiply. For Benjamin, the authority of the object is jeopardized by reproduction, but paradoxically its authority is enhanced by the proliferation of translations that this process begets.

This notion of translation allows us to see transformation as an ongoing process. To use the metaphor of the journey, a translation never arrives at its destined port, it is forever conscious of its place of departure and unable to rest in any abstraction of its own destination. Never quite there, the translation continues to reinscribe itself in the process of journeying. These temporary reinscriptions, which are formed in the contestation between departure and arrival, are the signs with which diasporic communities enunciate themselves.

Homi Bhabha has also taken Benjamin's insight into the translational process as a guide for the negotiation of the in-between spaces and disjunctive temporalities of migrant experience.[32] The zone of cultural difference that Bhabha evokes is not bound by the assimilationist rhetoric of the dominant culture nor by the atavistic resurgence of minority cultures – both of which invoke the goals of purity and discreteness – but is rather a complex overlapping of differences. Identity is constituted through the oscillations between what can and what cannot be translated across difference. Translation is always an encounter with the resistance of the untranslatable. From this tension there emerges both a haunting sense of irresoluteness and the driving energy for further translation. The migrant's culture faces its own untranslatability, and in doing so must also return to the perpetual task of re-imagining the cultural contract between self and other. In similar tones, Sarat Maharaj has also drawn attention to the modern multicultural space as the 'scene of translations': 'In the 1990s we have come to see the international space as the meeting ground for the multiplicity of tongues, visual grammars and styles. These do not so much translate into each other as translate to produce difference.'[33]

Translation, Maharaj argues, is as much about producing correspondence as it is about producing dissonance. To translate is to carry a meaning from one language to another; it involves the recognition of the equivalence as well as the intransigence. In opposition to the everyday association of translation as the facilitative act of rendering other signs intelligible and transparent, Maharaj reminds us of the 'opaque stickiness' of untranslatability. This disrupts the political goals of liberal pluralism, which would prefer to define the field of multiculturalism as the arithmetic summation of cultural differences, with each culture defined by its distinct boundaries and with a transparent form of exchange between all. By shifting our attention from culture as product with fixed boundaries and a unique essence to a process formed through the interaction with difference, we also confront the limits of exchange. Consider Jacques Derrida's observation on the untranslatability of proper names: 'Understanding is no longer possible when there are only proper names, and understanding is no longer possible when there are no longer proper names.'[34]

Proper names become boundary markers to the limits of translation. The intermediary space is where translation is possible. Derrida also poses a number of other questions about the parameters of translation which are also relevant for cross-cultural debates. How is a text which is written in several languages at a time to be translated? Can the plurality that constitutes the scenes of transculturation be rendered by translation? In the literature of Salman Rushdie, for instance, there is already the acknowledgement that the original text is constituted by the dramas of colliding translations. These texts, with their multiple articulations of Englishness and Indianness, make the translation process buckle. There is no sense of one language being translated into another, rather it appears as if they are jostling and rubbing up against each other. If there is no original language which does not already bear the mark of another translation, what we are faced with is the irreducible multiplicity of languages competing together in the space of a single text. Following from Derrida, we can ask: if proper names remain untranslatable, and if the text originates out of a multiplicity of tongues and never coheres into a single tongue, is translation still possible?

This translation problem is most pressing in the cultural clashes of colonialism and in the politics of renaming space. Jimmie Durham, an artist from the Cherokee nation, has argued that language is the medium in which the ethnocidal legacy of colonialism is most apparent. It is not just a matter of correcting ignorance and misrecognition with 'proper' translations, but rather facing a deeper incapacity, which Durham calls the 'un-understanding'.[35] The mutual misconceptions are not just between Indians and non-Indians but even among Indians. Understanding can be as much snared by those who resist colonialism by seeking to preserve native traditions within the closed space of the past, as by those who believe that the only way forward is to make a clean break with the past. Traditionalist and modernists are caught in a face-off.

Durham is conscious that a neutral space or a home ground from which one could speak with security and certitude has already been colonized. 'I feel fairly sure that I could address the entire world if only I had a place to stand. You [white Americans] have already made everything your turf.'[36] The politics of representation are compounded by a refusal to conform to the stereotypical images that precede his own identity and a gritty reluctance to deny the fragmented traces of his heritage. The available options are restricted: 'We're either not supposed to refer to our own people and our situation at all, or we're supposed to exclusively refer to that.'[37] The pincer effect of this binary between being authentic or suspect is echoed by Shonibare and his own attempt to shake off the exotic label:

What I've found, making work in Britain, is that when you make work about your origins, all it can be about is your origins. But if you don't make work about your origins, people will say you're an African artist who doesn't make work about African subjects, so your identity becomes suspect.[38]

To be able to speak back against the violence of colonialism and assert his own agency within the here and now, Durham has established a series of allegories about translation as appropriation and questioned the process of self recognition through the adoption of the persona of the 'noble savage'. In his exhibition *Original Re-Runs* (Institute of Contemporary Art, London, 1994), which was an ironic tour through the congested scrapyard of neo-colonialism, he adopted the Shakespearian guise of Caliban and declared: 'I don't know what I look like. Since Dr Prospero came there has been nothing that reflects me.' With such ironic clues Durham leads us into the silvering within the mirror of translation. When traces of the past are gone, when there is not even a memory of the language that is lost by colonialism, how can translation proceed other than by holding up the silences in the two languages? Gayatri Spivak has observed that all translation relies on the erotics of submission. The seduction of translation is that it enables the reciprocity between self and other to become a form of mutual extension. 'It is a simple miming of the responsibility to the trace of the other in the self.'[39] Spivak recognizes, like Durham, that the ethical space of love in translation is dependent on the recognition of the limits of equivalence. Within the very act of translation there is also the gesture of withholding. What Durham signifies in his portraits is the passage of identity through the marks of untranslatability. This should not be confused with a pure negation of self. Durham is not alluding to some form of historical self that is buried and waiting to be affirmed through excavation; rather there is the identity that is passed on through the silence of scars and in the furtive glances of misrecognition.

In *Acha que minto, nao, que ideia, alias, nos mentimos, quando e preciso limitamo – nos a usar as palavras ques mentem* (1995) Durham mounts a sign on a piece of wood. Translated from Portuguese the message reads, 'Do you say I am lying? Of course not, we have never lied to each other; when precision limits us we use words that will lie for us.' The piece of wood is like an elbow with a ring screwed into the middle that keeps it suspended on the wall. The mixed message of honesty and deceit leans at one end, while at the the other a luminous seashell rests above a steel bracket. At one end the wood has forked into two branches. Two sticks are joined on to the metal bracket to make an inverted T-shape. Like all of Durham's sculptures, this work has a precarious symmetry. Everything is fastened tight like a clamped prosthesis. The words speak of trust deeper than treacherous words can ever honour. Yet they also suggest the disingenuous gesture of conveniently knowing the limitations of translation. An escape clause? Perhaps, for the other signs are heavy with hints of broken treaties, contracts and promises. The seashell, with its alluring lustre, suggests the lover's ear still waiting for the beloved's response in the waves of faraway sounds. Below it two hooks dangle idle, ready to swing or fasten their catch. The gesture of acknowledgement, which links the foreign message and the beckoning ear, is both open and hard, like the joints bolted on to the branches. As in two earlier works, *Death* (1991) and *We Have Made Progress* (1991), the conjunction of found wood and scrap metal almost produces the spark of dialogue.

Durham's artwork is rooted in the strategic reclamation and contemplative resignification of junk. The two figures of Paolo Friere and Marcel Duchamp stand as the twin sentinels that not only mark out the forces that govern Durham's aesthetic orientation but also signify the type of political conjunctions from which his convictions are born. From Duchamp there is the enduring lesson that sculptural meaning and irony are found in the simple act of displacement, and from Friere is the reminder of the cost of alienation in 'specialism'. Throughout his writing, Jimmie Durham refers to the concept of tolerance. The suggestion is that tolerance is not testament to the limits of acceptable differences, for difference is not an exotic option: it is a basic fact and therefore also a constitutive force of everyday life. What we find *in*tolerable is the index of our intelligence and imagination. Tolerance, when faced with the sign of the intolerable, is not just the incorporation of difference into the structures of the known – as it is conceived in liberalism – but becomes part of the translational process of reaching out into the unknown. It involves understanding through extension, an active engagement with others rather than a passive detachment. Through one of his most familiar personas, Durham declares the limits of his own tolerance:

> Oh, I wish I could cease being such a savage. My intention like Attakulakula's, is always to be a person in the world: the entire world as it is. . . . All that we know we know by direct action – such as a bee sting – or by metaphor. Language is metaphor, as much as are dreams.[40]

Durham's appreciation of the sting of colonial metaphors is made more evident in a series of signposts which were part of *Original Re-Runs*. In *Veracruz/ Virginia* Durham assembles four sculptures, with the words Virginia, Veracruz, Veracity, Voracity displayed on each like road signs, and both turns it against the colonial practice of renaming colonized space, as if it were unoccupied and virgin, and twists it towards the relationship that Derrida posed between proper names and translation. How can the name of a place be translated into different languages, which presuppose different historical attachments, competing claims of membership and conflicting semiotic associations? Proper names can only be grasped in terms of their specific and exclusive designations. It is at this point that the limits of translation noted by Derrida cross with Lyotard's concept of the *differend*. The translation of proper names always produces a *differend*. Lyotard suggests that, unlike words whose meaning shifts and can refer to different things in different sentences, proper names are 'rigid designators'.[41] The proper name retains its value and refers to the same thing irrespective of how it is uttered. In this sense, proper names cannot be translated. The impossibility of re-wording a proper name would beget another form of semiotic transmutation. Who decides on the form of this transmutation? Should we gloss over all that simply does not fit, or dismiss the untranslatable as the failure of a proper translation?

In *Not Lothar Baumgarten's Cherokee* (1990), and in the drawings of *Six Authentic Things* (1989), Durham presents the viewer with texts written in Cherokee. By his own account, the puns and jibes in these works are not available for translation. Part of the meaning of these works, for a non-Cherokee-speaker, is the experience of non-comprehension. 'What I want them to know is that they can't know that.'[42] The refusal to translate these texts is not so much a visible display of the stubborn untranslatability of linguistic puns but a political response to the appropriation of the Cherokee language by non-Indian artists. Seeing how Baumgarten used the Cherokee writing system in his work, Durham responded, 'I felt appropriated and sort of cancelled.'[43]

The residue that does not pass neatly from one language to another, and the supplement that cannot be contained by the terms of either language, are crucial elements in the identity of 'the hybrid'. According to Maharaj, the hybrid is not just an incomplete stage in translation but is the creative response to the dual task of translation. A hybrid is composed of the impossible reconciliation between the transparent and opaque features of different languages. For instance, to say that my identity is Greek-Australian is not a declaration of the two constitutive parts. The most telling feature may be neither the addition of a Greekness upon a prior Australianness, nor the conflict between them, but rather the energy that comes from conjunction and juxtaposition. From this perspective the identity of the hybrid is not found in the sum of its parts but from the power of the hyphen. It is thus neither the negative result of partial definition nor the triumphal synthesis of opposites. It is an energy that tends towards identity, taking the leftovers and the collisions between languages as the source for its own construction. The hybrid has no prior or ultimate identity, and this makes it seem potentially treacherous and constantly unstable, for it acknowledges that all identity is forged out of the ongoing interaction between the elements of difference that are the grist of translation.

The restless process of the hybrid's identity formation is linked to what Derrida calls the 'genealogical indebtedness' of translation.[44] Transparency of meaning, universal application and fixed identity are the impossible conditions upon which the language of colonial violence rests. The strength and weakness of colonialism rested on its own univocity, manifest in its dogged assumption that perspective does not alter perception, its rigid insistence on how meanings should be translated into all contexts, and its mania for renaming all the colonized spaces in its own self-image. In the earlier example of the *differend* between the mining company and the aboriginal community, in which conflict was born out of the refusal to acknowledge the differing values and links between the concepts of belonging, stewardship, entitlement, possession and inheritance in each other's language, we can see that colonial dispossession was executed by the belief that indigenous people had no means of claiming, communicating and transferring ownership of land. If the indigenous people did not really own it, then the colonizer did not take it. They renamed the 'virgin' land not only as a way of asserting their own identity, but as the means of effacing the prior naming and sense of belonging to the land. This colonial deafness short-circuited the translation process. The colonizers disowned their debt to the other's language. Had the colonizers entered into genuine dialogue with indigenous people, the very process of translation would have exposed the limits of their authority.

A translation constantly undoes and disperses the authority of the original. In 'Mr and Mrs Andrews without their Heads' (1998) Shonibare takes this strategy to its logical conclusion. This museum display of English aristocrats painted by Gainsborough in 1748, re-dressed in African patterns, would take John Berger's critique of the quintessential representation of the proprietorial attitude,[45] and Steven Bell's picture postcard substitution of Mr Reagan and Mrs Thatcher,[46] one step back and two steps forward. Shonibare's ambition to ethnicize those symbols of taste and decorum, which are meant to be above judgement, hits its target, as it directs our attention to the dirty politics of empire. The duplicities and unintended consequences of colonialism are brought together in this work. For here we witness how the preservation of landscape in the home country was gained at the expense of exploiting the colonies. And colonialism which presupposed the distinct separation of races also laid down the routes which brought into contact people of diverse places. Dress codes have always been very strict for the aristocracy, but in the contact zones of transnational and postcolonial space, Shonibare's inversions and re-dressings open a new symbolic attack. Without their heads, the icons of colonialism not only lose their authority but are re-dressed to signify a new order. Colonialism has been formally dismantled, but while the relations of domination have not been substantially transformed the forms of cultural critique have altered. The icons of the centre can no longer assume unquestioned authority. Images circulate with greater frequency. Subjects are on the move and meanings are transformed by these unstable relations.

The meaning of an original always shifts by the very process of being translated. Translation becomes a permanent debt, and hybridity an endless search. To translate one's relationship to the land in terms of living obligations – belonging, stewardship, inheritance – would be unthinkable in a language which has alienated land into an exchangeable commodity. How can we now bridge these historical chasms? To leave the differences apart is like leaving the wound open. If a translation is to be seen as part of an ongoing stream of juxtapositions rather than a hierarchical superimposition, then the gesture of invitation and the words that lie for us may be acknowledged. We could say that once we face the opaque mirror of translation, language and identity can no longer be the same.

7

Philosophical Frameworks and the Politics of Cultural Difference

Cultures are always in some state of interaction. This process is never neutral. The motivation for contact may vary from military invasion, to economic exchange and intellectual curiosity. Whatever the form of this interaction, cultures are always transformed by these complex and ongoing processes. No culture can sustain itself, or at least not for long, through isolation or exclusion. The recent debates on the cultural impact of colonialism have sharpened our appreciation of both the destruction wreaked on non-western cultures by the colonizer, and the complex forms of cultural survival expressed by those who were formerly colonized. The options were never as stark as the complete obliteration of the 'old' and the uncritical adoption of the 'new'. The attention paid to the tremendous oppositional forces that were unleashed in the cultural clashes of colonialism tended to make people overlook the more subtle forms of interplay between the colonizer and the colonized.

The complex patterns of cultural exchange and transformation have become a contentious subject in postcolonial studies. While this new approach has provided a more detailed account of the losses and gains associated with either colonialism and modernization, it should also draw our attention to the conceptual frameworks for representing cultural difference. What was the perspective with which one group viewed the other? How did they attempt to grasp their respective differences and communicate their commonalities? What were the parameters within which cultural representations were formed? Such political and historical questions cannot be answered without recourse to philosophical assumptions about language and interpretation.

The two dominant, if not always acknowledged, traditions which are utilized to frame the historical debates on colonialism, and the contemporary representation of multiculturalism, are universalism and particularism. The universalist perspective presupposes that all cultures have a common foundation and that, while some have evolved to a higher stage than others, there are clear standards against which all cultures can be measured. The particularist view opposes the notion that there is either a common pool or an evolutionary hierarchy, and claims that all cultures have to be judged by their own terms and that they should not be prejudged by looking at them from our own exclusive vantage point. This epistemological dispute over the 'truth of the other' and the authority of witnesses is a recurring feature of post-colonial studies and was the central theme in the debate between Ernest Gellner and Edward Said. In his review of *Culture and Imperialism*[1] Gellner attacked Said for his wholehearted alignment with those who fought against colonialism:

> European imperialism of the eighteenth and nineteenth century, formally dismantled in the twentieth but surviving in many forms, is in certain important ways unique. It wasn't simply a matter of one set of people dominating another, it involved a move from one kind of society to a profoundly different one. It is this deep metamorphosis and the difficulty of finding a viewpoint from which to judge it, which is the real problem of imperialism. It cannot be seen in terms of imperialist-baddies and resister-goodies. No amount of restraint or tolerance on the part of the rulers, no amount of pride, conservatism and stubbornness on the part of the ruled, could avoid at least some measure of transvaluation of values. By what standards can we judge this?[2]

It is this process of transvaluation – the qualitative shift in the construction of the social – which opens up the specific configurations of knowledge-power in colonialism and, as Gellner notes, we lack a cultural theory that attends to this process of transformation. Gellner has rightly observed that any account of colonialism is caught in an epistemological aporia. How do we measure the impact of social change? How do we distinguish the different levels of truth claims whose authority and authenticity come from 'knowledge about' or 'knowledge of' something? These questions of perspective, position and experience have challenged the presuppositions of social investigations. No representation of colonialism is entirely objective. Each carries within it a specific world-view and all the social and cultural predispositions that this would entail. Said was surely right to condemn those imperialist texts which conformed to the nineteenth-century theory of cultural evolutionism. Clearly the Eurocentric hierarchy which ranked all cultures in ladder formation has to be rejected. However, as Gellner observes, what often follows the abandonment of this vertical hierarchy is a 'post modernist pan-relativism' which places all cultures on an open and horizontal plane. In Said's counter-response to Gellner, he rejects both positions. Neither an absolutist nor a relativist, how is Said to sustain his truth claims?

Said's subsequent replies shift from the bold assertion that the truth comes when the 'author writes from within his subject', to the qualification that truth is not the monopoly of those who have a 'privileged insider status'.[3] Between these two moves we see the epistemological aporia that surrounds the positions of both the engaged critic and the detached observer. Priority is given to neither. Gellner's criticism of Said's position established the difficulty of defining the precise grounds for mounting either a defence of, or an attack on colonialism. Said's contradictory and guerrilla-styled responses may have stimulated the need to rethink the conditions in which knowledge of others is produced. Yet it has not resolved the deeper epistemological questions. The binaries of insiders and outsiders, subjectivism and objectivism, and the ability of individuals to move between these positions, frame much of the discussion of cultural politics. Like the exchange between Said and Gellner, these frameworks repeat rather than overcome the conceptual deadlock. However, within cultural theory the concept of translation has focused attention on both the multiple levels of meaning in a language and the broad processes by which knowledge of the self is always an interrogation of the other. It is now worth considering whether philosophical investigations into the concept of translation can also add to our understanding of cultural transformation.

Translation and the truth of the other

The limits of translations have always figured in the philosophical discourses of truth claims in universalist and particularist perspectives. The gulf that lies between these two perspectives can be seen in the ambivalent role of translation in the philosophical debates between holism and relativism. Donald Davidson, one of the strongest exponents of holism, argues that the meaning of each sentence is dependent on grasping both its specific structure and the general language in which it features. Thus he concludes that a specific meaning is not comprehensible without the whole of its language: 'Different points of view make sense, but only if there is a common co-ordinate system on which to plot them: yet the existence of a common system belies the claim of dramatic incomparability.'[4]

From this perspective it is impossible to consider the coexistence of a multiplicity of languages and a conceptual scheme which addresses the incommensurability between languages. According to Davidson, translation does not offer an alternative schema. Translation is confined to a form of equivalence or correspondence, because a language can incorporate only that which is not other than itself. If something remains untranslatable, then it is no longer part of language. There is no space for the untranslatable, it is reduced to silence. Holism would reject that there are ever other ways, or even partially overlapping ways, of seeing the world. This theory of translation confines the dynamics of cultural exchange to either assimilation or exclusion. Foreign views can only be grasped if they are made compatible with, or seen as being equivalent to, the already familiar concepts, and therefore, are not seen as representing a fundamental difference. Difference is thus reduced to either a variation on the same, or excluded as a form of incomprehensible non-sense. Such a punishing framework would allow little space for understanding transformation as a process that occurs through the interaction with difference. The counter-position to holism is relativism.

Relativism has gained considerable intellectual and popular appeal in a political climate that has sought both to protect the boundaries and to encourage a selective form of exchange between cultural differences. Relativism, to an extent, facilitates the acknowledgement of cultural incommensurability. It recognizes that there is at least a contest over truth claims, and at its most radical level, it dismisses any absolute or inherent claim to truth. From this perspective, truth claims are not posed in terms such as 'There is only one way of seeing the truth', but rather they would necessarily be qualified in expressions like 'the appearance of truth varies according to your position'. The shift from a universalist to a particularist perspective enables relativism to offer a more open and tolerant attitude to cultural transformation. But this has not necessarily advanced the understanding of the processes of exchange and mixture that occur across such boundaries. Nor has it addressed the problem of how to decide between competing claims when two codes clash.

In the context of diasporic communities and global migration, the contest between universalist truth claims in holism and the particularist perspectives of relativism is not simply an academic exercise. Multiculturalism has emerged as a social policy for managing cultural difference, and it is therefore necessary to consider the philosophical frameworks in which it operates. The very recognition that other cultures are different, and that this difference has value in and of itself, marks a shift in the relationship between dominant and minority cultures. For instance, if minority cultures are seen not just as inferior, irrelevant or latent forms which need to be either improved or discarded, but as viable alternatives with their own inbuilt mechanisms of interpretation and representation, then this very recognition is only possible if the concept of cultural difference is already linked to the relativist position of truth claims. Relativism does debunk the authority upon which a singular viewpoint is constituted as the universal. While respecting the different truth claims of other positions, however, relativism can only maintain its calm call for tolerance as long as it maintains a distance from the conflict. Relativism may allow for the recognition of the legitimacy of the other claims, but it does not provide the means for breaking the deadlock between two claims. Conflict is not resolved by this process of recognition; at best it can suggest that differences must be respected and that they find a separate space in which coexistence is possible.

In the overlapping and abutting scenarios of the multicultural city, such a discrete space – within which differences are maintained but kept apart from each other – may seem like a false haven. If the multicultural experience is characterized by the constant jostling for space, the negotiation over jagged and loose cultural boundaries, then it is not clear how relativism will allow us to go beyond a mere tolerance of difference, and into a dynamic and inclusive reconfiguration of cultural practice.

The dilemmas that emerged during the Rushdie affair are an instance of this.[5] The two sides in this struggle were locked in conflict over the boundaries of cultural interpretation. Rushdie's interpretation of the Koran was premised on the assumption that it could be interpreted as if it were *a* text. This form of logic was also a displacement of the Koran from its context as *the* text. The shift from the universalist to a particularist view of the text is also marked as a shift from the religious to a secular domain. It could be argued that it was this displacement, and the divergent potential translations of the Koran that this activated, which inspired the Ayatollah Khomeini to issue his *fatwa*. How is freedom of speech to be weighed against a demand for reverence before a sacred text? This moral dilemma was compounded by the uneven boundary between modernity and tradition. Most of the commentators in this debate tended to polarize the two positions. Rushdie became a symbol of the modernist author who challenges tradition, while Khomeini was portrayed as the maniacal and intolerant despot of the Orient. Yet, Rushdie is not a conventional modernist author, just as Khomeini was not simply a feudal despot mired in atavism. Both were engaged in some form of cultural mixture. The dispute was actually over the limits of these mixtures. Rushdie presupposed that he had the general right to interpret the Koran within the context of a novel, and Khomeini responded with the judgement that this particular interpretation was blasphemous. Rushdie's interpretation was mobilized within the literary and political discourses of liberalism, whereas Khomeini's operated in the context of Islam. Both discourses had access to the global circuits of the media. The *differend* between these two positions emerges once we recognize the process of displacement that occurs in the very act of interpretation and translation.

How would a relativist deal with the conflicting views in the Rushdie affair? For relativism even to recognize the difference between these rival claims, it must offer distinctions and judgements about both positions. This, in itself, undermines the neutrality of the process. A relativist who operates from a western liberal democratic background would have a clearer appreciation of Rushdie's secular claim than of Khomeini's claim for Islam and the boundaries of the sacred. One of the conventional criticisms of relativism is that by its very mode of comparison, it introduces absolutism through the back door. To judge between two positions, the relativist must take one position as his or her subject position, and hold the other as an object. The very hierarchy which relativism seeks to dismantle is thus established through its own process of making descriptions of differences. Malcolm Bull has argued that holism exposes this failure of relativism to relativize itself. He argues that to make sense of the other position, the relativist would have to make a distinction between subject and object and then hold one of them static so that the other can be described as relative to it. Bull concludes that if the intelligibility of relativism depends on an exception to the principle of relativity, then it is not really a theory of relativism at all.[6]

Holism and relativism have distinctive ways of addressing the meanings that emerge from cultural interaction. Holism forecloses and excludes any internalization of difference other than through the logic of the same, whereas relativism can never overcome an inherent bias, nor specify the criteria by which it judges between differences. Both philosophical frameworks ultimately imply a judgement between differences and expose limits to the ability to engage with the hybrid reality that enjoins both positions. The borderline between different cultures in the diasporic context is not necessarily clear-cut, and the tension is not just oppositional. In such cases, the necessary decisiveness of judgement that relativism glosses, and the prescriptive distantiation that holism maintains, would neither address the complexities of the interactions that occur, nor provide an adequate basis for cross-cultural judgement. The ethical paradox of multiculturalism is that it grants to each culture the fullness of moral choice while sundering the universal framework which structures each moral order. If universal acceptance does not underpin each moral order then the responsibility of ethical practice is thrown back onto the individual. As Bauman has noted, in relation to the more general ethical condition of postmodernity, morality has been privatized:

> In a cacophony of moral voices, none of which is likely to silence the others, the individuals are thrown back on their own subjectivity as the only ultimate ethical authority. At the same time, however, they are told repeatedly about the irreparable relativism of any moral code. No code claims foundations stronger than the conviction of its followers and their determination to abide by its rules. Once embraced, the rules tell what one must do; but nothing tells one, at least convincingly, why these rules (or any other rules for that matter) should be embraced in the first place.[7]

Beyond relativism and holism

Philosophers as divergent as Alasdair MacIntyre, Charles Taylor and Chantal Mouffe have turned to various philosophical traditions to develop suitable responses to the crisis of judgement in the age of cultural differences. Having observed that the old political strategies which privileged material struggle over cultural affirmation are no longer tenable, they have called for new moral perspectives which will be able to confront both the growth of socio-economic inequalities and the persistent forms of cultural domination. These philosophers are all aware of the limitations of the dominant materialist and idealist paradigms for explaining social change. Class interest can no longer be raised above other social divisions like gender and race. Nor can the consciousness associated with identity politics be elevated beyond its socio-economic context.

These three philosophers, however, by no means represent a new school of thought. While they may be responding to a common social problem and share a number of political principles, what is significant is the way they articulate different philosophical responses. MacIntyre, although mistakenly referred to as a communitarian, is concerned with the way rival traditions of morality are situated within specific communities. Taylor also shares the conviction that philosophical ideals are embedded within a social context and is thereby often at odds with the dominant order. However, his aim is to redefine the conceptual framework within which liberal rights can be secured. For Mouffe, liberalism occludes the politics of difference, and she favours a more radical postmodern theory of agonism. These three perspectives represent the key trajectories in the philosophical responses to the issues of cultural difference. It is clear that the progressivist ideologies of modernity have not in themselves furnished the conceptual apparatus for understanding the interactions that have occurred in its own context. This chapter will, in the first instance, focus on the work of Alasdair MacIntyre because it represents the most explicit attempt to formulate an alternative to cultural relativism.

Alasdair MacIntyre's work is worthy of a close reading, not because he has succeeded in steering a clear path between what he calls the Marxist and 'post-Nietzschean' perspectives, but for his sustained effort to overcome the limitations of particularistic forms of rationality without resorting to a universal moral vocabulary. One of the questions that recurs throughout his writing is: if our moral vocabulary is specific to our cultural context, then who is to judge between rival codes? This question, he claims, can only be answered either philosophically through rational argumentation, or politically through the brutal imposition of will. Assuming the superiority of the philosophical method, he asserts that the existence of incompatible traditions does not entail that their differences cannot be resolved:

> How and under what conditions they can be resolved is something only to be understood after a prior understanding of the nature of such traditions has been achieved. From the standpoint of traditions of rational enquiry the problem of diversity is not abolished, but it is transformed in a way that renders it amenable to solutions.[8]

To grasp the significance of cultural differences MacIntyre acknowledges that subjective factors will always affect judgement. Cultural interactions cannot be understood outside the interplay of such subjective processes. Contrary to the view proposed by holism, MacIntyre argues that the ideal position from which to understand rival claims is not that of the informed insider, for he notes that the limits of a cultural system are best witnessed by a bilingual speaker. Gaps within a cultural system are exposed more precisely in a boundary situation. The bilingual speaker in the boundary situation is, however, not always a bridging person. Recognition of differences does not always facilitate the flow of traffic across the boundary, it can also involve the recognition of an abyss that separates incompatible world-views. The process of translation may recognize the similitude and differences between rival concepts but it does not always provide a mechanism for defining compatibility:

> when two such distinct linguistic communities confront one another, each with its own body of canonical texts, its own exemplary images, and its own tradition of elaborating concepts in terms of these, but each also lacking a knowledge of, let alone linguistic capacities informed by, the tradition of the other community, each will represent the beliefs of the other within its own discourse in abstraction from the relevant tradition and so in a way that ensures misunderstanding. *(p. 392)*

Within this schema MacIntyre shows that conflict between rival cultural positions, without having to be wilful, is neither accidental nor occasional – rather, it is inevitable. For when the modes of interpretation, the sources of ideas and the contexts of meaning are alienated, then the barrier to cross-cultural exchange is not just a lack of knowledge. The very difference in the means for representation and the mode of interpretation will preclude mutual understanding. Translation, even when it is operating in terms of a search for equivalence, or consciously setting out to bridge the gaps between languages, also creates the possibility of alternative meanings. Translation is, as MacIntyre reminds us, never a neutral practice. There is always the disruptive effect of non-correspondence, oblique referentiality, silent resistance and excessive signification. Thus the sign of bilingualism, paradoxically, rests on the ability to discriminate between what remains untranslatable in the very process of translation. To go beyond the very impasse that bilingualism reveals MacIntyre argues that a third position is necessary. However, the introduction of this position is only possible if the respective combatants are prepared to cede the last word to an external source:

> For the only standards of truth and justification made available within the two communities are those between which a choice has to be made. And the only resources afforded for the members of each community to represent the concepts, beliefs and standards of the other ensure that from the point of view of each its own concepts, beliefs and standards will be vindicated and those of its rival found wanting. *(p. 394)*

From this perspective, MacIntyre notes that the price the bilingual speaker pays for living in the two worlds simultaneously, is the necessity to transform his or her understanding of truth. Suspended in an *aporia*, MacIntyre deduces that such a person would by *rational choice* be forced to be relativist. The absolute claim to truth purported by both sides cannot be sustained by this in-between figure. He or she will not be able to form the same conclusions as the other members whose understanding of the conflict is confined to the language and conceptual outlook that is internal to a particular community. Being located on the border between the two languages, the bilingual speaker is granted a perspective that reveals the relativity of truth claims. From the bilingual speaker's position, both sides have their version of what is true and neither has an absolute claim on the truth.

From the way MacIntyre unfolds his argument we can see that the position of the bilingual speaker is an uncomfortable one, and more generally he is implying that there is a sort of hierarchy in the modes of resolution of conflict. At the brutal edge of politics, as with colonialism, he notes that a conflict of will is generally resolved by coercion. When one side is determined to impose its will on the other, the relativist has only limited means for establishing a truce. The relativist is witness to an irreconcilable antagonism and yet has no access to other standards against which the two parties can be measured to facilitate a rational judgement. To overcome the deadlock, for which relativism is no real solution, MacIntyre proposes the learning of a third language. For the bilingual person to choose between the positions which are in conflict, he or she must *step* into another language. MacIntyre characterizes the third language as one which is equidistant from both, has no prior allegiance to either, and possesses the conceptual range to comprehend accurately and represent the two other competing languages. This third language must have the rare attribute of recognizing that meaning and truth are not absolute but are constituted in their specificity.

The question that now remains is: what is this third language? Using the convenience of ideal types, MacIntyre offers us a surprisingly bold answer. The third language is any one of the three twentieth-century, internationalized languages of modernity: English, French and German. This choice is validated by the claim that 'the belief system of any and every culture, or almost of any and every culture, can thus be accurately represented within our own.' The faith in these languages of modernity is premised on the belief that these languages are in some sense 'encyclopaedic'. They are at once the 'acretic' repository and the framework into which all other knowledges have been assembled and incorporated. The canonical texts and modes of interpretation of other languages have all in some sense passed into the frame of these languages of modernity. This answer must not be confused with MacIntyre's general criticism of the smug sensibility that underwrites the modernist presumption of omniscience. While attacking the illusion that our culture is somehow capable of understanding all other cultures, and his prior debunking of the predatory mode of understanding intellectual transference as merely a matter of translucent accessibility and consumerist acquisition, MacIntyre never relinquishes the idea that rational means can be found to resolve the conflict between rival traditions. For while he accepts that the existence of cultural diversity discredits any singular claims of rational neutrality or superiority, he insists that this does not make all cultures equal or absolve us from the need to judge.

Given his awareness of the asymmetry of exchange between two languages which are locked in conflict, the turn to a third language can only be sanctioned if it can demonstrate its independence from both. Yet which of the global languages of modernity is not complicitous with the violence of colonialism? Even if it were possible to establish the independence of the global languages of modernity, why is the status of third position reserved for them? This claim could only be sustained if the cultural outlook of the global and local positions were codified according to the binaries of modern/traditional; open/closed. Such a code is implicit in MacIntyre's claim that while traditional languages have meanings which are embedded only in one context, modern languages have developed systems of meaning through the incorporation of signs from other languages. In this way, the depth and complexity of a concept in a modern language may be richer than the original because it has been translated with the knowledge of other views which were unavailable to the original source. This expansive, dynamic and multi-perspectival frame is attributed solely to modern languages. In contradistinction, the traditional concept is seen as static and bound to a particular community or time. The distinction implies that in modern languages meaning has been disembedded from its originary context and is subsequently constituted *in* the encounter with the incommensurable. It appears that the framework for judgement and the mechanisms of violence are too deeply enmeshed in any of the proposed third languages and that they would fall before the dual criteria of independence and comprehension.

MacIntyre is conscious of the impossibility of the third language constituting a transcendental position and warns that the bilingual person will not find an absolute reconciliation in this language. The framework for reconciliation within which the languages of modernity operate is not bounded by distinct spaces, nor do they offer a structure within which identities assume a discrete location and follow a precise order. Rather than offering the satisfaction of resolution and integration, there is the admission of the ongoing difficulty of dealing with doubt and conflict as they are negotiated through the supposedly impersonal and neutral standards of rationality:

> [what] he or she will in fact learn from acquiring this new language is that it is a central feature of the culture whose language it is that rationally founded agreement as to the nature of the justification required is not to be obtained. *(p. 401)*

MacIntyre's promise of going beyond the limits of relativism is thus a paradoxical one. When solutions are proposed the justifications which support them are not founded on a universalist view of language. There is no prior code which determines values and measures outcomes. MacIntyre's solution to the conflict between rival positions is, at best, a strategic one: it proposes an alternative language that is informed by the very heterogeneity of languages. The standards proposed as rational and neutral do not exempt them from contestation. For instance, with the annexation of other civilizations, 'Eastern', 'vernacular', or 'pre-literate', the languages of modernity have produced a possibility for the multiplication of rival standpoints. Incommensurability is the central feature, not the limit, of this language. MacIntyre concedes, however, that the active incorporation of the incommensurable into the languages of modernity offers no guarantee of an external and neutral standard from which to establish a rational justification that is capable of breaking the deadlock.

It is here that MacIntyre's quest for cross-cultural understanding leads towards a refutation of relativism. While accepting that in the culture of modernity it appears that 'relativism is inescapable from certain particular points of view' (p. 405), he still insists that 'it does not follow that relativism cannot be transcended.' In his earlier remarks on the limits and resilience of a moral tradition, MacIntyre discussed the possibility of an accumulated knowledge which may, in itself, be an inadequate resource for explaining one's own condition. This may therefore compel either a switch or a re-excavation which revalues and reprioritizes internal and external ways of seeing. This incorporation of 'alien traditions' in ways which enable us to identify and to understand the limitations of our own tradition is a key feature of MacIntyre's argument. Here he lays stress on the way rationality is formulated in our tradition, so that it is capable of recognizing a limit that in turn enables a transgression. MacIntyre is not simply establishing the shifting axes of knowledge/power exchanges, but attempting a reformulation of the Platonic distinction 'between "is true" and "seems true to such and such person" ' into the establishment of a tradition that recognizes the *truth in relativism*. He recognizes that though there is no guarantee of an objective standard to establish rational justification, there is still the need to recognize the particularism from which judgement is made. The existence of a moral tradition built out of rival standpoints forces us to seek the truth in its very relativity, which MacIntyre claims is distinct from the relativist claim that 'there is *no* truth', or that 'everything is *relatively* true'.

From this perspective we can appreciate both MacIntyre's critique of the universalizing tendency in relativism which reduces the essence of all cultures to a variation of our own, and his general claim that the disjunctiveness of cultural difference leads to cultural transformation. It is not, however, clear whether this provides a sufficient basis for grasping the dynamics of cultural exchange in the diasporic context.

Multiculturalism without essentialism

Global migration has stimulated the scattering of cultures; however, this has also involved a form of regrouping under foreign skies and the rebuilding of communities with different members and neighbours. This shift in context, and the presence of others, creates new questions about the boundaries of identity and provokes new demands for representation. To succumb to a politics of representation, whose identity is confined to reproducing the past, and to making visible the identity which racist discourse sought to repress, is to enter an arena where the standards of authentication pay little attention to the dynamics of emergence. When diasporic cultures accept the affirmative discourses of anti-racism, there is the danger that they are also accepting the burden of representing themselves within categories which make their minority status more visible, without flushing out the invisible order that secures the dominant culture in its place. The dominant culture has always defined its own identity through the racialized discourse of the Other. To repeat Sartre's famous dictum, 'if the Jew did not exist, he would have to be invented.' By making the Other visible through projected fears of dirt, fantasies of depravity and threats of decline, the order, health and superiority of the dominant self remain implied. If multiculturalism is to correct this false image of the Other, then it must not only project images which glorify a minority culture's past, or highlight its achievements in the present, but also address the invisible links which determine the contours of the dominant self.

The limitations of multiculturalism are not to be measured against its failure to eliminate racist practices from everyday life, but in its failure to develop a critique of the very process of the cultural. Even if multiculturalism enjoyed the unequivocal backing of all the state apparatus and found infinite corporate sponsorship deals, the most rigorous implementation of existing multicultural policies would, at best, guarantee a stronger representation of the substantive contents of different cultures. It would do little to highlight either the simultaneous processes of differentiation that occur between cultures, or the complex processes of transformation within the cultural.

The pluralist model that dominates the politics of multiculturalism has done a great deal to identify new constituencies within the structures of society. It has empowered new subjects to make different claims about the priorities and trajectory of social change. However, this model has not challenged the very structures by which we see the process of identity as being formed across differences.[9] It encourages the interplay of cultural differences only insofar as they do not disrupt or challenge the institutional procedures of the dominant society. Slavoj Zizek makes the strong claim that multiculturalism reduces the sign of cultural difference to a spectacle that satisfies the liberal gaze:

Liberal 'tolerance' condones the folklorist Other deprived of its substance – like the multitude of 'ethnic cuisines' in a contemporary megalopolis; however any 'real' Other is instantly denounced for its 'fundamentalism', since the kernel of Otherness resides in the regulation of its *jouissance*: the 'real Other' is by definition 'patriarchal', 'violent', never the Other of ethereal wisdom and charming customs.[10]

Multiculturalism thus fails to disrupt the racist constructions of the Other; it merely brings forward the palatable roles while pulling back the threatening images of alterity. The space of tolerance is thus always threatened by the vengeful return of the repressed. This form of cultural politics postulates difference only as the line of separation and as the marker of competition for access to resources. The Other may compete within the game of pluralism but has no right to question the rules. To cross this boundary is to unleash the full armoury of liberal scorn, making the Other no longer a contestant in the game but the unruly outsider. There is a need to develop a perspective on cultural identity that goes beyond an oppositional model in which the battle for representation is locked into a zero-sum game.

Sarat Maharaj's image of the multicultural as the 'space of translation' draws attention to the fluidities of difference in the process of cultural transformation. Before we return to the space of translation in cultural difference, it is also necessary to consider the relationship between the part and the whole of a culture. Does a translation only occur when a whole culture encounters another, or when the part of a culture – which is representative of the whole – is in contact with the whole of another culture? Or can there be a more radical proposition, where translation occurs through and with the fragments of different cultures, and whereby the totality of these fragments that are in translation does not add up to the whole of a culture? If the translational process were confined to the interaction between distinct cultural forms, this would turn our attention away from an interplay with multiple differences and towards models that presuppose unitary identities. Interaction would be restricted to a series of binary oppositions and would overlook the more subtle exchanges that occur in the diasporic context. Binary constructions of cultural differences are caught in a paradigm of purity and contamination. The concept of identity in a binary model is defined by privileging the formative role of internal and exclusive experiences. Interaction is also limited to a series of negotiations between discrete entities across predetermined boundaries. It is no coincidence that many ethnic leaders endorse this mode of thinking about cultural difference, as if a diasporic culture could be represented as the bejewelled fragment of a larger mosaic. For this coding reinforces the cultural boundary between different cultures and restricts the practice of political negotiation to a repositioning within the hierarchy of centre and periphery.

In MacIntyre's rejection of the moral ambiguity of relativism there is a promise of a new basis for the resolution of conflict through a deeper understanding of the traditions in which differences are articulated. Yet, it is the determination of this category of tradition, which may obscure the more subtle and mixed processes of exchange that constitute the field of cultural difference, as a zone of differential interconnection rather than polarized opposition. In one sense, we can see that MacIntyre's sensitivity to the absence of a singular and absolute objectivity against which all subjectivities can be measured, and his stress on the individual responsibility to derive meaning from a specific tradition of moral thought, are symptomatic of the disenchantment that comes with segmentation in modernity. What his theory fails to grasp, however, is the possibility of identity being formed through the interconnection of partial languages and fragmented cultures.

Recognition and partial blindness

How do we judge between cultures which have not yet claimed an equal space in the discursive field of representation? Can the culture constituted by the processes of displacement be compared with one which has historically enjoyed the structures of settlement? If the mutual understanding of the truth claims in other cultures can only proceed when both cultures have equal space to ground their traditions, how will a diasporic culture, which lacks the conditions of grounding, enter into dialogue? The very concept of dialogue needs redefinition in order for us to appreciate that in every representation of cultural difference there is a fluid and unstable zone, in which identity is produced through the constant negotiation *between* past and present, here and elsewhere, absence and presence, self and other. The identity of the diasporic community does not arrive fully formed. It is not an identity that has been constituted elsewhere and is transposed intact. The passages between places, and the translations that have occurred in time suggest that identity does not exist outside the sphere of representation. Thus it is more accurate to argue that diasporic identity is produced within the 'ambivalent' space and in the 'double' time of cultural translation. This more complex and hybrid form of identity seems to baffle those models of translation that presuppose a binary distinction between different groups.

A parallel observation about the process of representation was made by Homi Bhabha in his critique of Charles Taylor's account of multiculturalism and the 'politics of recognition'.[11] Bhabha noted that Taylor, when attempting to define which cultures should be recognized in the field of cultural difference, excluded the presence of partial cultures. In Taylor's argument, the only cultures which are worthy of admiration and respect are those which are derived from 'whole societies over some considerable stretch of time'.[12] I would like to turn to Taylor's theory of recognition in order to consider whether a contemporary defence of liberalism can also accommodate the dynamics of cultural difference.

From a relativist's perspective this qualification would be seen as a marker of arrogance and ethnocentrism. By what standards will one cultural value be compared with another? Who determines the parameters of social wholeness and the fullness of historical time? How can you predefine which cultural forms are worthy of recognition without imposing patterns of prejudice and authority? How can you evaluate the forms of other cultures, when it is our own cultural perspectives which have destroyed and deformed their institutions of representation? These are difficult and demanding questions; like MacIntyre, Taylor is not prepared to accept that relativism has the last word. He challenges the view that all knowledge is merely interpretation and therefore ultimately value-laden. Taylor insists that the task of philosophy is to discriminate between significance and worth, and that the 'truth of the other' can be discerned in terms of a movement of one interpretation to another.[13] He would claim that not all cultures are commensurate, attack the stance of disengagement and accept that philosophical concepts are mediated by their social context. In the process, he would also like to outline a framework within which the evaluation of other cultures shifts from the mere affirmation of difference, to a politics of recognition based on equal dignity. This process of evaluation is presented in terms of a philosophical critique which is capable of recovering and reactivating sources of self-interpretation and moral judgement that modernity has already closed. Therefore, the crucial question for Taylor is: does liberalism provide a suitable framework within which the conditions of cultural differences can be recognized?

Cultural rights, Taylor argues, can only be addressed when they are claimed on behalf of a group whose identity can be defined in terms of a specific historical evolution, with a given attachment to place, and representing a large number of people. This qualification in terms of who can enter the arena of cultural negotiation would automatically disqualify diasporic communities whose own history has never been fully recorded, who have been compelled to move away from their homeland and who have been dispersed in multiple directions. By offering recognition only to the established units of cultural identity, liberalism turns a blind eye to many groups which, despite the omissions of history and the ordeals of geography, are nevertheless constantly attempting to negotiate their own cultural identity. They are always developing strategies to articulate their experiences and aspirations. The questions that remain are: which language will speak their history, and why should they be excluded from the language of rights?

Taylor's theory of cultural recognition stumbles as it faces these decisive issues of identity and representation. He recognizes that multicultural societies pose a challenge to liberalism, yet his attempt to expand its procedures fails to resolve the underlying tension between collective and individual identity formations. At the centre of his model is the assumption that each culture has the right to equal respect, and the appreciation that all identity is shaped by recognition and that this process is dialogical. However, the prior qualifications on the definition of a culture and the privileging of the survival of the existing cultural units may conflict with the counter-claim of the individual's autonomy and obscure recognition of emergent cultural formations. The cultural critic K. Anthony Appiah has challenged Taylor's defence of liberalism on the grounds that he grants too much authority to the already existing forms of collectivity. This level of recognition would also carry a commitment to upholding forms of social reproduction which threaten the autonomy of individuals who are members of a collectivity but who do not wish to conform to the existing norms and regulations. Appiah gives the example of education within a minority and argues that if control were delegated entirely to that unit, then the ethics of education would be reduced to what was deemed permissible only within the boundaries of its own cultural practice. This effectively reduces the very condition of dialogue across cultural boundaries. Appiah concludes that in terms of identifying collective identities, Taylor is, even by his own terms, insufficiently dialogical, and at worst, at risk of 'replacing one kind of tyranny with another'.[14]

The dominant notions of identity in liberal politics have not always emphasized this dialogical process. The conceptions of identity which have followed Herder's definition of authenticity as 'one's original way of being human' have directed our understanding of self-realization through an inward-looking optic and measured the boundaries of identity from the putative radix of the inner self. Taylor is conscious that this monological notion of identity has generated considerable harm and chauvinism. In democratic cultures the dignity of minority groups must be not only privately tolerated but also publicly respected. This notion of identity has given rise to a politics of difference which stresses that, along with the recognition of universal equality, the politics of dignity require a recognition of the specificity and unique identity of individual groups. Yet, as we have noted, this presumption of equality is not positioned on a level playing field. Jürgen Habermas commences his response to this theory by posing this astute question: 'Can a theory of rights that is so *individualistic* in its construction do justice to those struggles for recognition which clearly appear to revolve around the articulation and assertion of *collective* identities?'[15]

The problematic definition of the subject, which is at the core of liberalism, is compounded by the unstable context of diasporic communities. The struggle for recognition is operating from a platform of neither known historical achievements nor organic structural formations, but out of a collective experience of violation and dispersal. How is it possible to gain recognition when the very resources and language for representation have been partially lost or radically damaged? Taylor has attempted to respond to this problematic by shifting the liberal principles of 'equal respect' away from an individualistic core and towards a judgement of a good life in society. Yet this move fails to overcome the pitfalls that marginalized groups have constantly faced within liberal societies. Habermas has argued that liberal societies have always adopted a paternalistic approach to minorities, implemented rights which have been ethically patterned by their own norms, and protected their own legal and political structures.

If multiculturalism contested these frameworks of evaluation and representation, it would also have the potential to expose the neutrality of liberalism. The resistance to this line of contestation is revealed once again in the philosophical discourse of cultural difference. The limitations of the liberal framework are found in Taylor's 'test of excellence' which, he suggests, must be passed before the right to equal respect is extended to other cultures. His aim is to balance the basic political principles of liberalism without the marginalization of other cultures. Yet, does this proposed balance, or what Gadamer calls the 'fusion of horizons'[16] between different cultures, disrupt the very dialogism which is necessary for recognition?

> As a presumption, the claim is that all human cultures that have animated whole societies over some considerable stretch of time have something important to say to all human beings. I have worded it in this way to exclude partial cultural milieux within a society, as well as short phases of a major culture.[17]

The presumption of equal value is thus confined to those cultures which have made a contribution to world civilization. But who is to measure 'contribution', and how do we define 'world civilization'? Modern societies are defined by and composed of multiple clusters of diasporic communities. These clusters have generated images which are so fragmented and hybrid that they have challenged the conventional notions of community as being grounded on the standards of ethnic purity and cultural homogenization. Taylor has no doubt that modern societies must rethink their frameworks of equality and freedom. He recognizes that the transformation of the self can only proceed through the understanding of the other. But his willingness to be open to comparative cultural study is bound by a restrictive binary model.

Bhabha also stresses that Taylor's criterion of whole cultures is out of time with the actual processes of cultural negotiation and interaction. Minority cultures cannot be defined as either fragments of an archaic culture, or as being merely in a transitional state en route to modernization. Their own identities emerge, not simply from the preservation of the past, or the belated attempt to grasp the present of modernity, but, as Bhabha argues, from being implicated in both worlds simultaneously. It is this 'in-between' position, or rather the dynamic process of oscillation between positions, which is difficult to comprehend within a liberal schema, and is all too often dismissed as incoherent, or, at times, not even registered as worthy of consideration. The disjunctive and double temporalities of partial culture are, Bhabha argues, not assimilable into the greater whole to which Taylor would designate them. This is the hubris of liberalism – it elevates the identity of the whole by subsuming the identity of its parts, and what is disavowed is the contestatory energy of hybridity that exists within and between cultures. In Taylor's schema, hybridity is not recognized in the arena for recognition of cultural rights. Hybridity is relegated to a transitional stage that occurs prior to the formation of a cultural identity.

Towards a critical multiculturalism

Hybrid forms of cultural identity and complex forms of collective representation in the context of multiculturalism have exposed the limits of liberal modes of recognition. To avoid a mere retreat into the pitfalls of relativism which, as MacIntyre noted, surround this debate, we need to develop an alternative philosophical framework. The identity of the migrant, the stranger, the other, cannot be defined in opposition to the dominant self. A critical multiculturalism would begin by shifting the terms of identity from an antagonistic struggle for purity to an agonistic process of identification and entanglement. All identity is defined in relation to difference. The notion of the 'constitutive outside', which has destabilized the claims of identity as being bounded by a binary of interior and exterior, can also provide a conceptual link between the politics of multiculturalism and the dynamics of hybridity. Chantal Mouffe points out that the limitations of liberalism are revealed by the necessary exclusions upon which its mode of consensus is based and by its restrictive construction of the subject. For a genuine form of multiculturalism to flourish there needs to be a radical commitment to the politics of difference. The political arena requires more than an extension of its prior notion of constituency and representation, but also a rethinking of the very principles of consensus. As Mouffe argues, the future of a critical multiculturalism rests on the need to break out of antagonistic contests, and move towards a zone of agonistic struggles. From this perspective multiculturalism would involve

> a clean break with the objectivism and essentialism which dominate political analysis. But liberal thought employs a logic of the social based on a conception of being as presence, and which conceives of objectivity as inherent to things themselves. This is why it is impossible for liberal thought to recognize that there can only be an identity when it is constructed as a 'difference', and that any social objectivity is constituted by the enactment of power. What it refuses to admit is that any form of social objectivity is ultimately political and must bear the traces of the acts of exclusion which govern its constitution.[18]

Liberalism's commitment to the ethic of self-realization would always reduce hybridity to a form of inferiority. Taylor's effort to define the principles of equality and tolerance in the context of multiculturalism stumbles at the point of defining entry. Excluding the process of hybridization from the field of recognition effectively limits the understanding of cultural transformation. It not only confines negotiation to a contestation amongst subjects and entities who already have a place and voice within the arena, but it also fails to see how new boundaries and different identities emerge in the very process of interaction. To presume that identities are defined prior to the interaction is to pincer the very possibility of cultural emergence into negative categories. Diasporic communities, in particular, are caught by this double bind. Their own experience of displacement is a testimony of loss and reconfiguration. To summon an identity of wholeness and continuity would be a denial of the violations and transformations that have led them to their present position, and yet to express the absences and contradictions of their identity would also undermine their claim to be recognized within the present. A different framework for representing identity is necessary. It requires that we must, in the first instance, acknowledge that the creation of any identity is also the affirmation of difference, but that this difference is neither immutable nor primordial. Differences are socially constructed, and the relationships between identity and otherness can be established in ways that open up the dynamics that a liberal schema would exclude or bypass.

On a broader level, Bhikhu Parekh has argued that the very categories that liberalism constructs for the representation of cultural identity are bound by an evolutionist model of cultural development, a utilitarian framework for defining political rights and a commitment to privileging the autonomy of the subject over communal and traditional ways of life. Parekh argues that these basic principles bear the legacies of a colonialist world-view and negate liberalism's claims to neutrality and universality.[19] Liberalism remains a distinctly European political philosophy which was deeply implicated in colonial rule, and was unable to develop a common language through which it might enter into dialogue with non-liberal practices, let alone identify the moral basis for universally shared experiences and aspirations. Zygmunt Bauman further argues that the liberal concept of toleration actively undermines any genuine dialogue with the Other:

> Toleration does not include the acceptance of the other's worth; on the contrary, it is one more, perhaps somewhat subtler and cunning way of reaffirming the other's inferiority and serving an advance warning of the intention to terminate the Other's otherness – together with an invitation to the Other to co-operate in bringing to pass the inevitable. The famed humanity of the toleration policy does not step beyond the consent to delay the final showdown – on condition, however, that the very act of consent would further strengthen the existing order of superiority.[20]

Tolerance requires more than the magnanimous gesture of accepting others in all their difference, because this gesture does not necessarily disturb a prior hierarchy of superiority and inferiority. To go beyond this potential humiliation of the 'tolerated', liberalism would need to develop mechanisms for both acknowledging the equal worth of other cultural systems, and also engaging with what Bauman calls their 'knowledge-producing discourses'. There is little evidence to suggest that liberalism has ever extended its conception of tolerance to such a dialogic form. According to Parekh, John Stuart Mill regarded non-European cultures as not only 'backward' but in a stagnant stage of 'nonage', and believed that the only way that they could progress was by accepting the strong hand of foreigners.[21] Non-European cultures were seen as mired in atavistic traditions and closed societies, whereas the strength of European cultures was justified by their love of individuality and diversity. Parekh accordingly argues that liberalism's philosophical framework for representing cultural interaction is the outcome of its limited conception of the relationship between the individual and its specific cultural setting. The autonomy of the subject was defined with a mechanistic view to self-regulation and control over destiny. The dynamics of cultural exchange were crude extrapolations of biological metaphors of grafting and cross-breeding. Throughout this discourse the priority of the western male's access to potency and rationality remained unquestioned. As a consequence, the foundations of liberalism have provided a particularly narrow view of subjectivity and cultural difference.

According to Parekh, contemporary liberal thinkers have not liberated themselves from the limitations of this philosophy. There is still no recognition of cultural identity as a primary goal in society. While the evolutionist model of cultural development may be discredited, the binary model for determining the differences between cultures remains deep-seated. There has been no sustained engagement with the philosophical traditions of non-European cultures. The ideal of individual autonomy also remains as the condition of human development. However, on an optimistic note Parekh concludes that the politics of multiculturalism has offered liberalism the challenge to rethink its foundations in order to realize its own goals:

> It needs to become more open-minded, more self-critical, more tolerant of its rivals, and far more sensitive to the diversity and complexity of human existence than it has been hitherto. It must reassess its Millian commitment to a single mode of human excellence and evolve a view of the world in which different ways of life, including the non-liberal, can converse as equals and enrich both individual and collective existence. A truly liberal society is characterized by diverse ways of life, both liberal and non-liberal, both secular and religious, both individualist and communitarian, and each in turn nurturing its own diverse forms. A true liberal state cherishes and gives public recognition to this diversity, provides such resources and conditions of growth as they need and cannot raise themselves, encourages a civil dialogue between them, and enforces norms that they have agreed upon and without which their peaceful coexistence is impossible.[22]

Working from a different philosophical perspective, Chantal Mouffe makes similar observations on the contours of democratic practice. Following from Derrida's concept of the 'constitutive outside', she notes that identity formation often implies a hierarchy, but if this is understood in relational terms rather than as a fixed opposition, then it opens up the field of contestation and enables the emergence of new forms of collectivity:

> So politics concerns public activity and the formation of collective identities. Its aim is to create an 'us' in a context of diversity and conflict. But to construct an 'us', one has to differentiate it from a 'them'. That is why the crucial question for democratic politics is not how to arrive at a consensus without exclusion, or how to create an 'us' which would not have a corresponding 'them', but rather it is how to establish this 'us' and 'them' discrimination in a way that is compatible with pluralist democracy. This presupposes that the 'other' is no longer seen as an enemy to be destroyed, but as a 'counterpart' who could be in our place in the future. The aim is to transform antagonism into agonism.[23]

Although coming from different philosophical traditions and presenting varying critiques of relativism and liberalism, MacIntyre, Taylor and Mouffe are all attempting to redefine the frameworks of political judgement in the context of cultural difference and globalization. There is still no consensus on the philosophical frameworks for representing either globalization or cultural differences. There is no ideal 'third language' which can not only intervene in the struggle between fundamentalism and liberalism, but also unsettle the more insidious appropriation of multiculturalism within the culture of transnational corporatism. The politics of agonism, which seeks to activate the rights of minority groups and forge new alliances across the traditional divisions of nation, class and gender, has not yet addressed the institutional context in which these political formations will be mobilized. Globalization has decoupled the exclusive links between minority groups and the nation-state, the neutrality of liberalism has been debunked, but the framework within which the universal rights of minorities can be asserted has not been secured. On what basis will minorities forge bonds that can endure the pressures of globalization, and before which tribunal will they seek resolution? Liberal states have justified restrictions on immigration in order to defend the practice of redistributing resources and benefits amongst their members.[24] But when the state increasingly relinquishes effective control of the socio-economic levers to transnational corporations, on what moral grounds will it determine rights of entry? As the gap between north and south opens further and further, how will cross-cultural exchange ever approach any semblance of equality? The urgency of answering such questions is undeniable. With grievous clear-sightedness Ashis Nandy has noted that, given the asymmetry in cultural resources and the absence of a shared framework in which dialogue can be posed, the dominance of global culture will proceed unchecked:

> When two cultures of unequal secular power enter into a dialogue, a new hierarchy inevitably emerges, unless the dialogue creates a shared space for each participant's distinctive, unstated theory of the other culture or, in its absence,

each participant's general theory of culture. The concept of cultural relativism, expressed in the popular anthropological view that each culture must be studied in terms of its own categories, is limited because it stops short of insisting that every culture must recognize it is constructed by other cultures. It is easy to leave other cultures to their own devices in the name of cultural relativism, particularly if the visions of the future of these other cultures have already been cannibalized by the worldview of one's own. It is less easy to live with an alien culture's estimate of oneself, to integrate it within one's selfhood and to live with that self-induced inner tension. It is even more difficult to live with the inner dialogue within one's own culture when it is triggered off by the dialogue with other cultures because, then, the carefully built cultural defences against disturbing dialogues – and against the threatening insights emerging from the dialogues – begin to crumble.[25]

This disruptive relationship between different cultures, and the multiplicity of perspectives from which judgement proceeds, have intensified as globalization advances. The multiple sense of belonging and the complex formations of identity that I have discussed have implications for how we interpret reality, and also for the foundations for building a moral order. While the concept of cultural translation has enabled us to understand both the dynamics and the limits to this process of exchange and formation, it has also exposed the uncomfortable prospect of constantly redefining the moral boundaries that guide ethical practices. The moral dilemmas of cultural difference are part of the constitutive features of modernity. However, this appreciation of the complexity of radical difference has also revealed that we lack a general theory of culture, which can define the condition of its own existence without presupposing an opposition to other cultures, or proposing a hierarchical mode of interaction. The ambivalence of cultural difference is deeply linked to the ontological contingency of culture.

8

Tracing Hybridity in Theory

In the last decade there has barely been a debate on cultural theory or postmodern subjectivity that does not acknowledge the productive side of hybridity and describe identity as being in some form of hybrid state.[1] This is a radical inversion of the historical status that has trailed this concept. For as long as the concepts of purity and exclusivity have been central to a racialized theory of identity, hybridity has, in one way or another, served as a threat to the fullness of selfhood. The hybrid has often been positioned within or beside modern theories of human origin and social development, mostly appearing as the moral marker of contamination, failure or regression. Yet, one of the 'achievements' of post-structuralist theory was to liberate the subject from notions of fixity and purity in origin. And in a social context where the political structures for mobilizing and integrating emancipatory projects were also fragmenting, it was almost a form of succour to remind ourselves of our 'multiple subjectivities'. Can we now have the confidence that hybridity has been moved out from the loaded discourse of 'race', and situated in a more neutral zone of identity?

The contemporary discourse of cultural criticism and critical theory has embraced a number of models for representing the supposed 'newness' of postmodern identity: along with the concept of hybridity there is the 'cyborgian' fantasy of fusion between man and machine, as well as the 'morphing' of one object into another. This incorporation of the concept of hybridity into mainstream cultural discourse has raised new problems. Hybridity has served as the organizing principle for international cultural initiatives, as well as entering the programmes of local social movements. Artists like Guillermo Gomez-Pena, who previously described both the subjectivity and form of his work as hybrid, are now increasingly suspicious of its utility. When Guillermo Gomez-Pena once used hybridity as an 'elastic metaphor' to address the process of contradiction and difference in cultural exchange, he did not expect that it would be stretched so far as to justify either its exclusivist territorializing in downtown LA or the expansionist policies of NAFTA.[2]

From art critics in popular art magazines like *FRIEZE* to influential social theorists like Zygmunt Bauman, the concept of hybridity has been adopted both to demonstrate the principle of aesthetic connection that occurs from kitsch to high culture, and to address the construction of identity in a context of ontological uncertainty.[3] As hybridity achieves a more popular status it has been called on to perform a bridging function which previous concepts have failed to achieve. Just as the old modernist ideal of cosmopolitanism begins to appear passé, and the idea of a 'new internationalism' is caught on the shabby horns of the 'new world order', hybridity is ushered forward as the specific identity which, paradoxically, is universally applicable. Hybridity is the most unlikely contender for this role as 'multi-purpose globalizing identity kit'.

Despite its historical association, which bears the dubious traces of colonial and white suprematicist ideologies, most contemporary discussions on hybridity are preoccupied by its potential for inclusivity. The dark past of hybridity rarely disturbs the more cheerful populist claims. One of the aims of this chapter is to contextualize the various trajectories of thought and traditions in which hybridity has been inserted.

A quick glance at the history of hybridity reveals a bizarre array of ideas. Hybridity has shadowed every organic theory of identity and was deeply inscribed in nineteenth-century discourses of scientific racism. Whether it highlighted physiological or cultural difference in identity, it served primarily as a metaphor for the negative consequences of racial encounters. These metaphors are mercurial. Even when the scientific basis of racism had been discredited, racist practices were not abandoned but rehoused in the discourse of social types. Indeed the enigmatic 'nature' of the hybrid may still lurk within contemporary uses of hybridity as a model for cultural identity. Cultural critics like Jean Fisher stress that the concept is too deeply embedded in a discourse that presupposes an evolutionary hierarchy, and that it carries the prior purity of biologism.[4] Gayatri Spivak also notes that the preoccupation with hybridity in academic discourse has tended to gloss over persistent social divisions of class and gender.[5]

Despite the pseudo-scientific analogies and negative history that trail in the semantic associations of hybridity, the term has gained considerable acceptance in cultural theory. Its current use is perhaps motivated by a perverse pleasure in taking a negative term and transforming it into a positive sign, 'to wear with pride the name they were given in scorn'.[6] Why should the nineteenth-century eugenicists be allowed to retain a patent on hybridity? Should we use only words with a pure and inoffensive history, or should we challenge essentialist models of identity by taking on, and then subverting, their own vocabulary?

The positive feature of hybridity is that it invariably acknowledges that identity is constructed through a negotiation of difference, and that the presence of fissures, gaps and contradictions is not necessarily a sign of failure. In its most radical form, the concept also stresses that identity is not the combination, accumulation, fusion or synthesis of various components, but an energy field of different forces. Hybridity is not confined to a cataloguing of difference. Its 'unity' is not found in the sum of its parts, but emerges from the process of opening what Homi Bhabha has called, a 'third space', within which other elements encounter and transform each other. Hybridity is both the assemblage that occurs whenever two or more elements meet, and the initiation of a process of change. This perspective is a crucial departure from the functionalist models of cultural exchange. It also breaks with the 'cooking paradigms' of 'mix and match' which recur in much of the multiculturalist and anti-racist discourses on identity. By charting a path between a number of key theoretical models and perspectives I hope to clarify the historical legacy and sharpen the conceptual apparatus for our understanding of these much maligned monsters of hybridity.

Eugenics and the hybrid body

As a starting-point for an outline of the concept of hybridity, I want to consider the collusion between the nineteenth-century populist mythology of miscegenation and scientific racism. The preoccupation with the question of genesis in the nineteenth century was symptomatic of a generalized state of unease over origin and identity. Imperialism, in its quest for a global economic system, produced concurrent cultural ruptures. New forms of colonial integration could only be achieved through the dislocation of peoples and values. These new encounters had profound and disturbing consequences in the self-imaging of both the ruler and the ruled. Among the Europeans this new anxiety could be witnessed in the new racialized theories of genesis. The debates about ancestry and classification drew inspiration from the prevailing notions of progress, seized on all the apparatus for quantification, and dressed themselves according to the residual norms of savagery and civilization. Each theory was a potent mixture of narcissistic white supremacy and the Enlightenment logic of linear development.

The emerging theories of hybridity were for the most part normative prohibitions, rather than biological diagnoses or scientific prognostications. The two dominant views on the origins of humanity – monogenesis and polygenesis – were also ostensible attempts to explain the status of the perceptible differences between races.[7] According to the theory of monogenesis, all races were members of a single species and had a common origin. Differences between them had to be attributed to differing physical and social environments. While putative differences in forms of morality and levels of intelligence were explained by context rather than innate qualities, it was still presumed that the white race was both the superior form of development, and the original norm, from which others degenerated. Hence the notion of equality between the races was either backdated to the point of origin or postponed to an appointed time when everyone else had *turned* white.

By the middle of the nineteenth century the contrary theory of polygenesis began to gain ascendancy. George Morton and other members of the American school of ethnology argued that each race represented a distinct species, and that white supremacy was simply a 'gift of nature' that had not been bestowed on inferior races. To prove their argument, these scientists proceeded to gather data like historical variations in the thickness of skulls, breadth of noses and length of penises. Each physical measurement was interpreted as an indicator of intellectual development and moral stability. One craniologist got so excited with his methods and tools that he managed to take over a thousand measurements from another person's head.

Scientific claims about the distinctness of the races reinforced the pro-slavery ideology and gave grounds for the belief that the hybrid was either a monstrous or a debased offspring, and would inevitably be weaker and less fertile than either parent. The popularized naming of hybrids as mulattos was based not only on the difference in species between the horse and the donkey, but also on the sterility of the mule. Morton's theory of hybridity eventually shifted from interspecific sterility to diminished capacity for reproduction. This theory of hybridity, which was founded on selective readings from botany and supported by the spurious facts of Morton's 'experience', lent itself ideally to the pro-slavery ideology. At best, blacks deserved to be domesticated under slavery, whereas the unfortunate hybrid offspring inspired pathos and loathing.

A whole mythology about the status of mulattos followed from the assumption that they were incapable of reproducing amongst themselves and that therefore their fertility was dependent on 'artificial contrivance', or by an 'unnatural act of mating'. There was also the sense that they were both 'effete' – lacking the physical endurance of blacks, and 'flighty' – lacking the moral fortitude of whites. They remained apart from both races. Caught in the no man's land of the neither/nor category, hybrids were subjected to the whole battery of accusations that follow an anxiety over an anomalous identity. Perhaps the most bizarre twist in the collusion between popular mythology and scientific knowledge was expressed by a group of neurologists, who argued that electrical signals in the bodies of whites and blacks flow in opposite directions, and therefore mulattos would suffer from confusion as their systems were tangled up in a state of multidirectional conflict. As Joel Williamson noted, the mulatto was potentially disruptive of the existing social order. Hence the function of this 'muleological' discourse was to neutralize anxiety that the mulatto might actually suggest a more viable alternative to the polarized view of black against white:

The myth of the mulatto demise functioned to relieve the Southern white mind of a great irritation. Whites chafed under the continued mulatto presence. Just as free Negroes and mulattoes per se before the war jarred the white man's conception of himself in a neat free white–black slave universe, the simple universe of mulattoes after the war militated against the white man's sense of identity.[8]

The debates on the 'origins of mankind' and the 'constitution of society' were framed in various metaphors connoting organic unity and racial purity. Hybridity always threatened these evocations of social order. The 'messy reality' that hybridity represented undermined fundamental beliefs in the basis and trajectory of progress. The presence of the hybrid was the persistent thorn in the side of the white ideologies of domination and purity. A third identity is one which would also disrupt the very basis upon which prior identities were granted. This disruption followed because the unknown identity was not simply additional and commensurable to previous identities, but was rather, to use Derrida's term, a supplement that disrupted the order for naming. This ambiguity and unfixed identity fanned hostile speculation. The deep-seated anxieties over miscegenation and fervent hostility to difference were most fancifully revealed in the prediction about the destiny of hybrids. Speculation over interspecific sterility or diminished reproduction, with eventual disappearance after three or four generations, is an illustration of how hybridity was always more a marker of the fictive limits of the racial imaginary than a site for scientific observation.

The advent of Darwinian principles on the origins of the races dealt a decisive blow against the foundations of the polygenist views. However, Darwinian theory only served to reinstate the old hierarchies that supported the dominant theories of hybridity. The crucial twist that was presented in Darwin's theory was that the notion of species was not a static construct. Species evolved, differences were formed and variations in types emerged. The border between races was thus shifted, and anxieties over hybridity re-entered. 'Darwinism displaced some racial ideologies but replaced them with others.'[9] Although the Darwinian paradigm was premised on the notion that survival was linked to mutation, the hybrid was constructed negatively because it was presumed to be less able to adapt, and was therefore a risk to the whole process of human adaptation. Darwin's follower Brace effectively reinstated the hybrid as flawed and sterile offspring by stressing that the inherent incompatibility of the parents with 'their mutual differences and varying constitutions would naturally render the surviving of the first offspring somewhat doubtful'.[10]

The developmental hypothesis in Darwinism promoted the view that differences between races emerged out of separate lines of evolution, and that these differences had reached the point where the races were now incommensurable. Differences could be explained in terms of paths of development, with some varieties producing inferior strains which were in the process of becoming separate species. For, if Darwin sought to demonstrate that divergences in paths of evolution eventually produce an absolute difference, then it was inevitable that these separate paths of evolution would be interpreted as evidence of degeneration, and the black race would be defined as an 'incipient species'. Thus the essence of polygenist racialism is compatible with the Darwinian framework. For while Darwinism discredited notions of plurality and absolute difference in the origin of human species, it nevertheless stressed that the process of transformation through adaptation and variation would generate a differentiation of types. His followers could thereby allocate the position of each type according to 'its peculiar office and duty in the world's destiny'.[11]

The racism that entwined the popular view of the hybrid as a product of the fall of whiteness into sin, with scientific theories which sought to demonstrate the superiority of the white race's evolutionary path, found its most pernicious voices in the eugenic movement.[12] In 1883, Francis Galton, a cousin of Darwin, coined the term *eugenic* to describe the science of using genetics to improve racial quality. Ability was once again presumed to be hereditary and, as this was an age of maximization, successful adults were encouraged to breed. Campaigns were commenced to sterilize the poor, insane and feeble. With the aid of instruments like callipers and craniometers, it was thought that intelligence could be measured and criminal tendencies detected. Echoes of current investigations into the criminal gene!

Eugenics was the science of 'good breeding' and it became the most sophisticated justification for the maintenance of purity in the white race. Thirty years before Hitler assumed power, the German Racial Hygiene Society issued the slogan: 'Remember you are German! Keep your blood pure.' Eugenic theories were being linked to immigration policies in the USA, and in 1912, amongst the scientists and enthusiasts who attended the first international congress of Eugenics at London University were Alexander Graham Bell and Winston Churchill. Prominent writers like H. G. Wells, Virginia Woolf and T. S. Eliot were attracted to eugenicist ideas.[13]

It would be a comfortable illusion to presume that the discrediting of the extreme eugenist ideology has also eliminated the stigma and prejudice against hybridity. However, unconscious forms of racism are not always displaced by rational argument. The persistence of hybrid discourse can be traced throughout twentieth-century thought on the maximizing of power, and it was to find its most blood-curdling and barbarous climax in Nazism. Hitler's theory of racial purity reclaimed the view that interbreeding reduced the chances of survival. The conduit of power across time was blood, and hence this 'transmitter' must not be corrupted. With great assurance Hitler announced that 'All great cultures of the past perished only because the originally creative race died from blood poisoning.'[14]

While scientific racism reached its apotheosis in the Nazi movement, the other white races started to edge away from these ideas in small steps. It is no coincidence that it was not until 1939 that the American scientist E. Franklin

Frazier 'proved' that hybrids were as fecund and as able as other people in similar circumstances.[15] Soon after the Second World War UNESCO issued a statement, supported by the scientific community, that 'no biological justification exists for prohibiting intermarriages between persons of different races.' However, the additional statement that 'available scientific knowledge provides no basis for believing that the groups of mankind differ in their innate capacity for intellectual and emotional development' did not find unanimous approval among leading biologists. The belief that intelligence and superiority are hereditary has yet to receive its final rebuttal, and this keeps open eugenic probes into the status of hybrids. The recent resurgence of support for the belief that intelligence is genetically transmissible, and the use of the IQ test by Charles Murray to demonstrate the inherent inferiority of Blacks, is an indication that while science has seemingly rejected the dystopic ideals of Nazism, it still retains the utopian illusion that social problems can be eliminated through selective breeding. Perhaps even more disturbing is the selective, and often unintended, transferral of the physiological stigma in the identification of the hybrid as a special 'social type'.[16] The concept of hybridity has thus found many conscious and unconscious representations in the discourse of origin and differentiation within the nation-state.

Cultural hybrids and national reconciliations

Whenever the process of identity formation is premised on an exclusive boundary between 'us' and 'them', the hybrid, which is born out of the transgression of this boundary, figures as a form of danger, loss and degeneration. If, however, the boundary is marked positively – to solicit exchange and inclusion – then the hybrid may yield strength and vitality. Hence the conventional value of the hybrid is always positioned in relation to purity along the axes of inclusion and exclusion. In some circumstances, the 'curse' of hybridity is seen as a mixed blessing.

For Octavio Paz, Mexican national identity is undeniably hybrid. With considerable melancholy, however, Paz situates this hybridism in the damaged maternal representations of the 'Malinche complex' and the *chingada*, 'the violated woman'. The people of Mexico are all children of a primal violation, that of conquest. Malinche represents the Indian woman who gave herself to the conquistadors. Cortez took her as his mistress, and she supposedly betrayed her people, first by learning his language and then becoming both his lover and his guide. She revealed everything until there was nothing else to take; then she was abandoned.

The ancestral drama for Mexico is thus poised between a traitor and a violator. The father figure of Cortez is wrapped in the cloak of the conqueror and somehow escapes the moral gaze, but the mother, as *chingada*, who is left to give birth to the hybrid nation, is seen as a victim who facilitated violence. The identification of Malinche with the *chingada* reinforces the dominant ideology of rape as it shifts moral attention away from the man and focuses on how she provoked her own violation. The figure of the mother as *chingada* reduces her to abject passivity. She becomes an inert heap of bones, blood and dust. All identity is gutted. The mother is maligned for her submission, her wounds are reminders that the children are the 'fruit of violation'. Disgust and self-hate compound and provoke further bitterness: 'Mexican people have not forgiven *La Malinche* for her betrayal.'[17]

Paz sees in this rejection of the violated mother by the unforgiving child, both a cry for purity in origin, and a demand for another mother who would rather die than suffer contamination. Rejecting Malinche, the Mexican rejects hybridity in the past and refuses engagement with difference in the present. The rejection of the violated mother serves as a negation of origin, by preferring the phantasmagoric exile of solitude and the impossible nostalgia for the uncontaminated womb. With stern invocations, Paz turns back to his people, urging them to face up to the traumas of the 'fallen' mother and to embrace the ambivalence of Malinche.

Racial classifications and the mythology of white supremacy reached their zenith in justifications of slavery and imperial conquest. Notions of superiority were often premised on alterity, exclusivity and purity. The comforts of ideology, however, failed to constrain a parallel ideology of conquest through sexual penetration. Hence the paradox of conquest: distanciation *and* penetration. In Latin America desire and disavowal were most palpably embodied by the presence of hybrids. The unspeakable distaste for – and yet the undeniability in the presence of – hybrids is reflected by the compulsive classifying of gradations of blackness. Each word carried a different status and specified the elements in the union.[18] These names included mulatto, half-breed, half-caste, mixed breed, quadroon, octoroon, sambo, mango mestizo. Up to one sixty-fourth black could be distinguished.[19] In Brazil, despite its cultural hybridity, it took time before the word *hybrid* was not spoken as a curse. Gilberto Freyre's celebrated account of Brazilian culture, *The Masters and the Slaves*, begins with the confession, 'Of all the problems confronting Brazil there was none that gave me so much anxiety as that of miscegenation.'[20] The rest of the book, as is foretold in an introductory anecdote, seeks to give light to the shadowy status of the hybrid:

Once upon a time after three straight years of absence from my country, I caught sight of a group of Brazilian seamen-mulattoes and cafusos crossing Brooklyn Bridge. I no longer remember whether they were from Sao Paulo, or from Minas, but I know that they impressed me as being the caricatures of men, and there came to mind a phrase from a book on Brazil by an American traveller: 'the fearful mongrel aspect of the population'. That was the sort of thing to which miscegenation led. I ought to have had some one to tell me what Roquette Pinto had told the Aryanizers of the Brazilian Eugenic Congress in 1929; that these individuals whom I looked upon as representative of Brazil were not simply mulattoes or cafusos but *sickly* ones.[21]

In the early records of the colonial encounters, the ambiguity surrounding the hybrid was wrapped in ambivalence. On the one hand, hybridity was blamed for causing bad health. The symptoms included fatigue and indolence. Economic inertia, moral decadence and even syphilis were also effects that hybrids supposedly brought to the New World. But on the other hand, Freyre reports that the colonizer's and the priest's preferred mistress was the mulatto woman, and he provides countless examples of their desire for the 'lascivious hybrid woman'. For Freyre, the negative associations given to hybridity were not the result of a deeply internalized ideology of purity but, rather, a confusion of subject positions. The disastrous consequences of the first contact, he argued, had been falsely projected onto the offspring. Once the genuine causes of disease and disorder were identified, Freyre believed that the hybrid's advantage would be restored and would establish a firm grounding for a 'racial democracy'. Moral repugnance would dissolve as the society was enlightened by its own potentialities. In this new, celebratory myth, which was defined in opposition to the polarities of race relations in the USA, hybrids were conceived as lubricants in the clashes of culture, they were the negotiators that would secure a future free of xenophobia.

Freyre had found a resolution to his anxiety over miscegenation; he would no longer see himself as belonging to a civilization whose origin was 'sickly'. He became convinced that a hybrid society creates a new social order through the principle of synthesis and combination of differences. Nevertheless, he retained uncritically the hierarchy that privileged the white race through its positive association along the poles of public versus private, culture versus nature, masculine versus feminine, throughout his celebration of hybridity.

Freyre's Eurocentrism prohibited him from questioning the paradigms of savagery and primitivism. The conceptual world of the other was rarely entertained; it was simply their virility and domesticity that was embraced, and in this sense his account bears a disturbing resemblance to some integrationist discourses which promote otherness merely in terms of 'black macho' or 'ethnic cuisine'. This is no coincidence, for the model that Freyre is expounding is drawn from European modernism, while his narrative of incorporation is coded in terms of a sexualized arousal and submission. The shock of the Other serves to stimulate seduction and to smarten consumption via ingestion and absorption. The useful is extracted and the rest is excreted. The modernist in the New World cannibalized the Other, but something troublesome always remained. The hybrid social space that Freyre evokes still privileges the colonizer's aspirations – even as it incorporates the most 'useful' and 'desirable' elements from the 'savage' and the 'slave'. It was also clear, however, that a hybrid society which admits to the vagaries of its origin and does not seek to define itself through 'absolute ideals' and 'unyielding prejudice', a society that proclaims a loose and open-ended cultural identity, while opening a space for tolerance of difference, does not necessarily guarantee a universal extension of social justice.

So although Freyre seems to have demonstrated that a hybrid society is not necessarily one in decay or invariably riven by conflict, his anxiety over miscegenation is still evident in his proclamation that the hybrid is not a disavowal of the European identity: '[It] tends to become more and more extra-European though in no sense anti-European.'[22] The hybrid is transformed into a sign for the extension of the European spirit. The mixing of blood shifts from being a stain or a stigma to an aesthetically pleasing and virile combination. Yet the success of the hybrid depends on a particular recipe: potency is secured by the implanting of the white seed in the nurturing indigenous womb. A modernist fantasy of appropriation through insemination is repeated throughout Freyre's narrative of the assimilation between European culture, Indian domesticity and Negro virility.

By privileging the role of mixture, Freyre's account of cultural development clearly distances itself from the nineteenth-century theories of natural law, evolution and racial purity that dominated the romantic constructions of nationhood. Hybridity succeeds not in its blind conformity to the European model, but in the application of European systems and ideals in a 'new world'. Progress in the New World is marked by the dialectic of adaptation and transformation. The hybrid's progress is therefore linked to a Eurocentric model of maximization. Mixture is celebrated in Freyre's narrative, but at a secondary level, because it is through mixture that a new order can be realized that will integrate and maximize the Eurocentric 'spirit'. Mixture overtakes purity because it can outperform it. Once again, hybridity is justified, not by 'love of humanity' but by the logic of maximization.

The limitations in Freyre's model of hybridity can be further exposed by considering his acknowledgement of being methodologically influenced by Picasso.[23] The ambivalence of hybridity in early modernism is seldom examined in terms other than a celebration of the western capacity for integrating 'raw' forms of the Other into the dynamic body of metropolitan culture. The difficulties of conceptualizing hybridity can be witnessed in an essay by Max Raphael where he sets out to examine the means by which Picasso contributed to the 'break' in the European tradition. Raphael argues that Picasso's affinity for 'Negro Art' represented a potential trespass of what was conceived as the border between reason and non-reason, while also signifying a reversal in the exchange of cultural influence from the periphery to the centre.

Raphael's account of the evolution of artistic practice, while ambiguously referring to Lévy-Bruhl's controversial anthropological distinction between the mentality of western and primitive peoples, remains convinced that the nationality of the former can assimilate the spirituality of the latter. While not commenting on the commensurability between these different cultural and philosophical forms, and despite his attention to the brutalities of colonialism, he seemingly endorses the privileges of western rationality. With these limitations in mind, I would like to examine the process of incorporating non-western cultural forms into modern art that Raphael offers:

> The integration of Japanese art was the loophole by which traditional artistic rationalism found its way to an artistic sensualism closer to nature. The incorporation of Negroid art, on the other hand, turns against rational and sensory contents in favour of metaphysics and the irrational, and at the same time creates a new, completely Non-European rationalization of form.[24]

Thus he suggests that the integration of 'Japanese' and 'Negroid' art follows the same principle but proceeds through diametrically opposed categories: 'Japanese' art enters through the door of European rationality in order to beckon the west towards its own objectives – that is, to find its way back to nature; 'Negroid' art, by contrast, is projected into the anarchic zone of irrationality. The presence of the two forms is at first perceived as both indigestible and incomprehensible. Yet it is this confrontation with otherness, albeit via latent or marginal concepts, that yields a new form. In both cases the foreign is incorporated in order to confirm or extend the conventional values. Raphael argues that Picasso, in incorporating foreign elements, fails to question the ruptures within metropolitan culture because he leaves the prior distinction between spiritual value and material production untouched. Picasso's example provides a template upon which Raphael can address what he regards as the great contradictions between early modernity and colonialism:

> Psychically emptied and over-rationalized, man discovers in the natives of his colonies a vast traditional domain, and this discovery accelerates his own rapid and continuing flight from Reason. But it also consolidates his humanity in the face of the machine, and activates his hitherto passive mysticism.[25]

Raphael's account of the reconciliation of the modern split between body and soul proceeds *not* through a critique of the existing relationship between material production and spiritual value, in which the modern self is already inscribed, but through an argument about the consumption of the idealized Other. Raphael argues that the non-European forms were assimilated back into the European tradition through the mediation of historically prior traditions. The reactivation of latent forms is the lever which allows the entry of the Other, and facilitates a form of moral and normative rejuvenation:

> European art assimilated Negroid influences by introducing: (1) the principle of corporeality, and hence, the Greek tendency, during the period of cubist objects; (2) the mysticism of the soul, and hence, the Gothic, during the period of the cubist field.[26]

This critique of the utilization of non-western elements in Picasso's art gives us an indication of an underlying pathos in the motivation for incorporating foreign elements, and also a surprising insight into the simplicity with which the foreign was understood within modern culture. I say that this insight is surprising because most critics associate the concept of modernity with an increasing complexity in the structures of everyday life, and assume that the cultural processes that accompany such structures are equally sophisticated. As Don Miller wryly observed, 'an idea like "simple modernity" would be seen as a blatant contradiction.'[27] But this is precisely what we do witness in the cultural dynamics that Raphael traces. He argues that the west's success in material production was achieved at the expense of hollowing out western spiritual values. However, the turn to primitivism in modern art was not a wholesale critique of material production, but simply another extension of the prevailing logic of appropriation and displacement. In primitivism we witness not only the commodification of other spiritual values, but also the domestication of this otherness as it is translated back into the familiar western forms of 'corporeality' and 'mysticism'.

By demonstrating Picasso's paradoxical appeal to western reason and non-western spirituality, and in the shift from realism to abstraction, Raphael attempts to probe the flaws in modern rationality, as well as to address the unresolved paradoxes between form and content in modernism. His account of Picasso's achievement is significant not just for its evaluations but also for its construction of a model of cross-cultural assimilation. According to the dynamics of this model, for the Other to be domesticated it must also be doubled, it must have one face that turns inwards, conveying a sense of belonging, and the other face that turns to the exterior, pointing to the beyond. It is this duality, he suggests, which secures a sense of extension and bridging; thus, for every foreign element to be accepted, there must be both a centrifugal and a centripetal force, a narcissistic sense of inclusion and a transgressive sense of extension. For the non-western to enter the west it must do so in the guise of the cultural hybrid: the non-western westerner.[28]

Hybridity in colonialism

The clash of cultures that colonialism invariably provoked, rather than producing an absolute bifurcation between the colonizer and the colonized, encouraged the formation of new cultural hybrids. Ashis Nandy's account of the levels of consciousness which at first sustained and then undermined the colonizing project, stresses that the conventional binarism which represented the colonized as victim, and the colonizer as victor, overlooks that both were caught up as players and counter-players in the dominant model of universalism. Shifting his attention away from the obvious sites of conflict and violence, Nandy focuses on the actual interfaces, such as the processes of negotiation between opposing groups, the means of resistance expressed by urban westernized Indians and the degrees of degradation experienced by the English colonizer. Agency is never the monopoly of one player, he suggests, for both are locked in a dyadic relationship in which the colonizer becomes a self-destructive co-victim.

> And even that White Sahib may turn out to be defined, not by skin color, but by social and political choices. Certainly he turns out to be . . . not the conspiratorial dedicated oppressor that he is made out to be, but a self-destructive co-victim with a reified life-style and a parochial culture, caught in the hinges of a history he swears by.[29]

Colonialism produced new losses and gains, allowed new forms of identity to ascend, and debased or crushed others. This trajectory was always at least dual. It was one of the peculiar features of English colonialism that the subjects that induced the greatest discomfort, and were the victims of the most bitter attacks, were the hybrids. The repulsion that was genuinely felt towards the hybrids was, according to Nandy, deeply connected to the repression of the antonyms and oppositional dualisms that jostled for position in the colonizer's sexual identity and political ideology. Perhaps no other figure articulated these contradictions so exquisitely as Rudyard Kipling. The very man who so persistently criss-crossed the tremulous line between 'westernized Indian' and 'Indianized westerner' was also the one who insisted that 'west' and 'east' could never be reconciled. For Nandy, Kipling displayed the qualities of the hero who 'interfaced culture' and kept open the feminine side in masculinity, while also being able to despise the effeminate hybrid who lacked a clear sense of self. Kipling's capacity to project his own self-hatred is thus taken as an index of the underlying repressions in colonialism:

> Kipling distinguished between the victim who fights well and pays back the tormentor in his own coin and the victim who is passive-aggressive, effeminate and fights back through non-cooperation, shirking, irresponsibility, malingering and refusal to value face-to-face fights. The first was the 'ideal victim' Kipling wished to be, and the second was the victim's life Kipling lived and hated living. If he did not have any compassion for the victims of the world, he did not have any compassion for a part of himself either.[30]

The conflict of interests between the colonizer and the colonized was also a conflict between the parts and processes of identity. It promoted a self-image and form of consciousness that was defined in opposition to the putative characteristics of the 'eastern man' and exaggerated the qualities of hardness, distanciation and responsibility. A self was fashioned that was not only more congruent to the needs of the colonial machine but intolerant of the inherent mixtures in oneself and others. The acknowledgement of his own androgynous biculturalism was – according to Nandy – Kipling's most disturbing dilemma, and his solution, which accords with the dominant model, was to opt for absolute choice. He should be *either* western *or* Indian. It was inconceivable to be *both*, for the path of progress was opposed to those meandering oxymorons and perambulating paradoxes.

While a reordering of the colonizer's consciousness, and a distanciation from that of the colonized, was central to the success of the colonial project, it was also – as Nandy suggests – the cause of its rigidity that ultimately facilitated its own demise. Kipling could never reconcile *both* his western *and* Indian selves, yet, in everyday life such conjunctions were both practical, and continuous with the syncretic processes which constructed Indian identity. The relentless quest for purity and the historical burden of superiority never allowed Kipling to grasp the resilient dynamism of hybridity, and so he remained slightly detached from even his most beloved subjects. Crucial to the transformative processes of Indian tradition was what the colonizer dreaded most, a critical engagement with the other:

> India has tried to capture the differentia of the West within its own cultural domain, not merely on the basis of a view of the West as politically intrusive or as culturally inferior, but as a subculture meaningful in itself and important, though not all-important, in the Indian context.[31]

Kipling's personal failures are history lessons for Nandy, because each expression of moral repugnance and political outrage was so utterly framed by the Enlightenment ideals of development through determinate sequences. Surveying the culture as if caught in the 'backward innocence of childhood', the Indian identity slipped in and out of the determinacy. It was this indeterminateness which Kipling hated, yet it was the key to survival under colonialism and to the creative space that ensured cultural transformation.

For Nandy, all encounters produce change. The perversity of colonialism is thus measured not just in terms of the extreme exploitation of the other, but also in the contortion and constrictions of the self that were necessary to enforce such a relationship. Nandy explains this process of cultural co-optation in two ways. First he demonstrates the homology between sexual repression and political dominance which led to an internalization of self-images of hardness and detachment as the appropriate 'manly' modes of colonial rule. Second, he reveals that the initial identification with the aggressor was not just an attempt to seek salvation by means of mimicry but also a resurrection of latent self-images which could be made compatible with the ideology of colonialism.

A version of Indian hyper-masculinism would thus not only mirror back the ruler's wishes but also serve as 'new, nearly exclusive indicator of authentic Indianness'.[32] Under colonialism both the ruler and the ruled produced new self-images which were selectively drawn from earlier forms of social consciousness. Colonialism found legitimacy because it elicited a set of codes that were common to both cultures, and because it was thereby able to privilege components that were previously subordinate or recessive in these cultures. The seeds for this foundational colonialism were already contained in the consciousness of both parties, and central to its legitimacy was the valorization of the pure and the denigration of the hybrid – that is, of sexual and spiritual androgyny.

Nandy's account of colonial modes of exchange through the psychic mechanisms of projections and introjections, and his celebration of the 'superior' resilience of hybridity, leave one central question unanswered: does the encounter with the Other presuppose a replaying of old identities or the invention of new ones? Nandy systematically elaborates the principles of exchange as a rupture in prevailing cultural codes and priorities, and the establishment of new modes of self-presentation and social management. The rupture is not seen as a total upheaval but as a radical shift of emphasis, which leads to the highlighting of aspects of the self which had been kept dark, and a promotion of previously recessive components of culture.

Although there is no explicit theory of hybridity in Nandy's narrative, this process of rupture and regrounding outlines the dynamism of exchange. Nandy is able to link the denials and repressions in, say, Kipling's consciousness to both an inability to keep in play the contradictory forces and a tendency to create a distorted and untenable self-image. Similarly, he praises the 'Indian's' humble capacity to include aspects of the Other without losing his or her original cultural checks and balances. However, in order to consolidate the argument that distanciation inevitably leads to atrophy and identification secures survival, one also needs a closer theory of the dynamics of exchange. Moreover, to understand both the disturbing anxiety generated by cultural hybrids and the productive and enabling force of hybridity, there needs to be a closer scrutiny of the creation of differences, precisely when there is a renewed circulation of equivalences, or an exaggerated outburst of hostility towards the 'intimate enemy'. For this theorization of difference we must turn elsewhere, and move on from the history of culture to consider the semiotics of culture.

The semiotics of hybridity

Bakhtin's attention to the mixture of languages within a text, which both ironizes and unmasks authority, demonstrates a new level of linking the concept of hybridity to the politics of representation.[33] The language of hybridity becomes a means for critique and resistance to the monological language of authority. The hybrid text always undoes the priorities and disrupts the singular order by which the dominant code categorizes the other. In Bakhtin's theory the 'doubleness' of hybrid voices is composed not through the integration of differences but via a series of dialogical counterpoints, each set against the other, allowing the language to be both the same and different. This clearly constitutes a turning-point in the debates on hybridity. This turning-point is most evident in the current appeal of Bakhtin's theory of heteroglossia and the carnivalesque. However, while there has been a greater appreciation of the subversive potential of language, attention to difference in literary and critical theory has been mostly confined to a representation of its products rather an engagement with its processes. To overcome this limitation it would be useful to turn to the work of Yuri Lotman, a Russian semiotician who both drew on Bakhtin's theory of hybridity and extended it into the semiotics of culture. If the concept of hybridity is to go beyond a mere celebration or denigration of difference, then Lotman's theory, which outlines the dynamism of difference within culture, may provide a valuable framework.

Lotman's approach to the semiotics of culture goes beyond conventional concerns with the uses of signs for the communication of content. In his work, culture is defined as a system that mediates the individual's relationship to his or her context, the mechanism for processing and organizing the surrounding signs. The way we deal with inputs, how decisions are made, priorities established, behaviour regulated, models envisaged and questions posed in the 'communicating dialogue' with the outside world, is all expressive of a particular sense of culture. This dialogue always comprises relatively individualized languages which are in a state of interdependence and are transformed by their specific historical conditions. Lotman stresses this interdependence and avoids any movement towards analytical abstraction, for culture is never a mere summation of separate and discrete languages. Therefore the formation of a cultural system cannot be seen to resemble the overlapping leaves of an 'onion'. In Lotman's theory, the form of culture is defined via references to motion rather than by comparison to a static or bounded object. Hence it is seen to be more like a river with a number of currents moving at different rates and intensities. The aim is to see how culture operates as a whole, in a state of constant 'creolization' or what he calls the 'semiotic physiology' as opposed to the 'atomistic approach'.

The name Lotman gives to this dynamic process of influence, transformation and coexistence within the space of culture is the semiosphere.[34] The semiosphere is the totality of semiotic acts, from squeaks to sonatas, from blips on the radar to burps at the dinner table. It also includes all acts past and present, possessing a 'memory which transforms the history of the system into its actually functioning mechanism, this includes the mass of texts ever created and . . . the programme for generating future texts'.[35] While the value and position of elements in a language shift and change, and the set of languages in a cultural field intersect, fragment, diversify or realign, the whole of the semiotic space remains constant. Thus the semiosphere refers to the totality of the cultural system, and also the condition for the development of culture.

To illustrate the heterogeneity of elements and the diversity of functions which are contained in the semiosphere, Lotman uses the example of the museum as a model for the representation of difference within a single system. The museum, he argues, is a single space containing exhibits from different periods; each exhibit bears inscriptions in languages which may or may not be decipherable, there are instructions, explanations, guides, rules and plans which, to some degree, regulate the responses of visitors and staff. Within this single space, Lotman stresses, we have to remember that all the elements are dynamic, not static, and that the correlations between terms are constantly changing. In a context where the construction of the museum as an encyclopaedic repository of culture's diversity is deeply contested, this may seem a flawed example. Nevertheless, it remains a paradigm of staging difference within contemporary culture.

In the model of the museum we can at least see how Lotman's conception of the semiosphere recognizes oppositions and tension, for it does not presuppose either that this binarism leads to a single point of antagonism, or that positions are mutually exclusive and immutable. His representation of the system of communication recognizes that binarisms constantly undo their own fixity. It describes a system in which there is a constant conflict between resolute and opaque codes, compatible and contradictory practices. The relationship between centre and periphery in the semiosphere is not explained by either the functionalist paradigm of mechanical interaction, or the dialectical model for the overcoming of antagonisms, but rather by attention to the dynamics of contestation over the *fit* between the language of the code and the language of practice. At one stage he tries to evoke the incalculable flux of intellectual energy in the semiosphere by saying that it 'seethes like the sun'.[36] However, with this metaphor, which suggests both organic thrust and chaotic dispersal, there is the sense that the principle of power cannot be contained neatly in the acts of cultural exchange. In some sense this energy of transmission, that he refers to as central to the semiosphere, bypasses the political questions of power and overrides the co-ordinates of morality.

The structure of the semiosphere can be crowded and chaotic, possessing languages with different levels and forms of representation. Lotman consciously idealizes the opposition between centre and periphery in terms of codification and indeterminacy, in order to articulate the constant tension in the definition of norms, customs and laws which are generated to legitimize the extension of one language over the whole semiosphere. He is astutely conscious of the counter-productive consequences of a hegemonic language. In the semiosphere, the expansion of one language is only achieved by its rigidification and its severance from the milieu of dynamic interaction. To expand in a unified manner is to become more and more prone to disintegration. For the periphery never passively accepts conversion. It is this tension, between the code of the centre and its (in)ability to reflect the practices on the periphery, that produces a dissenting language. Lotman describes the contradictions that await 'the proselytizing mission' of the centre thus:

If in the centre of the semiosphere the description of texts generates the norms, then on the periphery the norms, actively invading 'incorrect' practice, will generate 'correct' texts in accord with them. Secondly, whole layers of cultural phenomena, which from the point of view of the given metalanguage are marginal, will have no relation to the idealized portrait of that culture.[37]

This uneven terrain of cultural production and the stochastic distribution or multi-vectorial transmission of culture are also stressed by Michel Serres. In his complex analyses of cultural dynamics he persistently questions the transparency of the laws of determinism and challenges the conventional passage from the local to the global.[38] The productive tension between local and global, noise and dialect, that Serres notes, is similar to Lotman's tracking of the flux of energy that follows every criss-crossing of a boundary. For Lotman, the semiosphere is in a constant state of hybridity. It always oscillates between identity and alterity, and this tension is most evident at its boundaries:

> Paradoxically, the internal space of a semiosphere is at the same time unequal yet unified, asymmetrical yet uniform. Composed as it is of conflicting structures, it nonetheless is also marked by individuation. Its self-description implies a first-person pronoun. One of the primary mechanisms of semiotic individuation is the boundary, and the boundary can be defined as the outer limit of a first-person form. This space is 'ours', 'my own', it is 'cultured', 'safe', 'harmoniously organized', and so on. By contrast 'their space' is 'other', 'hostile', 'dangerous', 'chaotic'.
>
> Every culture begins by dividing the world into 'its own' internal space and 'their' external space. How this binary division is interpreted depends on the typology of the culture.[39]

An archetypical example of this type of differentiation between US and THEM, a relationship of non-relationship whereby the exterior Other is defined by the logic of the inversion, is the designation of the Other as Barbarian. The crucial marker is, in this instance, language: a Barbarian is simply the person who does not speak Greek! However, the Other that is within the semiosphere is not perceived by such an *a priori* categorization, but is identified through the processes of translation. The construction of the exterior Other, by the logic of inversion, is designed to preclude dialogue, whereas the presence of an other who speaks different languages within the semiosphere interacts through translation, and thus facilitates both dialogue and transformation. Because the different languages within the semiosphere do not have mutual semantic correspondences, translation presupposes asymmetry. Once the other's utterances stop sounding like muttering 'bar bar bar', and he or she is deemed to speak 'Greek' properly, he or she is no longer just a Barbarian. But this difference, as Lotman emphasizes, has to be perceived as both necessary and desirable. For the precondition of dialogue is the mutual attraction of the participants.

Lotman outlines the mechanisms by which dialogue occurs in the context of difference – that is, how information is generated from the tension between a language and its contact with a foreign text – and he describes this process of interaction in five stages. This enables us, I suggest, to reflect on Raphael's explanation of Picasso's success and Nandy's account of exchange within colonialism.

First, a text arrives from the outside; it appears in its original form, in its own language, its strangeness is intact; it is not considered a threat or a problem because it is presumed to be superior and therefore will offer a positive contribution.

Second, a transformation at both ends begins to occur – that is, the imported text and the receiving culture begin to restructure each other. The foreign text is idealized because it offers the local culture the opportunity to break with the past. Here the foreign text is imbued with salvific qualities. However, there also emerges a counter-tendency in which the foreign text is linked to a submerged element in the receiving culture; the foreign thus activates a dormant component, and is therefore interpreted as an organic continuation or a rehabilitation of the familiar culture.

Third, there emerges the tendency to deprecate the source from which the text originated, and to emphasize that the true potential of the text is only realized by being integrated into the receiving culture. Reception has not only led to transformation but is also a form of transcendence. Before, it was crude and particularistic; now it has the grace of fullness and universality.

Fourth, after the imported text has been fully assimilated, its distinctive presence has been dissolved, and has led to the production of a new model. Now that the receiver has internalized the text and restructured its own axioms and values, the local becomes producer of the new and original texts.

Fifth, the receiver is now a transmitter – or, in Lotman's words, it 'issues forth a flood of texts directed to other, peripheral areas of the semiosphere'.[40]

Lotman was conscious that this dialogue – or what he calls this process of 'infection' – could only be realized under favourable historical, social and psychological conditions. But Serres adds another dimension, which locates the interruptive moment and the potential for innovation not singularly in the dialogue between the interlocutors, but in what he sees as the alliance against the disruptive third man:

> Such communication [dialogue] is a sort of game played by two interlocutors considered as united against the phenomena of interference and confusion, or against individuals with some stake in interrupting communication. These interlocutors are in no way opposed, as in the traditional conception of the dialectic game; on the contrary, they are on the same side, tied together by a mutual interest: they battle against noise. . . . They exchange roles sufficiently often for us to view them as struggling against a common enemy. To hold a dialogue is to suppose a third man and to seek to exclude him: a successful communication is the

exclusion of the third man. The most profound dialectical problem is not the Other who is only a variety – or a variation – of the same, it is the problem of the third man.[41]

Where Lotman defines the semiosphere as the resultant and the condition of possibility of the system of communication, Serres invokes the third man – or what he also referred to as the parasite. Lotman's theory acknowledges the fluidity and the perpetuity of cultural interaction. Serres highlights the previously unacknowledged vectorial forces of a third element which emerges whenever two subjects enter into a dialogical relationship. Both approaches break with the functionalist models for understanding the incorporation of difference in terms of, either assimilation, or amalgamation. Both theorists are intensely conscious of the role of the hybrid and creolized, and draw attention to the various levels of splitting and interference in the dissemination of languages. This new theoretical perspective leads towards a re-evaluation of the position, role and function of strange and foreign cultural ideas in the formation of cultural knowledge. Yet both theories say little about the carriers of these concepts, that is, the strangers and the foreigners, nor do they confront the politics of acceptance, given the theoretical precondition of mutual desire, or the disposition to relegate the stranger to the position of the third man. Are these structural questions simply left as the invisible bias of history?

The problem with the semiosphere is that it does not directly address the politics in the distinctions between language and silence, between coherence and babble, between comprehension and confusion, the determining patterns of selection that influence which languages will be learnt, and what thresholds between the axioms of transparency and opaqueness in language will be sustained in order to stimulate particular forms of knowledge and to permit the emergence of particular claims. In other words, it does not address the politics by which the margin is hierarchized, appropriated, tokenized or fetishized to serve the interests and maintain the order constructed by the centre. For all his attention to the fluid dynamics of the semiosphere, Lotman appears to have overlooked the specific forces of access and exclusion. The levels of travelling and the process of transmission discount any degree of loss or mutation in the course of the journey. Meaning begins only once the text enters the space of the semiosphere, but what traces are there of the meanings, prior to this encounter? The arrival of a foreign text is never a perfect isomorph of another culture; it, too, is formed by the travails of travelling. The strength of the theory of the semiosphere is not in measuring the symbolic changes that occur as cultural practices shift from one context to another, but rather in accounting for the semiotic forms of transformation within a single cultural system.

From this perspective it appears that the primary tendency within the semiosphere is towards the acculturation of the foreign text and subtle modification of the dominant language. Lotman's followers, who have used his theory of semiotics for the study of 'ethnic culture texts', have accepted this limitation on the grounds that ethnic culture is a 'subset of culture in general'.[42] This mapping of cultural interaction presupposes levels of structural equivalence which may be untenable, and it overlooks the dynamic transformation that occurs prior to the entry into the semiosphere. In order to witness the innovative potential of the foreign text, or the restructuring of the dominant language according to the laws of the Other, we will have to measure the resilience of the foreign code and examine the impact resulting from the insertion of the foreign text. Are some cultural texts more mobile than others? How significant is the transitional stage? What are the available spaces within a given culture for receiving foreign cultural texts? If the interruptive force of hybridity is ultimately smoothed over, as it is incorporated into the semiosphere, then we must question whether this theory of dynamic transformation is sufficiently attentive to either concept of difference or the contemporary crisis within culture.

Hybridity in postcolonial theory

The most vigorous debates on the dynamics of difference in contemporary culture have occurred in the field of postcolonial theory. Given the extremities of social and psychic upheaval generated by colonial encounters, it is no coincidence that the most radical critics of modern transformation have come from places that have experienced these global changes most brutally. After Fanon's detailed and passionate argument that the violence of colonialism has to be measured according to the west's philosophical consciousness of right as much as its military display of might, and with Ngugi wa Thiongo's clear awareness of the ongoing processes that reshape cultural priorities, redirect political directions and rewrite historical scripts in ways that split the internal operations of social mechanisms and bind them to neo-colonial structures, it is necessary to re-examine the concept of hybridity in relation to the ongoing colonizing of the mind and the destruction of traditional social forms to be overlooked.

In the context of rupture and violation, communication and identity are always problematical. For as Stuart Hall argues, the emergence of 'other histories' in contemporary discourse is synchronous with the radicalization of the notions of identity, history and language. If the experience of displacement has become the paradoxical starting-point for understanding the parameters of belonging in the modern world, then this entails a challenge to the conceptual framework for understanding identity and culture. On the one hand, there is still the romantic claim that identity can retain the essential distinctiveness of a culture. On the other, the process of constructing identity through the mixing and engaging with the Other has been given, as we have seen, a far more critical perspective. Recent writings in postcolonial theory routinely cite the work of Stuart Hall, Homi Bhabha and Gayatri Spivak as authorizing hybrid identities.

At the broadest level of conceptual debate there seems to be a consensus over the utility of hybridity as an antidote to essentialist subjectivity. However, Spivak sharply dissents from Bhabha's and Hall's suggestion that hybridity has purchase in both the Third World postcolonial arena and in the diasporic condition of minorities in the First World.

According to Stuart Hall, cultural identity is always hybrid, but he also insists that the precise form of this hybridity will be determined by specific historical formations and cultural repertoires of enunciation.[43] Homi Bhabha notes the rising influence of once excluded voices now challenging the boundaries of what is seen as a Eurocentric project. The affinity of these interruptive voices, Bhabha suggests, offers the basis for rethinking the process of change and the subjects of modernity:

> For the demography of the new internationalism is the history of postcolonial migration, the narratives of cultural and political diaspora, the major social displacements of peasant and aboriginal communities, the poetics of exile and the grim prose of political and economic refugees.[44]

Hybridity may be a condition that is common to all who have sharp memories of deprivation but – as Bhabha also reminds us – it seems an insufficient basis to consolidate new forms of collectivity that can overcome the embeddedness of prior antagonisms. Nevertheless, Bhabha's work has focused on the psychic processes of identification and the cultural practices of performance to highlight the hybridization that is intrinsic to all forms of radical transformation and traditional renewal. Gayatri Spivak is not so quick to embrace such a demography of postcolonials; she draws a sharp distinction between the diasporic communities in the First World and the subaltern in the Third World. The subaltern and the diasporic are in her view incommensurable worlds, and projecting the concept of hybridity into the former is not only a misreading but also akin to providing an alibi for global exploitation. By charting how hybridity is variously defined by Hall, Bhabha and Spivak we can break with the naive assumption that hybridity is itself a stable concept or that one perspective is interchangeable with another.

In Stuart Hall's writing the term hybridity is integral to the Bakhtinian–Gramscian perspective that he brings to bear on his representations of social transformation. Nowhere in his work is there a theoretical model which could be transferred to particular sites of struggle and used to 'read off' examples of hybridity. Hall's understanding of the process of transformation is never constructed in terms of either an absolutist oppositionality – where one position demolishes its antagonist – or a neat succession, with each stage being a clean break from the one before. Transformation is seen as occurring in a more 'generative' way: as ideas, world-views and material forces interact with each other, they undergo a process of being internally reworked until the old ones are displaced.

From this perspective, hybridity can be seen as operating on two levels: it refers to the constant process of differentiation and exchange between the centre and the periphery, and between different peripheries, as well as serving as the metaphor for the form of identity that is being produced from these conjunctions. Hall's representation of hybrid identities as always incomplete does not imply that they aspire to a sense of wholeness and that they invariably fall short of becoming a finished product, but rather that their energy for being is directed by the flows of an ongoing process. This anti-essentialist perspective on identity has had a significant impact on the debates over the 'politics of representation' and has been utilized by Hall like a spiralling coil to turn the concept of ethnicity out of its anti-racist paradigm, where it connotes the immutable difference of minority experience, and into a term which addresses the historical positions, cultural conditions and political conjunctures through which all identity is constructed. So ethnicity becomes a positive concept for the 'recognition that we all speak from a particular place, out of a particular history, out of a particular experience, a particular culture . . . We are all, in a sense, *ethnically* located and our ethnic identities are crucial to our subjective sense of who we are.'[45] By initiating such a contestation over the boundaries of ethnicity Hall opens up a mode for understanding identity which is paradoxically both inclusive and specific.

With the revelation of the multiple others in the self – or rather understanding the history of the self 'as composed always across the silence of the other'[46] – and when language is framed by a broader politics of articulation, embedded, that is, within 'an infinite semiosis of meaning',[47] this opens the space for the process of reidentification and reterritorialization of experiences previously deemed too 'marginal' to be worthy of representation. Hall describes this rearticulation of the symbolic order through the Gramscian theory of hegemony and counter-politics. The margin challenges the centre via a three-pronged strategy: first, through an opposition to the given order; second, via recovery of broken histories and the invention of appropriate narrative forms; and third, through the definition of a position and a language from which speech will continue:

> You could not discover, or try to discuss, the Black movements, civil rights movements, the movements of Black cultural politics in the modern world, without that notion of the re-discovery of where people came from, the return to some kind of roots, the speaking of a past which previously had no language. The attempt to snatch from the hidden histories another place to stand in, another place to speak from. . . . Ethnicity is the necessary place or space from which people speak.[48]

Hall's perspective presupposes that translation across cultural difference is always possible. But, how do we map a culture whose own references do not correspond to the co-ordinates of another culture? How do we represent a culture whose historical memory and conceptual apparatus have been so damaged by the colonial encounter that the very possibility of exchange or dialogue seems no longer to exist? These questions are central to Gayatri Spivak's essay, 'Can the Subaltern Speak?' With characteristic bluntness, Spivak has answered her own question in the negative: she has stated that the subaltern cannot speak. Between posing the question and the negative response lie profound implications about the languages of resistance, the structures of oppression and the role of the intellectual. Spivak argues that there are two sides to the meaning of representation, the political and the rhetorical, which are articulated by Marx with separate terms, like proxy and portrayal. This observation serves as both a rebuke to the tendency to conflation by western intellectuals, and a corrective to any suggestion that there can be a representation of the real subaltern's consciousness. This is because any representation of authentic condition is always premised on 'contestatory replacement as well as an appropriation (a supplement) of something that is artificial to begin with – "economic conditions of existence that separate their mode of life" '.[49]

Who knows how best to manage the Other? Spivak again casts a suspicious glance at the possibly benign identification with the subaltern, the well-meaning gesture of solidarity with a constituency that First World intellectuals neither appreciate nor could find the language to address. Against all those facile claims of unity, she reminds us that subalternity is not a condition to be desired. Taking the rural and landless poor of India as her example, Spivak points out that the question of understanding is not confined to the linguistic problem of translation, for how would you translate a culture whose 'responsibility-based ethical systems have been for centuries completely battered and compromised'[50] into the other culture's notion of democratic rights and civil society? The incommensurability between these two orders is such that the gaps and silence would be more significant than any utterances. There is no clear process by which the realities and experiences of the Indian subaltern can be translated into western categories. Spivak insists that in this instance there is no prior space that can facilitate a dialogue between the west and its Other.

The moment the subaltern has stepped into the arena of representation and negotiation is the first mark of a movement away from the position of the subaltern. The ability to 'speak up' to the hegemonic forces is a step towards becoming an organic intellectual. However, to become such a representative is already a movement away from the condition that is being represented. The subaltern condition cannot even bear the privilege of its own 'organic intellectuals'. Spivak repeatedly warns against the presumption that subaltern experiences are texts that are available for translation. This prognosis is aimed particularly at radical historians:

> When we come to the concomitant question of the consciousness of the subaltern, the notion of what the work *cannot* say becomes important. In the semiosis of the

social text, elaborations of insurgency stand in the place of 'the utterance'. The sender – 'the peasant' – is marked only as a pointer to an irretrievable consciousness. As for the receivers, we must ask who is the 'real receiver' of an 'insurgency'? The historian, transforming 'insurgency' into 'text for knowledge' is only one 'receiver' of any collectively intended social act. With no possibility of nostalgia for that lost origin, the historian must suspend (as far as possible) the clamor of his or her consciousness, (or consciousness effect, as operated by disciplinary training), so that the elaboration of the insurgency, packaged with an insurgent consciousness, does not freeze into an 'object of identification', or worse yet, a model for imitation. 'The subject' implied by the texts of insurgency can only serve as counterpossibility for the narrative sanction granted to the colonial subject in the dominant groups. The postcolonial intellectuals learn that their privilege is their loss. In this they are a paradigm of the intellectuals.[51]

Spivak's reminder of the need for added reflexivity over the precise status of who is speaking in place of the subaltern, and who would be able to listen to the subaltern, is a precaution against both false delegation and idle identifications. For as she reminds us, to be in a position to speak for the subaltern is both impossible and unenviable. The poverty and brutalized conditions of the subaltern imply that the very step towards representation involves, at first, a move *out* of its own context. Alienation is the price of every representation. This is the extreme edge of Benjamin's observation that no translation can find exact correspondences between different languages. Thus we could say that, unlike Hall's attention to the 'politics of representation', Spivak is more concerned with the 'violence of silence'. In this way Spivak, unlike Hall, seems to limit the concept of hybridity as a metaphor for cultural identity.

In Homi Bhabha's writing the concept of hybridity is initially used to expose the conflicts in colonial discourse, then extended to address both the heterogeneous array of signs in modern life and the various ways of living with difference. Hybridity becomes an interpretative mode for dealing with what Bhabha calls the juxtapositions of space, and the combination of 'time lag' out of which a sense of being is constructed that constantly oscillates between the axioms of foreign and familiar. Bhabha suggests that, in order to apprehend contemporary structures of agency, we need to shift our attention away from the concrete production of discrete objects and consider, rather, the restless process of identification. Bhabha places great stress on the 'fact' that identity is never fixed once and for all, it never coheres into an absolute form. For instance, he describes minority discourse as emerging from the 'in between of image and sign, the accumulative and the adjunct, presence and proxy'.[52] However, the refusal to accept the primacy of an originary essence, or the inevitability of an ultimate destiny for identity, is not an invitation to celebrate liberation from substantive strictures. The theoretical qualification on the processes of identity formation in no way implies that identity is constructed out of a political and cultural vacuum. To elaborate the elasticity in the trajectory of identity is not a vindication of the claims that the horizons are boundless, access is free and the past is without weight or shape. According to Bhabha, attention to the process of identification requires a finer recognition of the strategy of negotiation. Identity always presupposes a sense of location and a relationship with others. However, this attention to place does not presuppose closure. For the representation of identity most often occurs precisely at the point where there has been a displacement.[53]

The stress that Bhabha gives to the belatedness in the representation of identity is also connected to a deeper problematic of the partiality of representation in general. The status of representation is defined more by its limitations and distortions than by its ability to capture an 'elusive' spirit or hold the totality of presence. Therefore any theory of agency must also include the process of 'bricolage'. Identity is always conceived in the 'twixt of displacement and reinvention'. By stepping between Benjamin and Bhabha, we could say that representations of identity are at best a 'rear-view' of a part of the past that is pushing us forward into the future. For Bhabha, Jameson's attention to pastiche, Said's appreciation of the contrapuntal, Deleuze and Guattari's tracking of nomadology are parallel metaphors for naming the forms of identity which emerge in a context of difference and displacement:

> The process of reinscription and negotiation – the insertion or intervention of something that takes on new meaning – happens in the temporal break in-between the sign, deprived of subjectivity, in the realm of the intersubjective. Through this time-lag – the temporal break in representation – emerges the process of agency both as a historical development and as the narrative agency of historical discourse. . . . It is in the contingent tension that results, that sign and symbol overlap and are indeterminately articulated through the 'temporal break'. Where the sign deprived of the subject – intersubjectivity – returns as subjectivity directed towards the rediscovery of truth, then a (re)ordering of symbols becomes possible in the sphere of the social. When the sign ceases the synchronous flow of the symbol, it also seizes the power to elaborate – through the time-lag – new and hybrid agencies and articulations.[54]

Bhabha clearly differentiates his use of the term 'hybrid' from earlier evocations which defined it as the diabolical stain or the harmonic transcendence between different races. Bhabha has divorced the term hybridity from the context of miscegenation by placing it at once in both the semiotic field of discursive reconfiguration and in the socio-political domain of deterritorialized subjectivity. The exilic drives that underline our understanding of language and identity in modernity are thus made available to highlight the complex structures of agency.[55] The misfit between the formal structures that confer identity in fixed terms like nation, class, gender, race and more fluid practices by which identity moves across certain positions and manoeuvres around given borders is not taken as an index of modern freedom but rather highlighted in order to draw attention to the complex dynamics of agency.

Referring to the process of linguistic hybridization in the renaming that Guillermo Gomez-Pena stages in his performances and texts, Bhabha argues that their potency is not based on their capacity to hold together all the earlier parts or fuse together all the divergent sources of identity, but is found in the way they hold differences together. Like Bakhtin, he notes the sense of separateness and unity in a single semantic field. Hybrid identity is thus not formed in an accretive way in which the essence of one identity is combined with another and hybridity is simply a process of accumulation. 'Hybrid hyphenations emphasise the incommensurable elements – the stubborn chunks – as the basis of cultural identifications.'[56] The hybrid is formed out of the dual process of displacement and correspondence in the act of translation. As every translator is painfully aware, meaning seldom moves across borders with pristine integrity. Every translation requires a degree of improvization. The hybrid, therefore, is not formed out of an excavation and transferral of foreignness into the familiar, but out of this awareness of the untranslatable bits that linger on *in* translation. In this respect Bhabha would be critical of Raphael's model of appropriation.

In many ways Bhabha's strategy for understanding the formation of culture and identity by focusing on the interstitial and liminal moments of articulation and the proposal of terms like hybridity are both timely and effective counters to the essentialist views and organic models which are still common in the social sciences. Certain projects which are defined under the concept of multiculturalism uphold the hegemonic view that new cultures simply emerge from the process of accretion and synthesis. These arguments at best confuse the constituency of cultural difference by quasi-demographic pluralism, and at worst collapse the status of minority culture to a commodity that the dominant culture can safely consume. Bhabha's strategy is not a redemptive one. His strongest work is neither a chronicle of the strategies of political resistance; rather, it focuses on the more general processes through which the tactics of survival and continuity are articulated. Hence his theorizing of hybridity is distinct from Freyre's theory of amalgamation which attempts to re-evaluate the historical legacy and lend prestige to the contemporary status of cultural hybrids.

Bhabha's attention to hybridity must also be distinguished from Nandy's theory of co-optation. Bhabha does not confine transformation to the alteration in the position of discrete values, and project the encounter as a synthesis of these differences. Instead, by grafting the Bakhtinian notion of the subversive and dialogical force of hybridity onto the ambivalence in the colonial encounter, Bhabha gives a new twist to the meaning of hybridity. Hybridity is both the process by which the discourse of colonial authority attempts to translate the identity of the Other within a singular category, but then fails and produces something else. The interaction between the two cultures proceeds with the illusion of transferable forms and transparent knowledge, but leads increasingly into resistant, opaque and dissonant exchanges. It is in this tension that a 'third space' emerges which can effect forms of political change that go beyond antagonistic binarisms between the rulers and the ruled. The case of hybridity is pressed because the process of translation is, in his view, one of the most compelling tasks for the cultural critic in the modern world. Yet – to paraphrase Spivak in her corrective notes to other prominent radical theorists – this evocation of hybridity is 'so macrological that it cannot account for the micrological texture of power'.[57] Indeed, if we are all hybridized subjects, but our encounters with otherness and our flexing of translation are not equal, we may well need to return to a theory of ideology to demonstrate how the gaps and slants of representation have various effects on the subject.

9

Conclusion: Clusters in the Diaspora

'I am here, because you were there!' declared a black man in response to racist assaults on his right to stay in Britain. He has remained. He has not forgotten where he came from and he is clear about all the historical cataclysms that propelled him to this place. Neither the memories nor the abuse have forced him to abandon the hope of making a new community for himself and the others around him. But how to build a new community when the ground is foreign? What will hold 'the people' together when their needs and dreams are always in the making?

The need to construct communities is deep, a universal feature of the human condition. One cannot live in isolation for long. While the compulsion to make a community seems like a permanent feature, the practice of making communities always varies in time and place. Community is often seen as a source of protection from the fears of isolation, conflict, vulnerability and estrangement. However, solidarity is not just a means of physical security, for it is out of the experience of connectedness that there is also a step towards making sense of the world. Giving meaning to the otherwise fragmented and disjointed experiences of everyday life is profoundly connected to an understanding of belonging. But it is the relationship between belonging and community which is also undone in the modern world. Communities are constructed today in a context where attachments are multiple and partial. People may feel a sense of belonging to more than one community, or they may participate in different communities in different parts of their lives. As they move on they also move out of communities. These interminable journeys and multiple attachments often generate suspicion and unease. What brings people together at one point may push them apart at another. Can there be communities without the guarantees of stability? Is the essence of a common language and shared history the only guarantee for a collective identity?

The ambivalence that surrounds the concept of community is a recurring theme in this book. In a world where people value their independence as much, if not more, than their interdependence, the matrix of desires and obligations that generate communities will always be renegotiated. However, without trust there can be no community. How do we form trust in a context of cultural difference? By focusing on the patterns of global migration, this book has also attempted to map the complex division of communities in contemporary society. The lines that separate one community from another are not always visible. Communities overlap, abut and adjoin to each other. What holds them together can rarely be identified by unique values or an exclusive set of characteristics. The horizontal divisions of class are cross-cut by other tangential lines, the most obvious of which are race and gender. Communities are thus formed for a number of reasons, which may vary from the pursuit of common interests to the identification of mutual values and practices. Communities are therefore not always defined by their territorial boundaries.

For over a decade, ideas of space, time, location, affiliation and belonging have been the subject of considerable debate in the broad field of social and cultural theory. This book has attempted to cleave open the 'bounded social science concepts'[1] of tribe, ethnicity, race and nation. These concepts had effectively confined our understanding of cultural identity by situating it within exclusive and discrete territorial and political boundaries. While the practices of cultural identity are constantly shuttling between deterritorialization and reterritorialization, hegemonic political discourse is bound within territorializing frameworks. As we have become more conscious of the complex relationships between globalization and migration there has been, in some circles, a growing awareness that the representation of cultural identity requires a redefinition of existing theoretical frameworks and the development of a new conceptual vocabulary.

In the process of mapping the turbulent patterns of global migration and examining the various modes for representing cultural difference, I have tried to generate a dialogue between the new concepts and methods that have emerged at the borders of philosophy, political economy, cultural theory and art criticism. I have focused on the conceptual parameters of the critical discourse in the visual arts, in order to demonstrate the gaps between theory and practice. For while they have been slow to address the questions of identity and belonging, the practices of many contemporary artists have taken transnational trajectories and created complex hybrid forms. This book has also sought to identify possible parallels between different voices as well as to encourage a dialogue between positions which are all too often kept apart. I do not presume that theories developed in one field can be automatically transferred to another, but I do believe that the deep and difficult questions which lie at the centre of one piece of work may be clarified by listening to formulations proposed by another. It all depends on our ability to define relations of proximity and distance.

The popular image of community is still framed in a romantic and rural setting. A place where there is a warm glow around the evening fire of the local pub, a place where people all recognize and greet each other by name. As a number of commentators have pointed out, this idealized image of community conceals the deep divisions that existed then, and glosses over the uneasy sense of change and transformation that is ongoing. Traditional life was never as cosy or as static as it is often presented in the present. The desire to return to such a space speaks more of our anxieties over security and stability than it conveys the realities of earlier forms of communal life. It is partly because modern life has created such unprecedented levels of alienation, as well as tantalizingly suggesting that the scope for reinvention is endless, that the concept of community has been elevated to sacral heights. In his passionate defence of how art can offer fellowship and self-understanding Tim Rollins has suggested that while a community 'can't change the world, it can keep me out of purgatory'.[2]

'Gated' communities can now be found in Sydney, Manila and Johannesburg, as well as Los Angeles. These mini-fortresses are both unlike and like earlier enclaves that protected foreigners within Imperial Shanghai and the merchant class in industrial Manchester. The premium of domestic security and the recent patterns of 'white flight' are not driven by a perceived hostility from a specific class or threats of a known enemy. Rather, there is the increasing feeling of unspecified anxiety and ambient fear due to a perception of the metropolis as unknowable and unpredictable. As Richard Sennett repeatedly argues, people fear 'exposure' in the modern city.[3] The metropolis is once again associated with deprivation, corruption and pollution. The renewed debate over communitarianism is one of the responses to the prevailing dis-ease within modern urban life.

In recent political debates the concept of communities has captured the attention of both the left and the right. Communities are constructed to represent both the sacred space of tradition and the multifarious networks of modernity. The contradictions between using the concept to define the social formations that occur in either the building of national institutions or the ruptures of globalization are often overlooked. Parallels are often drawn with the moral campaigns initiated in the Victorian period, when the concept of community was galvanized to counter the threats of alienation, immorality and chaos in the industrial cities of England. However, those projects were also pushed by groundswell demands for improved standards in literacy, health and welfare. The task of claiming communities was also linked to the project of building civil societies. In the contemporary discourse the concept of community is mobilized to combat a different malaise. In the disorganized and fragmented post-industrial cities of the west the idea of community has been made appealing for its defensive values. The community has become a 'walled-in' retreat with 'closed-circuit camera' security. Communities are increasingly defined as private zones where people can bypass or exclude others from the surrounding 'no go' zones.

The purpose of this book was not to provide a universal map or to plot the contours of a particular diasporic community. One of its main aims was to challenge the 'bounded' frameworks which defined communities in terms of exclusion and purity. I have argued throughout that patterns of global migration and hybrid cultural formations are producing spatial trajectories and identities that do not fit into the classical models of the social sciences. While these complex dynamics continue to have a transformative effect on communities, the inherited conceptual tools for representing the relationship between migration and social change have limited our understanding of the processes of flow and mutation. For instance, the diverse range of migrant positions has been blurred by the homogenizing definition of the 'migrant as victim', which fails to distinguish between degrees of mobility, levels of attachment, access to resources and forms of cultural capital amongst the multitude of people who are 'on the move'. It is impossible to propose a category like the migrant, when all its members do not share the same characteristics or belong to the same class. There is no single definition of migrant identity, as all forms of subjectivity are always situated within dynamic fields of power differentials. While more and more people are having direct experience of migrants or are participating in the radial processes of migration, there is a need to draw attention to the differences as well as the similarities between these levels of experience.

The transformations of community life have often been explained by emphasizing changes in the external environment, and advances in the technologies of transport and communication. There is no doubt that the possibilities for long-distance travel and instantaneous telecommunication have dramatically increased in recent decades. Although air fares have been slashed and mobile phones have an unashamedly promiscuous presence in metropolitan life, these new opportunities for contact and communication do not explain all aspects of social change. The availability of cheaper forms of travel does not explain either the motivation for migration, or the determination of a destination. Why people move and how they utilize their resources vary significantly. The dynamics of migration cannot be confined to monocausal and unidirectional models. Its radial energy emerges out of a matrix of social, psychological, cultural and economic 'forces'. Similarly, access to new forms of telecommunication does not explain the ways they are utilized by different groups. The multiple effects of these technologies remain an under-researched field in migration studies.

The concept of place has been central to sociological and anthropological studies of community. The structures, ideas and practices which distinguish one community from another are conventionally fixed within a bounded territory. Throughout the social sciences, the definition of community life has been linked with the demarcation of spatial boundaries. The 'stuff' of culture was meant to be contained within these boundaries. Hence the impact of migration was generally seen in negative terms because it was perceived as a form of intrusion and disruption. Migration was regarded as a threat when the balance of a culture was seen as dependent on its 'rootedness' within a particular place. The priority given to the internal parameters of cultural formation by these models meant that migration was rarely seen as a constitutive feature of the social. Even when the influence was recognized as a significant force that could bolster or complement the 'body' of the social, it was nevertheless represented as if it were merely a temporary contribution or a transitional phase. This presumed that after the initial impact was absorbed the constitution of the social would return to its normal functioning. Therefore the ongoing dynamics of migration and the constitutive tension between movement and settlement in the social were never fully explored.

Our understanding of identity, technology and place have taken new directions in the recent debates in cultural theory.[4] Some critics have observed that there is a crisis in conceptualization. There have been a number of strong calls for a new analytic framework to examine the emergence of new patterns of global migration.[5] The 'bounded concepts' of tribe, ethnicity, race and nation no longer reflect a sense of community with stable boundaries and a unilocality. Communities are increasingly being sustained and transformed as their members cross boundaries and mix cultural practices. Old identities are not shed as migrants move out or between places. We have become aware of the greater levels of mobility and the new forms of interaction, especially in contemporary visual arts, and yet much of the conceptual language in the social sciences still buckles as it attempts to grasp these processes, or is palpably rejected by agents who are taking an active role in the representation of multicultural spaces. The concepts of home, exile, host, sojourner, citizen, denizen, attachment and detachment are all in need of radical reconceptualization.

However, a new language for defining the formation is beginning to emerge. It is a hybrid language which has drawn its terms and concepts from a diverse range of sources and disciplines. As Doreen Massey argues, the space of communities is not like a fixed volume in which we are bound, but rather it is a space which is formed by the 'geometries of power'.[6] Communities need to be seen as a 'field' with porous boundaries and hybrid exchanges. We need to explode the myth of pure and autonomous communities, reject the earlier mechanistic and territorial models of community and present new perspectives on the concepts of space and time which can address the dynamic flows that make community life. There is a need for theories to take a more processual view of power and agency, to note that communities are not just dominated by rigid structures and fixed boundaries but are like a 'happening'.[7]

Kobena Mercer's observation, that the term 'community' is better understood as a verb than a noun astutely foregrounds the dynamic processes of its identity.[8] Community, he argues, cannot be totally defined in terms of ancestral claims nor distinctly mapped in neat geographic zones. It now transpires that it is the cultural and political decisions of their members that are more important than either their historical lineages or geographic positions. It is what people do and how they communicate with each other, rather than who they are or where they live, that may prove to be decisive. Hence, the future boundaries and levels of interconnection between different communities may be more complex than in the present.

By focusing on the significance of the invention of the printing press and the dissemination of texts which conferred a new sense of solidarity amongst different peoples, Benedict Anderson was able to demonstrate how the boundaries and membership of communities changed.[9] Communities were no longer confined to our proximate neighbours, that is people whom one saw on a day-to-day basis and with whom one had face-to-face relationships. This more intimate and, on the physical level, more 'real' sense of community, which had clearly defined sets of obligations, and whose membership could be traced along intricate genealogies, was overtaken by a broader and more abstract sense of belonging. Being part of a national community could not be founded on these more tangible social networks; it always requires the individual's relationship to the land and culture to be mediated through consciousness of common values or shared interests. The community that results from these abstracted relations is imaginary because it involves a sense of connection with a vast body of people with whom one can have little or no direct contact. Physical bonds were thus replaced by imaginary relations.

Anderson's book has provided a turning-point in the way we understand the structures that hold communities together. It is now impossible to think of the concept of nationalism without giving attention to the 'fictive', 'symbolic' or 'ideological' process of state-building and identity formation. Anderson's work has proved to be so influential not only because it gave a new insight into the ways in which communities are formed in the modern world, but also for its ability to reconfigure the sense of belonging in contemporary society.

The incisive turn in the understanding of the phenomenon of nationalism was thus found in seeing how the economic and political structures of social organization were related to cultural aspirations. Anderson turned his attention to newspapers and novels, and one could go further and look at other visual symbols of unity and belonging, such as flags and costumes. What becomes striking in the nineteenth century is that the question of self-representation, whether in terms of narratives or of icons, was increasingly restructured to fit the contours of a national identity. Local traditions became expressive of national forms of being. In most cases, competing traditions had to be suppressed, while others had to be smuggled in from elsewhere or invented overnight in order to confer a sense of timeless and continuous belonging. The individual recollection of things past was actually mediated through a politicized communion with the memory of the collective. This communion with history crucially shaped the present. National cultures were thus imagined as occupying exclusive and discrete territories. Boundaries were fixed around the space of these 'imagined communities'.

However, the assimilationist narratives which were mobilized to construct the 'imagined community' of the nation-state around the notion of a coherent and homogeneous culture are now being challenged by new narratives that reveal the fragmented and heterogeneous condition of all cultures.[10] These narratives no longer suggest a harmonious integration of dominant and minority cultures within the boundaries of the nation-state. Cultures split, spill over, and slip along boundaries. From individual aspirations to transnational corporate decisions, the prevailing pressures in contemporary society are motivated by the search for new opportunities elsewhere. The dominant trajectories are outward and away from the 'home' base. Whether because of international migration, or by means of 'virtual' escapism, the traditional links to place and the historical structures of solidarity are being rapidly undermined. Our sense of horizon and stability are undergoing radical transformation. Hence the stereotypical images of a job for life, three generations of a family under one roof, familiar neighbours – all this now seems remote and anachronistic. This leads us to the paradox which is at the centre of this book: does greater mobility entail more freedom? Can we construct identity without referring to essential and exclusive characteristics?

The great promise of multiculturalism was that it would liberate our understanding of cultural differences from the assimilative logic of the nation-state. Yet the commitment to a comprehensive recognition of minority cultures has been at best ambiguous. In most western democratic states there has been a growing tolerance of cultural difference in the private sphere. In the public sphere, the discourse of multiculturalism has at best stimulated the provision of additional services and selective incorporation of migrants. The belated and uneven delivery of these services, as well as the invisible racist 'ceilings' in the dominant institutions, has not left any doubt about the gaps between promises and realities. Nowhere have we witnessed an open acknowledgement of the need to develop multicultural institutions at all levels of everyday life, nor a radical commitment to redefining the traditional concepts of citizenship and belonging.

As the world is increasingly becoming a multi-ethnic space, with new and complex patterns of migration, there is a stronger imperative to link the concept of citizenship to migration. In the 184 recognized nation-states, it has been estimated that there are over 600 languages and 5,000 ethnic groups.[11] When countries demand that their citizens share a common 'mother tongue' and ethnicity there is an inevitable tension. The relationship between the individual and the state has been the central concern for the political tradition of liberalism. However, the assumptions that liberalism makes about the definition of the individual, the status it gives to groups and the way it privileges specific forms of belonging within the state, can prove to be as damaging as more overt forms of discrimination. Furthermore the criteria by which automatic rights to citizenship are conferred on one group of people, and the means by which others can be granted citizenship, have never been properly defined in liberal philosophy. Even among countries which claim to be liberal democracies, the space for strangers varies dramatically.

As Jacques Derrida has noted, the condition of exile is at the centre of the nation's culture: 'all national rootedness, for example, is rooted first of all in the memory and anxiety of a displaced and displaceable population.'[12] The conceptual linkage between exile and citizenship, self and other, which is often hidden from view by the sovereign discourse of nationalism, should be particularly stressed in countries like Australia. For the history of Australian citizenship is inextricably linked to the history of immigration. It has developed a number of strategies to encourage and incorporate strangers, as well as to exclude others and oppress indigenous peoples. In the last decade the world has witnessed greater flows of human movement than ever before in its history. It is now estimated that one-fifth of the world's population is excluded from citizenship rights.

Philosophically and politically the concept of multiculturalism has been a sort of amoeba term, which has been available to groups of conflicting ideologies as a means for articulating specific programmes for individual and collective affirmation. The formulation of multicultural policies by the state has not always corresponded with multicultural practices at the level of everyday life. Nation-states with strong welfarist programmes and pluralist political frameworks have been more active in recognizing the rights of minorities. In Australia, for instance, the transposition of cultural difference from a threat to a contribution to the national culture was also related to a complex cultural transformation.[13] The founding metaphors of the nation-state had to be reimagined. There was a metaphoric replacement of the image of a 'single body', into which all members had to assimilate, by a new conception of a 'diverse family' which could accommodate the distinctive identities of its members. For both the left and the right, the metaphor of the nation shifted to a 'family' which could embrace the 'children' of the world. As long as these 'children' could follow the unstated rule of the 'father' in public life, privately they were permitted to eat, dance and sing as they pleased. For the concept of multiculturalism to gain political legitimacy the constitutive concept of culture had to be stripped down to these folkloric and gastronomic elements. Hence, when multiculturalism was first promoted, the Australian government sponsored a series of advertising campaigns which showed children of all different 'races' joining in a circle singing the jingle, 'I am as Greek as a souvlaki, I am Irish as the stew . . . I am an Aussie, yes I am.'

Despite the extension of the national self-image from 'single body' to 'diverse family', this did not necessarily entail a further commitment to recognizing the way different communities not only 'needed' different forms of services but could also redefine the boundaries of the social. The dialogue between private and public life has always been an uneasy one in multicultural debates. The dominant image of multiculturalism did not go far enough towards challenging the 'bounded' frameworks which perceived the image of cultural difference as a temporary intrusion or a transitional disruption. Services to migrant communities only followed after protracted levels of activism by these communities, and were often limited and uneven in their distribution across the polity.

Multiculturalism was first proposed as a policy to respond to the specific migration patterns and forms of diasporic communities which have now effectively ceased or are institutionally blocked. The use of the term 'multiculturalism' is now increasingly promoted in a context where the authenticity of culture and the politics of struggle are simultaneously both slowly eroding and curiously bifurcating. This process of displacement, mixture and renewal exposes a problematic that remains unresolved in political theory: what is the future of the nation-state? Both multiculturalism and globalization work in and against the state. Liberals are nowhere in deeper conflict than in attempting to ascertain where lie the greater rights: in tolerance of difference or respect for autonomy.[14] Similarly, no contemporary defence of liberalism can proceed without reflection of the inherent ethnic bias in its own moral structures. Multiculturalism is caught on these liberal horns, it has been used to promote both openness and closure, the encourager and the protector of difference. One principle calls for dynamic patterns of cultural transformation through the inclusion of others, while a contrary but related principle is introduced to support the need for cultural exclusion and preservation of the self. When a conflict emerges between these contrasting positions, as in the Rushdie affair, the difficult questions will once again surface: Who will decide? From what perspective will decisions be made?

What the policies of multiculturalism have in general failed to address is the dynamic link between material needs and symbolic formations. The revolution of culture was confined to cappuccino rather than extended to what Stuart Hall defined as the exchange between conditions and consciousness. The belatedness of multiculturalism as a social policy does not necessarily mark a limit point in the process of cultural exchange. However, one cannot overlook that its inception in the late 1970s coincided with the end of the mass migration schemes. As multiculturalism gained greater popular appeal, by the 1980s the flow of migrants to places like Australia and Canada had been dramatically curtailed. When migrants did arrive in this period, the patterns of settlement were significantly different from those of migrants who had arrived a 'generation' earlier and formed distinct 'ethnic' communities.

Multiculturalism has most recently been represented as one of the few positive consequences of globalization. However, an uncritical association between globalization and multiculturalism elides a number of significant differences: the changing patterns of movement, variation in the identity of migrants, the socio-cultural forms of settlement and the legal-rational structures of integration. Multiculturalism does not spontaneously happen whenever migrants enter a geopolitical unit. Stephen Castles and Mark Miller conclude their carefully balanced survey of global migration and the various national policies for the socio-political integration of migrants with this hopeful statement: 'The globalization of migration provides grounds for optimism, because it does give some hope of increased unity in dealing with the pressing problems which beset our small planet.'[15]

On closer scrutiny multiculturalism has more links to the classical patterns of settler migration and the political mobilization of ethnic communities than it does with the new patterns of global migration.[16] If multiculturalism were given a broader definition, one that stresses the dynamic interaction between different cultures and heightens the ongoing process of cultural transformation, then this could be seen as a precursor of one of the progressive sides of globalization. However, while globalization has inevitably sharpened and intensified the 'contact zones' between different cultures, it has also largely done this from the position of promoting a given economic imperative as the unstated ground upon which all forms of culture must be subordinated. This 'ground' is never neutral in cultural terms. Thus multiculturalism has also been co-opted into the politics of selective incorporation, in which minority cultures are hierarchically and competitively aligned within the hegemonic framework. From this perspective an insidious parallel can be drawn between globalization and multiculturalism. While the concept of multiculturalism may have the aim of weakening divisions and highlighting the commonalities between peoples, we should also remain conscious of the ways it can be used to screen the structures of domination in the context of globalization.

The politics of multiculturalism needs to be examined from the perspective of the three key concepts of this book; globalization, deterritorialization and hybridity. Migration has had a crucial impact on the way communities are defined. In the sociological literature, it is now commonplace to consider the ongoing dynamics and new trajectories of global migration. Migration is a *process* which is not completed by the arrival of an individual in a foreign place. Arrival rarely means assimilation. Migrants are often transformed by their journey, and their presence is a catalyst to new transformations in the spaces they enter. Similarly their relationship to their original 'homes' is rarely erased. Departure seldom entails forgetting and rejection. The links between home and the new society need not contract and diminish; they may find new forms of connection and extension. These networks and circuits are, according to Eades, 'more like a "spider's web" than the conventional bipolar model of migration'.[17] The narratives of modern migration can assume intricate patterns of criss-crossing between various communities and across a number of generations. Migrants' sense of restlessness, insecurity and ambivalence, as well as their attachments and memories of 'home' are often transmitted to their children.

It is also important to stress that the directions that this process follows do not simply repeat the colonial axial routes that facilitated the early waves of migration. As western economies have restructured their industrial bases, large-scale migrations have also effectively ceased. The greatest flows of migrants are now occurring towards cities which are outside western Europe, the USA and Australia. The classic industrial centres like Manchester and Detroit have for the last half of the twentieth century experienced a steep decline in economic power and a contraction of their urban populations. The great metropolises like London and New York are still slightly expanding, but they are only recruiting migrants who can work in the unregulated financial and corporate services sectors. It is cities like Dubai, Kuala Lumpur, Shanghai and Mexico City which are experiencing the new waves of urban growth. It is within and towards the south that migrants are now heading.

These new trajectories, with their complex routing systems, have baffled social scientists who insisted that migration could be explained by the centre-and-periphery models that privileged the west, or by the push–pull factors of income differentials. The causation of contemporary migration is more variable, and the consequences are far more complex than such models anticipated. Not all contemporary migrants are peasants who have left their villages to work in factories in a distant country. Today many migrants are women from an urban background who support their families by working in the service industries of another city. The borders that are crossed are not always national ones. When they do cross national borders these migrants do not necessarily reproduce micro-nations within the ghettos of other communities. It is therefore more accurate to speak of the globalization of migration than of the internationalization of migration, because the nation-state no longer provides the parameters for regulating the dominant economies or for resisting or assimilating the cultural formations of migrant peoples. The concept of globalization can help us not only to track the dynamic process by which communities are reimagined, as a consequence of migration, but also can draw our attention to the shift in the trajectories and motivations for movement.

As J. K. Gibson-Graham have argued, the concept of globalization has been useful not only in drawing attention to the restless drive of capital and heightened forms of interpenetration between capitalist spaces, but also because of its implicit demand to articulate the 'other' of capitalism. By extrapolating a critical reading of the rape narrative on to the global hegemony of capitalism Gibson-Graham seek to identify forms of connection and dependency which challenge the dominant discourse of capitalist globalization. They have argued that the globalization script 'normalizes an act of non-reciprocal penetration',[18] leaving all forms of non-capitalism in the position of the damaged, violated and fallen subject. To avoid a textual repetition of this binarism, which is also blind to the 'third space' of hybrid economies, they call for a performative and counter-hegemonic discourse on globalization. The need to break out of the victim role is imperative. For the counter-productive effects of even the critical accounts of globalization are particularly evident in relation to immigrant economies, whose conceptual value, as they note, has all too often been reduced to exotic trading practices that reveal their own anachronism, and small family enterprises that document the persistence of traditional forms of solidarity. Such practices may also foreshadow the structures of survival that are neither temporary nor transitional. From Gibson-Graham's perspective, a critical reading of globalization will need not only to highlight the structural imbalances, but also to represent those hybrid practices which exist in the interstitial zone of relative autonomy. Attention to such forms may illuminate the multiple ways that migrant workers and entrepreneurs do not simply reproduce the structured patterns of capital flows when they enter the capitalist system.

The multiple displacement effects associated with globalization have had a radical impact on the way communities are 'grounded'. Communities are conventionally understood as being bound to specific places. Their identity and cohesion comes from relationships that are patterned within a given territory. The strength of community, it is assumed, is dependent on the density and intensity of these relationships. Hence, when people 'move out', it is thought that they have left that community, or at best that their active presence will be transformed into the more passive role of someone who just keeps 'in touch'. Membership of a community is thus seen in terms of proximity and contact with the centre of that space. The further away from the centre one is situated, the looser, more irregular, less connected one feels. The further towards the periphery one gets, the more one is regarded as a stranger. However, this concentric and territorial construction of community has been dramatically altered by the technological advances in communication and the multidirectional migrations of globalization.

The incessant flows of capital and symbolic forms across borders, and the routinized forms of dialogue by means of telephone or other media, have all altered our relationship to space. The ability to have a determining influence in a community is no longer dependent on having an ongoing presence in that space. Clearly these technological innovations have paved the way for transnational corporations to realign their control centres and extend their powers into the most remote corners of the planet. But as Nestor Garcia Canclini argues, this has also enabled new cultural developments.[19] Garcia Canclini, drawing on Roger Rouse's study of Mexican peasants who have migrated to California to work in the service sector of the computer industry, illustrates how the everyday life of these migrants is one of profound rupture and transition. Yet within these dislocations he traces the dynamic intercultural and economic movements that connect and redefine both the migrant community in California and the rural Mexican town of Aguililla from which they have come. He stresses that these two communities can no longer be seen as separate entities. The frequency of 'return' visits, the economic dependencies and the symbolic transfers are of such intensity that he argues that their culture has been deterritorialized.

Deterritorialization of culture refers to the ways in which people now feel they belong to various communities despite the fact that they do not share a common territory with all the other members. It also refers to the way that a national or even a regional culture can no longer be conceived of as reflecting a coherent and distinct identity. This attention to the way communities are connected despite distance, and redefined through exchange, has challenged earlier assumptions that cultures could be mapped into autonomous and bounded spaces. The authenticity of a cultural formation is no longer singularly linked to its physical proximity to a given cultural centre.

By constant movement from one place to another new components and different inflections are given to the cultural forms which were once seen as fixed and timeless. This process of transformation does not follow the functionalist models of adaptation or assimilation because the change that occurs does not always confirm the same identity and structures of the original form. And where there is a tension between the two cultural codes, this conflict does not necessarily lead to dysfunctional or destructive relations. Difference between cultures can be as enabling and as productive as similitude. For what is most noticeable in these exchanges is the way new meanings are forged, even when both positions are not totally and clearly represented. The change that occurs is not one of mere addition nor is it a form of absorption so that the new is indistinguishable from the old. In this interaction various bits of culture are grafted, inserted or rearranged to coexist, disrupt or revitalize the other. Hybridity is the name that is given to these startling and husky forms of cultural translation.

The concept of hybridity has often been received with suspicion by many cultural theorists because of the meanings attributed to it in other fields. There are three uses of hybridity – biological, anthropological and semiotic – which have informed its current application to cross cultural exchanges. Hybridity is often regarded as a dubious concept because in both the biological and anthropological disciplines it presupposes prior states of purity and authenticity. For instance, the mule which is the offspring of two other 'pure' species – the horse and the donkey – is the most often cited hybrid. It is a particularly infamous example, because its own infertility has served as a prohibition of mixture. Of course, as Darwin argued, some hybrids prove to be more resilient than their parents as they offer new lines of survival, but the word 'mulatto' demonstrates how a selective reading of biology can serve racist ideologies. In anthropological discourse hybridity is associated with the ideas of syncretism. Here hybridity refers to the cultural processes which fuse together two distinct religious orders. Hybridity is the space which occurs betwixt and between two other authentic zones, for instance the incorporation of Christianity into indigenous religions.

In both fields the hybrid is seen as comprising a mixture of opposites, but it does not signify a disruption of the prior purity or authenticity of these polarities.

A more radical view of hybridity can be derived from semiotics. From the work of the Russian literary theorist Bakhtin it has become more evident that hybridity is the fundamental condition of all forms of cultural innovation and exchange. This more radical claim dismisses the view that there are any prior states of purity from which the hybrid emerges. Instead, all cultures are always undergoing a hybridizing process.[20] Whether this is acknowledged or denied is a matter of ideology. From this perspective we could return to those anthropological sites of syncretic interaction and note that the very construction of the Christian religion as an authentic space is already a denial of its own pagan iconography. Similarly, the representation of indigenous religions as static and pure prior to contact with the west is to overlook their own histories of exchange and transformation.

The language for representing cultural difference in the context of globalization will need to continue the break with the mechanistic frameworks and bounded concepts that underpinned the social sciences throughout this century. As the exchange between fiction and theory intensifies and the academic boundaries begin to mutate, new perspectives will emerge. With a new set of concepts that attend to the transnational and hybrid practices it may be possible to understand multiculturalism as not just the affirmation of a diversity of national and ethnic cultures, but to stimulate our grasp of the dynamic flows of difference in all cultural processses. To achieve this we must now face the urgent task of rethinking the terms of collectivity and community. Under what conditions are groups formed? What is the relationship between an individual and the collective? How will different communities coexist within common spaces?

Arjun Appadurai has argued that hybrid identities and deterritorialized cultures resemble fractals and polythetic forms whose identity is constructed by overlapping but irregular structures.[21] Such analogies can also assist our attempt to discover new metaphors for collectivity and redefine the spatial configurations of community. The concept of community has been uneasily situated in the debates on the future of the nation-state. In the polarities of local and global, national and transnational, community has been figured as either the site of resistance or the zone of exemption. Rather than simply outlining strategies for protecting the integrity or extending the boundaries of a given community, it is now necessary to rethink the forms and processes by which individuals can participate within collectives.

At various stages in my life I have found myself working with other writers and artists. On the occasions on which we have recounted our life stories, we have often discovered the transpiration of common values despite the profound differences in our backgrounds and trajectories. Our collaborative ventures seemed to gain rather than suffer from these differences as our affinities resonate and rebound down the manifold corridors of experience. These groups were often temporary, or sustained by informal and unscheduled means. Despite their sparkling intensity and warm practicality, they never had an identity. In a context where formal communities like the nation-state, in which our sense of belonging is inscribed, it is these invisible gatherings which enable us to bridge the gaps between our unknown yearnings and our palpable frustrations. Through working in clusters of other 'like-minded' writers, activists and artists, I have often discovered the outlines of my own aspirations and clarified my position in this world.

From my experience I would define a cluster as a space in which various participants gather, and in the process of assembly the respective identity of each member is respected, but at the same time a motion, shape and energy are generated by their proximity.[22] Simultaneously a semi-porous boundary is formed and new sets of possibilities are established. Within such a space it may be necessary to hold a number of differences together, to arrange them in multi-directional and fluid orders, and, most importantly, not to reduce the identity of one as the negative of the other.

We need to break out of the stultifying narcissism that defines membership of a community through a series of self-reflecting mirrors. Within such schemes the space for difference was already determined by its contribution to a grander similitude. Difference was only tolerated and accepted when it contributed to a self-confirming image. Conversely, when these self-images were fragmented or agitated, the dominant attitude to difference within the community would be at best a form of resignation and, at worst, lead to violent acts of repulsion. Both approaches are ways of neutralizing the encounter with difference, the former by means of regulation and the latter via abjection. From this perspective there is no sense of the way otherness operates as a 'strange attractor', nor any appreciation that the consciousness of collective identity is always experienced at its own threshold.

It may be more illuminating to consider the bonds within a cluster not from the perspective of similitude but from difference. While the identity of a cluster is conventionally associated with commonality, it is possible to think of forms of attraction and modes of coexistence which do not rely exclusively on shared characteristics. In contrast to the formations associated with the nation-state, clusters are formed without the institutional mechanisms that conferred unity and cohesion. For instance, there need not be an appeal to a master narrative that established the roots of a common genealogy. Within a cluster, the cultural activity of translation is not regarded as the shadow but the condition of all communication, and there is an appreciation that every attachment to a territory is also a deterritorialization of that space. To participate in a form of belonging with others may not require that we all feel as one, that we have a common origin, or only speak in the same language. Unlike the dominant narratives of the nation-state, clusters are held together by their *inessential* features: their quality is found in the way relations are found between past and present, self and other, near and far. It is a form of hospitality which does not presume that the guest must be assimilable. The invitation must be made with an open hand, to allow the other to be as he or she is, acceptable and unexpectable, their identity never defined in advance, but always empty and waiting to be filled through exchange.

But how do we name the communities whose shape is formed by the dynamics of a cluster? Will such collectives be rendered impotent in a political landscape where recognition is dependent on discrete structures of belonging and representation? Such gatherings will not seek to represent a given constituency. Nor will they be bound to a precise terrain. There will be no essence which their gathering either reflects or magnifies. The holding force of a cluster is never so specific or as instrumental as the organizational principles that were previously identified by social theorists. Clusters have none of the attributes that the state demands before it offers recognition. Perhaps we need to define the cluster from another perspective. For it is precisely when the political form of community becomes absolutely established, where all the lines of being and the boundaries of belonging are rigidly defined, that the burden of identity becomes unbearable. For instance, in contemporary critical discourse any equation between artistic practice and community background is bound to provoke a backlash. Hence the overzealous attempt to fix the audience and connect meaning to specific communities has now alerted artists to the pitfalls of identity politics. Artists refuse to have the horizons of meaning in their work and their own cultural mobility restrained by any static and closed view of their origin.

Who declares their identity these days? Only those who are confronted by borders. In the presence of the euphemistically named 'customs officers' we display our passports and credentials in the hope that this will secure our rights of passage. Yet the declarations and the requests do not end at the frontier. Every institution is guarded by other forms of 'customs officer'. The discourse of contemporary art is well policed, particularly at the moment when it is confronting the ascendancy of non-western artists.[23] What is their identity? Where does their work belong? Recourse to the bounded concepts of identity and the modernist concepts of expression buckle when applied in the presence of these hybrid agents. Their identity and work demand a voice which can speak of a form of singularity that is determined neither by the root of their origin nor by any abstract sense of universalism. This singularity does not exclude interconnection with others, for it is in the context of a cluster that exile in language is most profoundly felt. This paradoxical bond, which at once unhinges one's relation to place and community and excludes any characteristic from being represented as a condition of belonging, is the strange attractor of clusters. They are always within the social but remain on the exterior of the state's operations.

Alberto Melucci named the actors who participate in new social movements as 'nomads of the present'. There are parallels between these collectives and my idea of the cluster. For the identity of these collectives is driven by neither the need to affirm a common origin, nor the pursuit of an alternative vision of the future. Rather, their gathering is sustained by a critical attention to the present which involves both the excavation of traditional, and experimentation with new forms of membership. It is in the process of participation that collective goals are defined. The processual form of organization challenges the conventional model for representing collectives. As Melucci argues, their image and function cannot be derived from either a Freudian account of psychic formation or a Marxist model of structuralist determination. These collectives do not have a centralizing subjectivity as either hero or villain. Nor are their responses explained by their access to economic resources and forms of political influence. These collectives emerge precisely because the institutional forms of representation are inadequate for articulating the needs of individuals. From the interstices of formal structures and the emergence of fluid networks of association, new modes of resistance and collective identities are being formed. While these identities do not have a home within the existing political structures, this does not necessarily render them invisible and impotent. On the contrary, it is the very gaps and failures in the dominant structures that have stimulated new forms of knowledge, action and communication. These systems, Melucci adds, are 'marked by a deep ambiguity':

> They develop networks of high density information, the participants of which require a measure of autonomy: without developed capacities for formal learning and action, the individuals and groups could not function as dependable, self-regulating components of the system.[24]

The refusal to be exclusively associated with specific communities is not always motivated by sheer individualism. There is also the deeper appreciation of the difficulty in genuinely defining the space in which you belong. Understanding where you are from may reveal a great deal about how you see the world, but it does not necessarily determine where you are heading. These journeys and the associations that form in their course are not as transparent as the identities that they gain with retrospection. While certain goals seem intelligible from the outset, it is not necessarily a particular object or specific place that is the desired destination.

Where do we belong? What is our identity? These questions are so often put together. The answer to one hitches on to the answer of the other. The being of our identity is transposed into the conditions of belonging, and vice versa. In every claim to identity there is a reclamation of territory. This equation has been used throughout modern times both to justify the most horrendous crimes against humanity and to hide our hybrid selves. To recognize our incontrovertible hybridity is no great achievement in itself. However, if identification shifts from a strict equation of identity and place, in which the properties that define both are neither replaced by a different set, nor transcended via the spirit of detachment, but are seen as being in a constant process of constitution, where no fixed identity or exclusive place of belonging is determined in advance, then the energy of hybridity can emerge in a way that resembles what Giorgio Agamben describes as 'lovable'. By drawing an analogy between the lover's attraction to the beloved and the condition of the individual's being in the coming community, Agamben describes the link between identity and community in terms of Plato's 'erotic anamnesis' – that is, 'the movement that transports the object not toward another thing or another place, but toward its own taking place – toward the Idea'.[25] It is along these uneven trajectories and scattered affiliations that communities may need to be defined. For the potentiality of gathering and the actuality of coexistence may not be a matter of a scheduled arrival and departure but an oscillational mode of 'shuttling in both directions along a line of sparkling alternation'.[26]

Notes

Chapter 1 Introduction: The Turbulence of Migration

1 Anthony Giddens, *The Consequences of Modernity* (Polity Press, Cambridge, 1990).
2 Manuel de Landa, *War in the Age of Intelligent Machines* (Swerve Editions, New York, 1991), p. 8.
3 Charles Taylor, *Multiculturalism and 'The Politics of Recognition'* (Princeton University Press, Princeton, 1992).
4 David Held, *Democracy and the Global Order: From the Modern State to Cosmopolitan Governance* (Polity Press, Cambridge, 1995).
5 Jürgen Habermas, 'Modernity – An Incomplete Project', in Hal Foster (ed.), *Postmodern Culture* (Pluto Press, London, 1987).
6 Marc Auge, *Non Places* (Verso, London, 1995).
7 Thor Heyerdahl, *The Ra Expeditions*, trans. P. Crampton (Allen & Unwin, London, 1971), pp. 321–3.
8 Mike Douglass, *Global Migration – Beyond Multiculturalism* (unpublished paper, 1997).
9 See the recent issues of *International Migration Review* and Mary Kritz, Lin Lim and Hania Zlotnik (eds) *International Migration Systems: A Global Approach* (Clarendon Press, Oxford, 1992), and for further discussion on the temporary and circular patterns of transnational migrants see Peter Stalker, *The Work of Strangers: A Survey of International Labour Migration* (ILO, Geneva, 1994).
10 Jacques Derrida, *Spectres of Marx: The State of the Debt, the Work of Mourning and the New International* (Routledge, New York, 1994).
11 Zygmunt Bauman, *Modernity and Ambivalence* (Polity Press, Cambridge, 1991), p. 11.
12 Zygmunt Bauman, 'From Pilgrim to Tourist, or a Short History of Identity', in Stuart Hall and Paul du Gay (eds), *Questions of Cultural Identity* (Sage, London, 1996).
13 Edward Said, 'Culture and the Vultures', *Times Higher Education Supplement*, 24

January 1992, p. 19.

14 Benedict Anderson, *Imagined Communities: Reflections on the Origin and Spread of Nationalism* (Verso, London, 1983).

15 Marshall McLuhan and Quentin Fiore, *The Medium is the Message* (Allen & Lane, London, 1967), p. 16.

16 Guy Debord, *Society of the Spectacle* (Black & Red, Detroit, 1983).

17 Paul Virilio, *Lost Dimension* (Semiotexte, New York, 1992), p. 16.

18 Scott McQuire, *Visions of Modernity* (Sage, London, 1998).

19 P. Baker, 'Clinton Calls for Dialogue on Race', *Washington Post*, 22 June 1997.

20 Guillermo Gomez-Pena, 'A Binational Performance Pilgrimage' (Cornerhouse Communiqué no. 2, Manchester, 1993), p. 5.

21 Scott Lash and John Urry, *Economies of Signs and Spaces* (Sage, London, 1994).

22 Derrida, *Spectres of Marx*, p. 83.

23 John Berger and Jean Mohr, *A Seventh Man* (Penguin, Harmondsworth, 1975).

Chapter 2   Mapping Global Migration

1 Paul Tabouri, *The Anatomy of Exile* (Harrap, London, 1972), p. 12.

2 Neal Ascherson, *The Black Sea* (Vintage, London, 1996), pp. 184–92.

3 Antigone Kefala, *The Alien* (Makar, St Lucia, 1973), p. 5.

4 Russel King, 'Migrations, Globalization and Place', in D. Massey and P. Jess (eds), *A Place in the World?* (Open University Press, Oxford, 1995), p. 10.

5 Paul Sweezy, 'Center, Periphery, and the Crisis of the System', in *Four Lectures on Marxism* (Monthly Review Press, New York, 1981), p. 71.

6 Roger Anstey, *The Atlantic Slave Trade and British Abolition, 1760–1810* (Macmillan, London, 1975).

7 Samir Amin, *Accumulation on a World Scale: A Critique of the Theory of Underdevelopment,* trans. Brian Pearce (Monthly Review Press, New York, 1974).

8 Anthony King, *Global Cities* (Routledge, London, 1990), p. 74. It is important to stress that while the scale has altered, emigration is not something of the past for British citizens. It has been estimated that between 1815 and 1945 1.5 million immigrants settled in Britain while it lost 11.4 million emigrants (Panikos Panayi, *Immigration, Ethnicity and Racism in Britain, 1815–1945* (Manchester University Press, Manchester, 1994), p. 23). Throughout the 1980s emigrants vastly outnumbered immigrants. Emmer has also calculated that between 1500 and 1914 approximately 65 million Europeans were involved in intercontinental migration, compared with only 15 million African and Asian migrants. See 'European Expansion and Migration: The European Colonial Past and Intercontinental Migration, an Overview', in P. C. Emmer and M. Morner (eds), *European Expansion and Migration: Essays on the Intercontinental Migration from Africa, Asia and Europe* (Berg, New York, 1992), pp. 1–12.

9 John Solomos, *Race and Racism in Britain* (Macmillan, London, 1993), pp. 40–7.

10 Teodor Shanin, *Defining Peasants* (Basil Blackwell, Oxford, 1990), p. 144.

11 William Thomas and Florian Znaniecki, *The Polish Peasant in Europe and America* (Dover Publications, New York, 1958), p. 1511.

12 King, *Global Cities*, p. 16.

13 Marcus Lee Hansen, *The Atlantic Emigration, 1607–1860* (Harper, New York, 1961), p. 288.

14 Patrick Leigh Fermor, *Roumeli* (Penguin, Harmondsworth, 1983), pp. 184–6.
15 Stephen Castles, Mary Kalantzis and Bill Cope, *Mistaken Identity: Multiculturalism and the Demise of Nationalism in Australia* (Pluto, Sydney, 1988), p. 81.
16 Stephen Castles, 'Contract Labour Migration', in R. Cohen (ed.), *The Cambridge Survey of World Migration* (Cambridge University Press, Cambridge, 1995), p. 512.
17 Panikos Panayi, *Immigration, Ethnicity and Racism in Britain, 1815–1945* (Manchester University Press, Manchester, 1994).
18 E. Pugliese, 'Restructuring of the Labour Market and the Role of Third World Migrations in Europe', *Environment and Planning: Society and Space*, 11 (1993) pp. 513–27.
19 Janet Abu-Lughod, 'Recent Migrations in the Arab World', in William McNeill and Ruth Adams (eds), *Human Migration: Patterns and Policies* (Indiana University Press, Bloomington, 1978), p. 226.
20 A. Phizacklea (ed.), *One Way Ticket: Migration and Female Labour* (Routledge, London, 1983).
21 S. Castles and G. Kosack, *Immigrant Workers and Class Structure in Western Europe* (Oxford University Press, London, 1973).
22 Michael Buroway, 'The Functions and Reproduction of Migrant Labour: Comparative Material from Southern Africa and the United States', in Robin Cohen, *The Sociology of Migration* (Elgar, Cheltenham, 1996), p. 39,
23 The argument on the cost and benefits of immigration has been an ongoing one between economists and social scientists. According to the 1997 report by the National Academy of Sciences (US), 'immigration benefits the US economy overall and has little negative effect on the income and job opportunities of most native-born Americans.' Yet two-thirds of Americans now believe that immigration should be restricted (John Cassidy, 'The Melting-Pot Myth', *New Yorker*, 14 July 1997, p. 40).
24 A. Rattansi, 'Race, Class and the State: From Marxism to Post-Modernism', *Labour History Review*, 60, no. 3 (Winter 1995), p. 23.
25 King, *Global Cities*, p. 65.
26 Colin Holmes, *A Tolerant Country? Immigrants and Minorities in Britain* (Faber & Faber, London), 1991.
27 Michael Piore, *Birds of Passage: Migrant Labor and Industrial Societies* (Cambridge University Press, Cambridge, 1979).
28 Calvin Goldsheider, 'Migration and Social Structure: Analytic Issues and Comparative Perspectives in Developing Nations', in Cohen, *Sociology of Migration*, p. 276.
29 B. Carter, C. Harris and S. Joshi, 'The 1951–55 Conservative Government and the Racialization of Black Immigration', *Policy Papers in Ethnic Relations,* No. 11 (University of Warwick, Centre for Research in Ethnic Relations, 1987).
30 Quoted in Solomos, *Race and Racism in Britain*, p. 55.
31 Quoted in Rattansi, 'Race, Class and the State', p. 29.
32 Ibid., p. 29.
33 Stephen Castles, *Migrant Workers and the Transformation of Western Societies*, Western Societies Program, Occasional Paper no. 22 (Center for International Studies, Cornell University, 1989), p. 106.
34 Stephen Castles and Mark Miller, *The Age of Migration* (Macmillan, London, 1993).
35 Alexandra Korol, 'Ukraine and National Identity' (unpublished Ph.D. thesis, Department of Sociology, University of Manchester, 1996).
36 Castles and Miller, *Age of Migration*, p. 260.

37 Mike Douglass, 'Culture and the City in East Asia: A Perspective for the 21st Century', in *International Conference on Cities in Transition: Towards a Creative and Cooperative Order* (Seoul Development Institute, November 1994), p. 5.

38 Allan Findlay, 'Skilled Transients: The Invisible Phenomenon?', in Cohen, *Cambridge Survey of World Migration*, p. 515.

39 European Commission Conference on Trafficking in Women, 10 June 1996.

40 Massimo Calabresi, 'Of Human Bondage', *Time* (February 1998), p. 26.

41 Michael Christie, 'Germany Urged to Tackle Sex-Slavery', *Reuter World Service*, 1 December 1993.

42 Victor Pope et al., 'Trafficking in Women', *US News & World Report*, 7 April 1997, p. 38.

43 Alice Leuchtag, 'Merchants of Flesh', *Humanist*, 55 (March–April 1995).

44 Alex Duval Smith, 'Foreign Bodies: Black Marketeers Trade in Women', *Guardian*, 13 June 1996, p. 4.

45 Quoted in Scott Lash and John Urry, *Economies of Signs and Spaces* (Sage, London, 1994), p. 176.

46 Richard Appelbaum, 'Multiculturalism and Flexibility: Some New Directions in Global Capitalism', in A. Gordon and C. Newfield (eds), *Mapping Multiculturalism* (University of Minnesota Press, Minneapolis, 1996), p. 298.

47 R. Walding, H. Aldrich and R. Ward (eds), *Ethnic Entrepreneurs* (Sage, London, 1990).

48 Chan Kwok Bun and Ong Jin Hui, 'The Many Faces of Immigrant Entrepreneurship', in Cohen, *Cambridge Survey of World Migration*, p. 525.

49 Étienne Balibar, '*Es Gibt Keinen Staat in Europa*: Racism and Politics in Europe Today', *New Left Review*, 186 (March/April 1991), p. 9.

50 Stefano Berterame has also argued that the causes for these migrations cannot be explained purely in the binary models of either individual choice or the structural force of the world economy. These models, which were once applied to explain migration from countries like Italy, are of limited value in the face of current movements. Italy is undergoing a transition from being a nation which was marked by mass emigration, to a stabilization in the number of emigrants and returnees, and is now a nation attracting immigrants from a diverse range of other countries. These migratory flows have been partly explained by economic differentials as well as a complex set of social, cultural and religious networks. In the absence of regulated and formal migration agreements, the management of migrant needs and issues has fallen on local trade union and voluntary organizations. The state has been belated or inadequate in its response, preferring to maintain the illusion that Italy is no longer a migrant society (S. Berterame, 'Immigrants in Italy: Problems of Racism and Integration', unpublished Ph.D. thesis, University of Manchester 1994).

51 S. Castles and G. Kosack, *Immigrant Workers and Class Structure in Western Europe* (Oxford University Press, Oxford, 1973), p. 31.

52 Robin Cohen, 'Introduction', *The Sociology of Migration* (Elgar, Cheltenham, 1996), p. xvi.

53 Ronald Skeldon, 'The Emergence of Trans-Pacific Migration', in Cohen, *Cambridge Survey of World Migration*, p. 536.

54 J. S. Birks, I. J. Seccombe and C. A. Sinclair, 'Labour Migration in the Arab Gulf States: Patterns, Trends and Prospects', in Cohen, *Sociology of Migration*, p. 100.

55 This view contrasts with the earlier views set out by John Rex in *Race, Colonialism and the City* (Routledge & Kegan Paul, London, 1973).

56 Avtar Brah, *Cartographies of Diaspora* (Routledge, London, 1996), pp 67–83.
57 Skeldon, 'Trans-Pacific Migration', p. 535.
58 Mark Miller, 'Illegal Migration', in Cohen, *Cambridge Survey of World Migration*, p. 537.
59 Ibid., p. 538.
60 M. Kritz and H. Zlotnik, 'Global Interactions: Migration Systems, Processes and Policies', in M. Kritz, L. Lim and H. Zlotnik (eds), *International Migration System: A Global Approach* (Clarendon Press, Oxford, 1992).
61 M. Douglass, *Global Migration – Beyond Multiculturalism* (unpublished paper, 1997). p. 8.

Chapter 3   The Ability to Move: Defining Migrants

1 Doreen Massey, 'Politics and Space/Time', in *Place and the Politics of Identity*, ed. M. Keith and S. Pile (Routledge, London, 1993), p. 146.
2 Ibid., p. 147.
3 Anthony Giddens, *The Nation-State and Violence* (Polity Press, Cambridge, 1985), p. 50.
4 Cited in Stephen Castles and Mark Miller, *The Age of Migration* (Macmillan, London, 1993), p. 3.
5 Jochen Blaschke, Introduction, *Globalization, Culture and Migration* (Eurofor Conference, Athens, October 1996).
6 Janet L. Abu-Lughod, 'Palestinians: Exiles at Home and Abroad', *Current Sociology*, 32, no. 2 (1988), p. 62.
7 H. Pick, 'World Refugee Crisis Spinning out of Control, UN Warns', *Guardian*, 21 November 1993.
8 Jacques Derrida, 'The Deconstruction of Actuality', *Radical Philosophy*, 68 (Autumn 1994), p. 35.
9 R. Williams, *Towards 2000* (Chatto & Windus, London, 1983).
10 P. Corrigan, 'Feudal Relics or Capitalist Monuments? Notes on the Sociology of Unfree Labour', *Sociology*, 2, no. 3 (September 1977), p. 445.
11 S. Castles, Mary Kalantzis and Bill Cope, *Mistaken Identity: Multiculturalism and the Demise of Nationalism in Australia* (Pluto, Sydney, 1988) pp. 84–5.
12 'The times are not good for the decolonization of metropolitan feminists. In the wake of the Cold War, there is a mood of triumphalist Americanism in the United States. The "democratization" of state capitalisms and their colonies to tributary economies of rationalized global financialization carries with it the aura of the civilizing mission of earlier colonialisms. The rationalization of sexuality, the invasive restructuring of gender relations, poor women's credit-baiting without infrastructural involvement in the name of micro-enterprise, the revision of women-in-development (modernization) to gender-and-development (New World Order) – all this is seen as global sisterhood.' (Gayatri Spivak, 'Of Poetics and Politics', in Catherine David and Jean-François Cherier (eds), *Documenta X – the book* (Cantz, Kasset, 1997), p. 764.)
13 N. Ascherson, 'Leaders who Shame us', *Independent*, 7 October 1993, p. 23.
14 A. Travis, 'Howard Promises Tough Immigration Bill', *Guardian*, 14 March 1995.
15 See special issue, 'Frontiers', *Oxford Literary Review*, 14 (1992); 'Krauts', *Granta*, 42 (1992).

16 Jochen Blaschke, 'German Peculiarities – German Models: A Contribution to the Discussion on Migration and Ethnic Relations', conference paper, *Culture, Communication and Discourse*, Manchester, 9–12 December 1992.

17 Alastair Davidson, *From Subject to Citizen* (Cambridge University Press, Cambridge, 1997).

18 Ibid., p. 13. A similar consensus was noted between the republican left and right in France when Mitterrand spoke of controlling immigration levels at 'a threshold of tolerance'. This discourse was not very remote from Le Pen's calls to protect 'the body of the nation'.

19 Lydia Potts, *The World Labour Market: A History of Migration* (Zed Press, London, 1990), p. 206.

20 Castles and Miller, *Age of Migration*, pp. 8–9.

21 Richard Appelbaum (ed.), *States and Development in the Asian Pacific Rim* (Sage, London, 1992).

22 Saskia Sassen, *The Mobility of Labour and Capital* (Cambridge University Press, 1988, p. 116.

23 Saskia Sassen-Koob, 'Notes on the Incorporation of Third World Women into Wage-Labour through Immigration and Off-shore Production', in R. Cohen (ed.), *The Sociology of Migration* (Elgar, Cheltenham, 1996), p. 160.

24 There are a number of important contributions, for instance J. Torrance, *Estrangement, Alienation and Exploitation* (Macmillan, London, 1977) and more recently Z. Bauman, *Modernity and Ambivalence* (Polity Press, Cambridge, 1991).

25 K. Marx, *Capital* (Foreign Languages Publishing House, Moscow, 1980), vol. I, pp. 784–90. On the applicability of the reserve army thesis for representing the conditions of labour migration see also S. Castles and G. Kosack, *Immigrant Workers and Class Structure in Western Europe* (Oxford University Press, Oxford, 1973), ch. 9, and S. Castles, *Here for Good: Immigrant Workers and Class Structure in Western Europe's New Ethnic Minorities* (Pluto Press, London, 1984), ch. 2.

26 E. Durkheim, *The Division of Labour* (Free Press, New York, 1956), p. 129.

27 E. Durkheim, *Suicide* (Free Press, New York, 1951), p. 250.

28 Castles, Kalantzis and Cope, *Mistaken Identity*, p. 83.

29 Robin Cohen, 'Introduction', *The Sociology of Migration* (Elgar, Cheltenham, 1996), p. xiii.

30 Quoted in David Frisby, *Simmel and Since* (Routledge, London, 1992), p. 66.

31 Georg Simmel, 'The Metropolis and Mental Life', in K. Wolff (ed.), *The Sociology of Georg Simmel* (Free Press, New York, 1950), p. 413.

32 Georg Simmel, 'The Stranger', ibid. For a more detailed discussion of this essay see my *Modernity as Exile* (Manchester University Press, Manchester, 1993) and special issue on Georg Simmel, *Theory, Culture and Society*, 8, no. 3 (1991). Contemporary interpretations of Simmel's work need to be distinguished from its earlier incorporation into American sociology. For instance, the Chicago School used Simmel's essay on the stranger as a starting-point to redefine modern society in terms of concentrated difference and to undo the negative association between marginality, deviance and migration. They were right to focus on the new forms of moral order that were constituted in the social space of the city. They also appreciated that outsiders would benefit most from the culture of difference, that the city not only encouraged but needed them for its own success. However, for all their efforts at revalorization and their acknowledgement of the positive contribution of strangers, they failed to reflect the depth of Simmel's dialectical insight into the objective

and subjective interactions in modernity, or to establish a theoretically enduring model of spatial relations in the modern city.

33 Quoted in Frisby 'Simmel and Since', p. 67.
34 Richard Sennett, *The Conscience of the Eye* (Faber & Faber, London, 1992), p. 128.
35 Ibid., p. 126.
36 Ibid., p. 132.
37 Elizabeth Wilson, *The Sphinx in the City: Urban Life, the Control of Disorder, and Women* (Virago, London,1991).
38 A similar framework is evident in Norbert Elias's study of a small English community where the insider/outsider division was marked by neither class nor race but simply in terms of the 'established' and the 'newcomer'. Elias notes that in 'Winston Parva the full armoury of group superiority and group contempt was mobilised in the relations between two groups who were different only with regard to the duration of their residence at this place' (p. xviii). The established group displayed all the forms of social stigmatization and prejudice against the newcomers. In order to protect their own positions and values against a group they considered dirty, lazy and corrupt – in short barbaric – they closed ranks, reserving for themselves a civilized identity which had higher values that were regulated by group-specific norms. Their superiority and exclusivity were thus defined by the axioms of barbarism (civility, nomic and anomic behaviour), and regulated by the mechanics of stigmatization which co-ordinated the process of identification, participation and gratification (Norbert Elias and John Scotson, *The Established and the Outsiders*, Cass & Co., London, 1965).
39 Sighard Neckel, quoted in Ulrich Beck, *The Re-invention of Politics: Rethinking Modernity in the Global Social Order*, trans. M. Ritter (Polity Press, Cambridge, 1997), pp. 76–7.
40 Julia Kristeva, *Strangers to Ourselves*, trans. L. Roudiez (Harvester Wheatsheaf, London, 1991), p. 1.
41 Ibid., p. 3.
42 Janet Wolff, 'The Invisible Flâneuse: Women and the Literature of Modernity', *Theory, Culture and Society*, 2, no. 3 (1985), p. 41.
43 Ibid.
44 Adrian Piper, *Adrian Piper* (Ikon Gallery, Birmingham, 1991), p. 26.
45 Walter Benjamin, *Charles Baudelaire: A Lyric Poet in the Era of High Capitalism*, trans. H. Zohn (Verso, London, 1973), p. 36.
46 E. Wilson, 'The Invisible Flâneur', *New Left Review*, 191 (January/February, 1992), p. 93.
47 Wolff, 'The Invisible Flâneuse', p. 40.
48 Wilson, 'The Invisible Flâneur', p. 110.
49 Zygmunt Bauman, *Modernity and Ambivalence* (Polity Press, Cambridge, 1991).
50 Germaine Greer, 'An Englishman's Home is an Illusion', *Guardian*, 15 October 1993.
51 Homi Bhabha, 'Dissemination: Time, Narrative and the Margins of the Modern Nation', in *Nation and Narration* (Routledge, London, 1990), p. 308.

Chapter 4   Globalization and Migration

1 Anthony D. King (ed.), *Culture, Globalization and the World System* (Macmillan, London, 1991).

2 Quoted in Eric Hobsbawm, *Age of Extremes* (Michael Joseph, London, 1994), p. 408.

3 S. Lash and J. Urry, *Economies of Signs and Spaces* (Sage, London, 1994), p. 4.

4 Ibid., p. 17.

5 Ulrich Menzel, *Globalization, Culture and Migration*, Eurofor Conference, Athens, (October 1996).

6 United Nations, *Human Development Report*, quoted in Victoria Brittain and Larry Elliott, 'World's Poor Lose out to Corporations', *Guardian Weekly*, 22 June 1997, p. 23.

7 Prabhat Patnaik, 'International Capital and National Economic Policy: A Critique of India's Economic Reforms', *Economic and Political Weekly*, 29, no. 12, 19 March 1994, p. 686. See also his *Economics and Egalitarianism* (Oxford University Press, Delhi, 1991), and *Accumulation and Stability under Capitalism* (Clarendon Press, Oxford, 1997).

8 Will Hutton, 'Sun, Sea, Wine and Loneliness Down Under', *Observer*, 2 November 1997.

9 Robin Cohen, *Global Diasporas* (UCL Press, London, 1997), p. 158.

10 Leslie Sklair, *Sociology of the Global System* (Johns Hopkins University Press, Baltimore, 1991), p. 49.

11 William Wolman and Anne Colamasco, *The Judas Economy: The Triumph of Capital and the Betrayal of Work*, quoted in R. Heibroner, 'Follow the Money', *Los Angeles Times Book Review*, 1 June 1997, p. 3.

12 Paul Hirst and Graham Thompson, *Globalization in Question: The International Economy and Possibilities* (Polity Press, Cambridge, 1996).

13 Stuart Hall, 'New Cultures for Old', in D. Massey and P. Jess (eds), *A Place in the World?* (Open University Press, Oxford, 1995), p. 184.

14 Stuart Hall, 'The Question of Cultural Identity', in *Modernity and its Futures* (Polity Press, Cambridge, 1992), p. 299.

15 Slavoj Zizek, 'Multiculturalism, or, the Cultural Logic of Multinational Capitalism', *New Left Review*, 225 (September/October 1997).

16 Malcolm Waters, *Globalization* (Routledge, London, 1994).

17 Saskia Sassen, *The Global City* (Princeton University Press, Princeton, 1991), p. 169.

18 Anthony D. King, *Global Cities* (Routledge, London, 1990).

19 The shift from a rural-based to an industrialized economy involved the absorption of a vast population in new urban centres. Pre-industrial societies had about 80 per cent of their population working in agriculture, whereas fully industrialized societies require only approximately 5 per cent of their workforce in farming. Although large numbers of workers have been displaced by the decline of manufacturing and the emergence of more efficient technologies, the transition to a post-industrial economy has not yet reproduced comparable scales of expansion and re-employment.

20 Lash and Urry, *Economies of Signs and Spaces*, p. 172.

21 M. Hepworth, 'Information Technology and the Global Restructuring of Capital Markets', in S. Brunn and T. Leinbach (eds), *Collapsing Time and Space* (Harper Collins, London, 1992), p. 141.

22 Masao Miyoshi, 'Borderless World?', in R. Wilson and W. Dissanayake (eds), *Global/Local* (Duke University Press, Durham, NC, 1997), p. 90.

23 Sassen, *The Global City*.

24 King, *Global Cities*, p. 142.

25 Cohen, *Global Diasporas* p. 175.
26 Ian Hunt, 'Walter Benjamin and "Qualitatively Distinguishable Times" ', in P. Buchler and N. Papastergiadis, *Random Access* (Rivers Oram Press, London, 1996).
27 P. Dicken, J. Peck and A. Tickell, *Unpacking the Global*, Manchester International Centre for Labour Studies, Working Paper no. 10 (February 1996), p. 7.
28 Félix Guattari, *Chaosmosis an Ethico-aesthetic Paradigm*, trans. P. Bains and J. Pefanis (Power Publications, Sydney, 1995).
29 Teodor Shanin, *Defining Peasants* (Basil Blackwell, Oxford, 1990).
30 Stephen Castles and Mark Miller, *The Age of Migration* (Macmillan, London, 1993), p. 123.
31 Mike Douglass, 'Culture and the City in East Asia: A Perspective for the 21st Century', in *International Conference on Cities in Transition: Towards a Creative and Cooperative Order* (Seoul Development Institute, November 1994).
32 Two-thirds of the 300,000 people providing live-in childcare in the USA are illegal immigrants (Douglass, 'Culture and the City').
33 Robin Cohen, *Frontiers of Identity: The British and the Other* (Longman, London, 1994), p. 7.
34 Peter Wollen, *Raiding the Icebox: Reflections on Twentieth-Century Culture* (Verso, London, 1993); Jean Fisher (ed) *Global Visions: Towards a New Internationalism in the Visual Arts* (Kala, London, 1994).
35 Peter Beilharz, *Postmodern Socialism* (Melbourne University Press, Carlton, 1994), p. 105.
36 Stuart Hall, 'Minimal Selves', in *The Real Me*, ICA Document 6 (London, 1987).
37 Edward Said, *Culture and Imperialism* (Chatto & Windus, London, 1993).
38 Scott Lash and John Urry, *The End of Organized Capitalism* (Polity Press, Cambridge, 1987), and *Economies of Signs and Spaces*.
39 *Economies of Signs and Spaces*, p. 24.
40 Nestor Garcia Canclini, *Hybrid Cultures,* trans. C. Chiappari and S. Lopez (University of Minnesota Press, Minneapolis, 1995), p. 232.
41 Guattari, *Chaosmosis*, p. 31.

Chapter 5   The Deterritorialization of Culture

1 Raymond Williams, *Towards 2000* (Chatto & Windus, London, 1983), p. 177.
2 Rupert Sheldrake, 'The Rebirth of Nature', in P. Buchler and N. Papastergiadis (eds), *Random Access* (Rivers Oram Press, London), 1996.
3 Doreen Massey, 'The Spaces of Community', in N. Papastergiadis (ed.), *Mixed Belongings and Unspecified Destinations* (INIVA, London, 1997), p. 38.
4 I. Prigogine and I. Stengers, *Order out of Chaos: Man's New Dialogue with Nature* (Bantam Books, New York, 1984), p. 2.
5 James Rosenau, *Turbulence in World Politics: A Theory of Change and Continuity* (Princeton University Press, Princeton, 1990), p. 8.
6 J. Briggs and F. David Peat, *Turbulent Mirror* (Harper & Row, New York, 1989).
7 Edward Said, *Culture and Imperialism* (Chatto & Windus, London, 1993), p. xii.
8 Nestor Garcia Canclini, 'Scenes Without Territory: The Aesthetics of Migrations and Identities in Transition', in N. Richard and B. Murphy (eds), *Art from Latin America: La Cita Transcultural* (Museum of Contemporary Art, Sydney, 1993), p. 13.
9 H. R. Wicker, 'From Complex Culture to Cultural Complexity', in P. Werbner and

T. Modood (eds), *Debating Cultural Hybridity* (Zed Press, London, 1997), p. 31.

10 Garcia Canclini, 'Scenes Without Territory', p. 14.

11 Raul Pertierra, 'Counterfactual Conditions of Culture and their Implication for Integration: A Philippine Example', *Pilipina*, 25 (Fall 1995), p. 50.

12 A. Gupta and J. Ferguson (eds), *Anthropological Locations; Boundaries and Grounds of a Field Science* (University of California Press, Berkeley, 1994).

13 Gillian Bottomley, 'Anthropologists and the Rhizomatic Study of Migration', *Australian Journal of Anthropology*, 9, no. 1 (1998), p. 32.

14 Trinh T. Minh-ha, *Woman, Native, Other* (Indiana University Press, Bloomington, 1989).

15 Homi Bhabha, 'How Newness Enters the World', in *The Location of Culture* (Routledge, London, 1994), p. 216.

16 Edward Said, *Culture and Imperialism*, p. 401.

17 Arjun Appadurai draws a similar conclusion at the end of his book: 'a framework for relating the global, the national, and the local has yet to emerge', *Modernity at Large* (University of Minnesota Press, Minneapolis, 1997), p. 188.

18 Claudio Gaulart, 'Postcards on the Road', *Third Text*, 18 (Spring, 1992), p. 76.

19 Geeta Kapur, 'The Centre–Periphery Model or How are we Placed? Contemporary Cultural Practice in India', *Third Text,* 16/17 (Autumn/Winter, 1991), p. 12.

20 Nestor Garcia Canclini, 'Modernity after Postmodernity', in G. Mosquera (ed.), *Beyond the Fantastic* (INIVA, London, 1995), p. 28.

21 Ibid., p. 32.

22 Stuart Hall, 'The Local and the Global: Globalization and Ethnicity', in A. D. King (ed.), *Culture, Globalization and the World-System* (Macmillan, London, 1991), p. 29.

23 Janet Wolff, 'The Global and the Specific: Reconciling Conflicting Theories of Culture', ibid., p. 171.

24 To give but a few examples, Nestor Garcia Canclini, *Hybrid Cultures* (University of Minnesota Press, Minneapolis, 1995); Celeste Olalquiaga, *Megalopolis* (University of Minnesota Press, Minneapolis, 1992); Gerardo Mosquera (ed.), *Beyond the Fantastic* (INIVA, London, 1996); Ella Shohat and Robert Stam, *Unthinking Eurocentrism* (Routledge, London, 1995); Mike Featherstone (ed.), *Global Culture* (Sage, London, 1990).

25 Olalquiaga, *Megalopolis*, p. 54.

26 A. D. Smith, 'Toward a Global Culture?' in Featherstone, *Global Culture*.

27 Benedict Anderson, *Imagined Communities* (Verso, London, 1983).

28 F. Anthias and N. Yuval Davis, *Racialized Boundaries* (Routledge, London, 1990).

29 H. Bhabha, *Nation and Narration* (Routledge, London, 1990).

30 Bottomley, *'Anthropologists and Migration'*, p. 35.

31 Phillip Mar, 'Just the Place is Different: Comparisons of Place and Settlement Practices of some Hong Kong Migrants in Sydney', *Australian Journal of Anthropology*, 9, no. 1 (1998), p. 59.

32 Mike Douglass, 'Culture and the City in East Asia: A Perspective for the 21st Century', *International Conference on Cities in Transition: Towards a Creative and Cooperative Order* (Seoul Development Institute, November 1994), p. 16.

33 Garcia Canclini, *Hybrid Cultures*, pp. 228–41.

34 Roger Rouse, 'Mexican Migration and the Social Space of Postmodernism', *Diaspora*, 1, no. 1 (Spring, 1991), p. 12.

35 Ibid., pp. 13–14.

36 Mar, 'Just the Place', p. 71.

37 See my 'Warring Ethnicities and Gendered Violations: Rape in Bosnia', in *Dialogues in the Diaspora* (Rivers Oram Press, London, 1997).

38 Nestor Garcia Canclini has also noted that one of the key tasks for cultural studies is to understand 'how the ideologies represented and solemnised by these two movements, fundamentalism and cosmopolitanism, manage to coexist' ('Rethinking Identity in Times of Globalization', in N. Papastergiadis (ed.), *Art and Cultural Difference* (Academy Books, London, 1995), p. 37).

39 John Hutnyk, 'Adorno at Womad: South Asian Crossovers and the Limits of Hybridity-Talk', in P. Werbner and T. Modood (eds), *Debating Cultural Hybridity* (Zed Books, London, 1997), p. 108.

40 G. Deleuze and F. Guattari, *Kafka: Towards a Minor Literature* (University of Minnesota Press, Minneapolis, 1986), p. 17.

41 See for instance Guillermo Gomez-Pena, *A Binational Performance Pilgrimage* (Cornerhouse Communiqué No. 2, Manchester, 1993) and Emily Hicks, *Border Writing: The Multidimensional Text* (University of Minnesota Press, Minneapolis, 1991).

42 Avtar Brah, *Cartographies of Diaspora* (Routledge, London, 1996), pp. 203–4.

43 Rosi Braidotti, *Nomadic Subjects* (Columbia University Press, New York, 1994), p. 5.

44 Caren Kaplan, 'Deterritorialization: The Rewriting of Home and Exile in Western Feminist Discourse', in *The Nature and Context of Minority Discourse*, ed. A. R. JanMohamed and D. Lloyd (Oxford University Press, New York, 1990), p. 361.

45 G. Deleuze and F. Guattari, *What is Philosophy?*, trans. G. Burchell and H. Tomlinson (Verso, London, 1994), p. 85.

46 E. Said, *Culture and Imperialism*, p. 403.

47 Appadurai, *Modernity at Large*, p. 166.

48 Ibid., p. 31.

Chapter 6   The Limits of Cultural Translation

1 Stuart Hall, 'New Cultures for Old', in D. Massey and P. Jess (eds), *A Place in the World?* (Open University Press, Oxford, 1995), p. 176.

2 Edward Said, *Orientalism* (Routledge, London, 1978).

3 Doreen Massey, 'The Spaces of Community', in N. Papastergiadis (ed.), *Mixed Belongings and Unspecified Destinations* (INIVA, 1997).

4 Lothar Baumgarten, 'Status quo', *Artforum*, 26, no. 7 (1988), p. 108.

5 Jean Fisher, 'Some Thoughts on "Contaminations" ', *Third Text*, 32 (Autumn 1995), p. 6.

6 Birgit Meyer, 'Beyond Syncretism', in C. Stewart and R. Shaw (eds), *Syncretism / Anti-Syncretism* (Routledge, London, 1994), p. 45.

7 Benjamin Whorf, *Language, Thought and Reality* (MIT Press, Cambridge, Mass., 1956); Edward Sapir, *Culture, Language and Personality* (University of California Press, Berkeley, 1956).

8 Mary Louise Pratt, *Imperial Eyes: Travel Writing and Transculturation* (Routledge, London, 1992).

9 Notable exceptions are: Ashis Nandy, *The Intimate Enemy* (Oxford University Press, New Delhi, 1983); Gayatri Spivak and Ranajit Guha (eds), *Selected Subaltern Studies* (Oxford University Press, New York, 1988).

10 See also the film by Gary Kildea, *Trobriand Cricket: An Ingenious Response to*

Colonialism (1975).

11 Myer, 'Beyond Syncretism', p. 45.

12 Ibid., p. 62.

13 Quoted in R. Schulte and J. Biguenet (ed.), *Theories of Translation* (The University of Chicago Press, Chicago, 1992), p. 4.

14 Walter Benjamin, 'The Task of the Translator' in *Illuminations*, trans. H. Zohn (Fontana, London, 1973), p. 76.

15 A similar point was made by Czeslaw Milosz: 'Experience shows that some excellent translations have been done by poets possessing only a limited knowledge of the language of the original or no knowledge at all, while some bad translations are the work of accomplished philologists whose perfect acquaintance with the language they translate from is unquestioned' ('A Symposium on Translation', *Threepenny Review* (Summer 1997), p. 10.

16 Paul de Man ironically observed that Benjamin's own comments on the impossibility of translation should be so literally confirmed by his own translators. In particular, de Man takes exception to Harry Zohn's rendering of the image of the amphora as a metaphor for the fundamental unity of language. He stresses that in the original the image suggests 'a metonymic, a successive pattern, in which things follow, rather than a metaphorical unifying pattern in which things become one by resemblance' (Paul de Man, *The Resistance to Theory* (Manchester University Press, Manchester, 1986), p. 90).

17 Ibid., pp. 78, 80.

18 J.-F. Lyotard, *The Differend: Phrases in Dispute*, trans. G. Van Den Abbeele (University of Minnesota Press, Minneapolis, 1988), p. xi.

19 Ibid.

20 These are questions that preoccupied me throughout my involvement with the journal *Third Text* and were the focus of a number of my essays in which I examined the strategies of selective representation, the paucity of contextualization, the uneven historical acknowledgement of marginalized practices and the limits of thematic constructions in 'global art' shows. See my *The Complicities of Culture* (Cornerhouse Publications, Manchester, 1994) and *Dialogues in the Diaspora* (Rivers Oram Press, London, 1998).

21 Both exhibitions attracted considerable debate about the pitfalls of identity politics. Critical responses tended to highlight the failure to contextualize non-western work in 'Magiciennes' and the appeal to non-aesthetic criteria for determining selections in the Whitney. (See the special issue on 'Magiciennes' in *Third Text*, 6 (Summer, 1989).) Consequently, the exhibits were dismissed as bad art or, as Luis Camnitzer described the Whitney, 'a festival of causes' (see L. Camnitzer, 'The Whitney Biennial', *Third Text,* 23, (Summer 1993), p. 128). The problems associated with the mode of critical assessment were acknowledged in the round-table discussion that the journal *October* initiated after the Whitney. Rosalind Krauss's concern was focused on the shift of attention from the meaning of the work to the origin of the author, a shift that she described as moving critical attention away from the signifier to the signified. However, what escaped attention was the need to evaluate the framework for interpreting cultural signs rather than privileging either the signifier or the signified. (See *October*, 66 (Fall 1993).)

22 Stuart Hall, 'Minimal Selves', in *The Real Me: Postmodernism and the Question of Identity*, ICA Document 6 (London, 1987), p. 44.

23 Both Terry Eagleton and Raymond Williams have noted that the canon of English

literature was formed by exiles and émigrés. See T. Eagleton, *Exiles and Émigrés*, (Chatto & Windus, London, 1970); R. Williams, 'When was Modernism?', *Politics of Modernism* (Verso, London, 1989).

24 Hal Foster, 'The Artist as Ethnographer', in J. Fisher (ed.), *Global Visions* (Kala Press, London, 1995), p. 12.

25 Gerardo Mosquera, 'Some Problems in Transcultural Curating', ibid., p. 136.

26 Jimmie Durham, 'A friend of mine said. . . . ', in *Global Visions,* ed. Fisher, p. 118.

27 John Lechte and Gill Bottomley, 'Difference, Postmodernity and Imagery in Multi-cultural Australia', in G. L. Clark, D. Forbes and R. Francis (eds), *Multiculturalism, Difference and Postmodernism* (Longman & Cheshire, Melbourne, 1993), p. 24.

28 Yinka Shonibare, 'Fabric, and the Irony of Authenticity', in N. Papastergiadis (ed.), *Mixed Belongings and Unspecified Destinations* (INIVA, London, 1997), p. 40.

29 Kobena Mercer, 'Art that is Ethnic in Inverted Commas', FRIEZE (November/December 1995), p. 41.

30 Kobena Mercer, 'Imagine all the People: Constructing Community Culturally', in N. Papastergiadis (ed.), *Mixed Belongings and Unspecified Destinations* p. 22.

31 Walter Benjamin, 'The Work of Art in the Age of Mechanical Reproduction', in *Illuminations,* trans. H. Zohn (Schocken Books, New York, 1968), p. 223. Bottomley and Lechte also draw on this element in Benjamin's essay in their elaboration of the concept of interweaving.

32 Homi Bhabha, *The Location of Culture* (Routledge, London, 1994), p. 224.

33 Sarat Maharaj, ' "Perfidious Fidelity": The Untranslatability of the Other', in Fisher (ed.), *Global Visions* p. 28.

34 Jacques Derrida, '*From* Des Tour de Babel', in R. Schulte and J. Biguenet (eds), *Theories of Translation* (The University of Chicago Press, Chicago, 1992), p. 220.

35 Jimmie Durham, *A Certain Lack of Coherence* (Kala Press, London, 1993), p. 12.

36 Jimmie Durham and Jean Fisher, 'The Ground has been Covered', *Artforum* (Summer 1988), p. 101.

37 Jimmie Durham quoted in Lucy Lippard, 'Jimmie Durham Postmodernist "Savage" ', *Art in America* (February 1993), p. 67.

38 Yinka Shonibare quoted in Mercer, 'Art that is Ethnic in Inverted Commas', p. 40.

39 Gayatri Chakravorty Spivak, *Outside in the Teaching Machine* (Routledge, London, 1993), p. 179.

40 Durham, *A Certain Lack of Coherence*, p. 146.

41 Lyotard, *The Differend*, pp. 57–68.

42 Conversation between Jimmie Durham and Jeanette Ingberman, in Jimmie Durham, *The Bishop's Moose and the Pinkerton Men* (Exit Art, New York, 1989), p. 31.

43 Jimmie Durham, 'Cowboys and . . .', *Third Text*, 12 (Autumn, 1990), p. 15.

44 Derrida, ''*From* Des Tour de Babel', p. 226.

45 John Berger, *Ways of Seeing* (Penguin, Harmondsworth, 1972), p. 106.

46 See Gillian Rose, 'Place and Identity: A Sense of Place', in D. Massey and P. Jess (eds), *A Place in the World?* (Open University Press, Oxford, 1995), p. 110.

Chapter 7   Philosophy and Cultural Difference

1 Edward Said, *Culture and Imperialism* (Chatto & Windus, London, 1993).

2 Ernest Gellner, 'The mightier pen?' *Times Literary Supplement*, 19 February 1993, pp. 3–4.

3 Edward Said, 'Culture and Imperialism', *Times Literary Supplement*, 19 March 1993, p. 15. See also Letters to the Editor, 19, 26 February, 5 March, 2, 16 April, 4, 11 June 1993.

4 Donald Davidson, *Inquiries into Truth and Interpretation* (Oxford University Press, Oxford, 1984), p. 184.

5 See special issue on the Rushdie affair, *Third Text*, 11 (Summer, 1990).

6 Malcolm Bull, 'Vision and Totality', *New Left Review*, 207 (September/October 1994), p. 143.

7 Zygmunt Bauman, *Intimations of Postmodernity* (Routledge, London, 1992), pp. xxii–xxiii.

8 Alasdair MacIntyre, *Whose Justice? Which Rationality?* (University of Notre Dame Press, Notre Dame, 1988), p. 9. This book can be seen as the sequel to his earlier investigation of the limits of relativism, specifically his most influential book, *After Virtue* (University of Notre Dame Press, Notre Dame, 1981). In this chapter I will concentrate on his essay 'Relativism, Power and Philosophy', in K. Baynes, J. Bohmen and T. McCarthy (eds), *After Philosophy: End or Transformation?* (MIT Press, Cambridge, Mass., 1987). Unless otherwise noted all further quotations from MacIntyre are from this text.

9 A similar line of argument is developed by Nancy Fraser when she distinguishes between the affirmative cultural politics of mainstream multiculturalism and the transformative cultural politics of deconstruction. The former recognizes the equal worth of cultural differences without disturbing the underlying framework that generates them, while the latter demands a transformation of the underlying cultural-valuation structure, whereby everybody's sense of belonging, affiliation and self is destabilized. See Nancy Fraser, 'From Redistribution to Recognition: Dilemmas of Justice in a "Post-Socialist" Age', *New Left Review*, 212 (May/June 1996), pp. 82–3.

10 Slavoj Zizek, 'Multiculturalism, or the Cultural Logic of Multinational Capitalism', *New Left Review*, 225 (September/October 1997), p. 37.

11 Homi Bhabha, 'Culture's In Between', *Artforum*, 32 (September 1993), p. 167.

12 Charles Taylor, *Multiculturalism and 'The Politics of Recognition'* (Princeton University Press, Princeton, 1992), p. 66.

13 Nick Smith, 'Charles Taylor, Strong Hermeneutics and the Politics of Difference', *Radical Philosophy*, 68 (Autumn 1994), p. 21.

14 K. Anthony Appiah, 'Identity, Authenticity, Survival: Multicultural Societies and Social Reproduction', in Amy Gutman (ed.), *Multiculturalism: Examining the Politics of Recognition* (Princeton University Press, Princeton, 1994), p. 163. This point must not be confused with the proposition that minorities should subordinate their cultural rights to the integrationist demands of the liberal state. Cultural rights are not necessarily defined in the antagonist mode as is assumed by Chandran Kukathas, 'Are There Any Cultural Rights?', in Will Kymlicka (ed.), *The Rights of Minority Cultures* (Oxford University Press, Oxford, 1995), p. 233.

15 Jürgen Habermas, 'Struggles for Recognition in Constitutional States', *European Journal of Philosophy*, 1, no. 2 (August 1993), p. 128.

16 Hans-Georg Gadamer, *Truth and Method* (Sheed & Ward, London, 1979).

17 Taylor, *Multiculturism,* p. 66.

18 Chantal Mouffe, 'For a Politics of Nomadic Identity', in G. Robertson et al. (eds), *Travellers' Tales* (Routledge, London, 1994), p. 106.

19 Bhikhu Parekh, 'Superior People: The Narrowness of Liberalism from Mills to Rawls',

Times Literary Supplement, 25 February 1994, p. 11.

20 Zygmunt Bauman, *Modernity and Ambivalence* (Polity Press, Cambridge, 1991), p. 8.

21 Parekh, 'Superior People', p. 12.

22 Ibid., p. 13.

23 Mouffe, 'For a Politics of Nomadic Identity', p. 108.

24 Rainer Baubock, 'Ethical Problems of Immigration Control and Citizenship', in R. Cohen (ed.), *The Cambridge Survey of World Migration* (Cambridge University Press, Cambridge, 1995).

25 Ashis Nandy, *Traditions, Tyranny and Utopias* (Oxford University Press, Delhi, 1987), pp. 16–19.

Chapter 8   Tracing Hybridity in Theory

1 In *The Complicities of Culture: Hybridity and 'New Internationalism'* (Cornerhouse Communiqué, no. 4, Manchester, 1994), I explored the incorporation of the term 'hybridity' in art criticism and curatorial practice. As an indication of how similar inroads have been made in literary and cultural theory, consider the recent overview by Iain Chambers, *Migrancy, Culture. Identity* (Routledge, London, 1994). For a most comprehensive account of the concept of hybridity in nineteenth-century scientific racism and British colonialism and its legacies in contemporary theory, see Robert J. C. Young, *Colonial Desire: Hybridity in Theory* (Routledge, London, 1995).

2 Coco Fusco, 'The Border Art Workshop/Taller de Art Fronterizo: Interview with Guillermo Gomez-Pena and Emily Hicks', *Third Text*, 7 (Summer 1989), pp. 53–76.

3 See M. Kwon, 'The Fullness of Empty Containers', *FRIEZE*, 24 (October 1995), and Z. Bauman, *Modernity and Ambivalence* (Polity Press, Cambridge, 1991).

4 J. Fisher, Introduction to special issue, 'Contamination', *Third Text*, 32 (Autumn 1995).

5 G. Spivak, 'The Narratives of Multiculturalism', ICCCR lecture, University of Manchester (January 1995).

6 S. Rushdie, *The Satanic Verses* (Viking, London, 1990), p. 93.

7 For a more detailed discussion on the ambivalence of miscegenation in the colonial context see Young's account of the different positions on hybridity that were articulated in nineteenth-century western scientific discourse. His useful typology includes: the *polygenist* view, which denies the viability of mixture; the *amalgamationist* thesis, which is a precursor of the melting-pot notion; the *decomposition* thesis, which allows for interbreeding but confirms the predominance of a single source for the constitution of the offspring; the *proximate and distant species* union, which restricts fertility to particular circumstances; the *mongrel* thesis, which promotes raceless chaos and degeneration. (Young, *Colonial Desire*, p. 18).

8 J. Williamson, *New People: Miscegenation and Mulattoes in the U.S.* (Free Press, New York, 1980), p. 95.

9 Young, *Colonial Desire*, p. 13.

10 Quoted in Williamson, *New People*, p. 235.

11 G. Fredrickson, *The Black Image in the White Mind* (Harper and Row, New York, 1971), p. 234.

12 J. Walvin, *Black and White: The Negro and English Society, 1555–1945* (Allen Lane, London, 1973).

13 C. Clay and M. Leapman, *Master Race: The Lebensborn Experiment in Nazi Germany* (Hodder & Stoughton, London, 1995), p. 16–21.

14 Ibid.

15 Williamson, *New People,* p. 123.

16 B. Tizard and E. Phoenix, *Black, White or Mixed Race?* (Routledge, London, 1994).

17 O. Paz, *The Labyrinth of Solitude* (Allen Lane, London, 1967), p. 77.

18 Parenthetically it can be noted that the origin of the word 'miscegenation', which is a transform of the Greek word *elaleukatio*, referring to the passing from 'black to white', connotes both moral cleansing and self-correction. The word first appeared in an anonymous pamphlet in 1864 which set out to satirize Abraham Lincoln by suggesting that the salvation of the American people could only be found in interbreeding between blacks and whites in order to produce a brown-skinned people. D. Aaron, 'The "Inky" Curse: Miscegenation in the White American Literary Imagination', *Social Science Information,* 22, 2 (1983), pp. 169–90.

19 Williamson, *New People*, p. xii.

20 G. Freyre, *The Masters and the Slaves*, trans. S. Putnam (Knopf, New York, 1946), p. xx. When referring to the general development of such a culture Freyre does not speak of a process of hybridity, preferring the term *mestizo*, and when addressing the specific formations of the Brazilian national identity he proposes the term '*Luso-Tropical*'.

21 Ibid. In Brazil Aryanization alludes to the absorption of the 'inferior' races by 'superior' ones (i.e. the white race) and the gradual shedding of hybrid characteristics.

22 G. Freyre, *The Gilberto Freyre Reader,* trans. B. Shelby (Knopf, New York, 1974), p. 87.

23 Z. Nunes, 'Anthropology and Race in Brazilian Modernism', in Francis Barker, Peter Hulme and Margaret Iverson (eds), *Colonial Discourse/Postcolonial Theory* (Manchester University Press, Manchester, 1994), p. 120.

24 M. Raphael, *Proudhon, Marx, Picasso*, trans. I. Marcuse (Lawrence & Wishart, London, 1980), p. 130.

25 Ibid., p. 131.

26 Ibid., p. 142.

27 D. F. Miller, *The Reason of Metaphor* (Sage, New Delhi, 1992), p. 120.

28 See also John Berger's account of Picasso as the 'vertical invader' in modern art in *Success and Failure of Picasso* (Penguin, Harmondsworth, 1965).

29 A. Nandy, *The Intimate Enemy* (Oxford University Press, New Delhi, 1983), p. xv.

30 Ibid., p. 68.

31 Ibid., p. 76.

32 Ibid., p. 7.

33 Robert J. C. Young, has drawn attention to the concept of hybridity in Bakhtin's theory of language and its broader implications for cultural theory. See *Colonial Desire,* pp. 20–2.

34 J. M. Lotman, *The Universe of the Mind*, trans. A. Shukman (Tauris, London, 1991), p. 123.

35 J. M. Lotman and B. A. Uspenskij, *The Semiotics of Russian Culture,* trans. A. Shukman (Michigan Slavic Contributions, no. 11, Ann Arbor, 1984), p. xii.

36 Lotman, *The Universe of the Mind,* p. 150.

37 Ibid.

38 M. Serres, *Hermes* (Johns Hopkins University Press, Baltimore, 1982), p. 80.

39 Lotman, *The Universe of the Mind,* p. 131.

40	Ibid., p. 147.

41	Serres, *Hermes*, pp. 66–7.

42	Irene Portis Winner, 'Some Comments upon Lotman's Concepts of Semiotics of Culture: Implications for the Study of Ethnic Culture Texts', in M. Halle et al., *Semiosis: Semiotics and the History of Culture* (Michigan Slavic Contributions, no. 10, Ann Arbor, 1984), p. 28.

43	S. Hall, *Stuart Hall: Critical Dialogues in Cultural Studies*, ed. D. Morley and Kuan-Hsing Chen (Routledge, London, 1996), p. 502.

44	H. Bhabha, *The Location of Culture* (Routledge, London, 1995), p. 5.

45	S. Hall, 'New Ethnicities', in K. Mercer (ed.), *Black Film, British Cinema* (ICA Documents 7, London, 1989).

46	S. Hall, 'Old and New Identities, Old and New Ethnicities', in A. King (ed.), *Culture, Globalization and the World-System* (Macmillan, London, 1991), p. 49.

47	Ibid., p. 51.

48	Ibid., p. 35.

49	G. C. Spivak, 'Can the Subaltern Speak?' in P. Williams and L. Chrisman (eds), *Colonial Discourse and Post-Colonial Theory: A Reader* (Harvester, London, 1993), p. 71.

50	Spivak, 'Narratives of Multiculturalism'.

51	Spivak, 'Can the Subaltern Speak?', p. 82.

52	H. Bhabha (ed.), *Nation and Narration* (Routledge, London, 1990), p. 307.

53	Bhabha, *The Location of Culture*, p. 185.

54	Ibid., p. 191.

55	In an earlier article I have examined in greater detail Bhabha's utilization of psychoanalytic and literary theory. See my 'Reading DissemiNation', *Millennium Journal of International Studies*, 20, no. 3 (Winter 1991).

56	Bhabha, *The Location of Culture*, p. 219.

57	Spivak, 'Can the Subaltern Speak?', p. 74.

# Chapter 9	Conclusion: Clusters in the Diaspora

1	L. Basch, N. Glick Schiller and C. Szanton Blanc, *Nations Unbound* (Gordon & Breach, Luxemburg, 1995), p. 30.

2	Tim Rollins, 'Art in the Construction of Beloved Communities', in N. Papastergiadis (ed.), *Mixed Belongings and Unspecified Destinations* (INIVA, London, 1997), p. 56.

3	Richard Sennett, *The Conscience of the Eye* (Faber & Faber, London, 1990).

4	John B. Thompson, *The Media and Modernity* (Polity Press, Cambridge, 1995) and Scott McQuire, *Visions of Modernity* (Sage, London, 1998).

5	James Clifford and George Marcus, *Writing/Culture: The Poetics and Politics of Ethnography* (University of California Press, Berkeley, 1986).

6	Doreen Massey, 'The Spaces of Community', in Papastergiadis (ed.), *Mixed Belongings and Unspecified Destinations*, p. 34.

7	Graham Crow, 'Community Time as Community's Fourth Dimension', ibid., p. 60.

8	Kobena Mercer, 'Imagine all the People', ibid, p. 20.

9	Benedict Anderson, *Imagined Communities* (Verso, London, 1983).

10	Homi K. Bhabha (ed.), *Nation and Narration* (Routledge, London, 1990).

11	Cited in Will Kymlicka (ed.), *The Rights of Minority Cultures* (Oxford University Press, Oxford, 1995), p. 4.

12 Jacques Derrida, *Spectres of Marx: The State of the Debt, the Work of Mourning and the New International* (Routledge, New York, 1994).

13 Alistair Davidson, *From Subject to Citizen: Australian Citizenship in the Twentieth Century* (Cambridge University Press, Cambridge, 1997).

14 See for instance the contrasting view of Kukathas and Green in Kymlicka, *The Rights of Minority Cultures*, pp. 228–75.

15 S. Castles and M. Miller, *The Age of Migration* (Macmillan, London, 1993), p. 275.

16 S. Castles, Mary Kalantzis and Bill Cope, *Mistaken Identity: Multiculturalism and the Demise of Nationalism in Australia* (Pluto, Sydney, 1988).

17 Jeremy Eades, quoted in Basch, Schiller and Blanc, *Nations Unbound*, p. 28.

18 J. K. Gibson-Graham, *The End of Capitalism (as we Knew it)* (Blackwell, Oxford, 1996), p. 125

19 Nestor Garcia Canclini, *Hybrid Cultures* (University of Minnesota Press, Minneapolis, 1995).

20 Homi Bhabha, *The Location of Culture* (Routledge, London, 1995).

21 Arjun Appadurai, *Modernity at Large* (University of Minnesota Press, Minneapolis, 1997).

22 Nikos Papastergiadis (ed.), *Art and Cultural Difference: Hybrids and Clusters* (Academy Group, London, 1995).

23 Nikos Papastergiadis, *Dialogues in the Diaspora* (Rivers Oram Press, London, 1998).

24 Alberto Melucci, *Nomads of the Present* (Hutchinson, London, 1989), p. 12.

25 Giorgio Agamben, *The Coming Community*, trans. M. Hardt (University of Minnesota Press, Minneapolis, 1993), p. 2.

26 Ibid., p. 20.

Bibliography

Aaron, D., 'The "Inky" Curse: Miscegenation in the White American Literary Imagination', *Social Science Information*, 22, no. 2 (1983).

Abu-Lughod, Janet L., 'Recent Migrations in the Arab World', in William McNeill and Ruth Adams (eds), *Human Migration: Patterns and Policies*, Indiana University Press, Bloomington, 1978.

Abu-Lughod, Janet L., 'Palestinians: Exiles at Home and Abroad', *Current Sociology*, 32, no. 2 (1988).

Agamben, Giorgio, *The Coming Community*, trans. M. Hardt, University of Minnesota Press, Minneapolis, 1993.

Amin, Samir, *Accumulation on a World Scale: A Critique of the Theory of Underdevelopment*, trans. Brian Pearce, Monthly Review Press, New York, 1974.

Anderson, Benedict, *Imagined Communities: Reflections on the Origin and Spread of Nationalism*, Verso, London, 1983.

Anstey, Roger, *The Atlantic Slave Trade and British Abolition, 1760–1810*, Macmillan, London, 1975.

Anthias, F. and N. Yuval Davis, *Racialized Boundaries*, Routledge, London, 1990.

Appadurai, Arjun, *Modernity at Large*, University of Minnesota Press, Minneapolis, 1997.

Appelbaum, Richard (ed.), *States and development in the Asian Pacific Rim*, Sage, London, 1992.

Appelbaum, Richard, 'Multiculturalism and Flexibility: Some New Directions in Global Capitalism', in A. Gordon and C. Newfield (eds), *Mapping Multiculturalism*, University of Minnesota Press, Minneapolis, 1996.

Appiah, K. Anthony, 'Identity, Authenticity, Survival: Multicultural Societies and Social Reproduction', in Amy Gutman (ed.), *Multiculturalism: Examining the Politics of Recognition*, Princeton University Press, Princeton, 1994.

Ascherson, Neal, 'Leaders who Shame us', *Independent*, 7 October 1993.

Ascherson, Neal, *The Black Sea*, Vintage, London, 1996.

Auge, Marc, *Non Places*, Verso, London, 1995.

Baker, P., 'Clinton Calls for Dialogue on Race', *Washington Post*, 22 June 1997.

Balibar, Étienne, '*Es Gibt Keinen Staat in Europa*: Racism and Politics in Europe Today', *New Left Review*, 186 (March/April, 1991).

Basch, L., N. Glick Schiller and C. Szanton Blanc, *Nations Unbound*, Gordon & Breach, Luxemburg, 1995.

Baubock, Rainer, 'Ethical Problems of Immigration Control and Citizenship', in R. Cohen (ed.), *The Cambridge Survey of World Migration*, Cambridge University Press, Cambridge, 1995.

Bauman, Zygmunt, *Modernity and Ambivalence*, Polity Press, Cambridge, 1991.

Bauman, Zygmunt, *Intimations of Postmodernity*, Routledge, London, 1992.

Bauman, Zygmunt, 'From Pilgrim to Tourist, or a Short History of Identity', in Stuart Hall and Paul du Gay (eds), *Questions of Cultural Identity*, Sage, London, 1996.

Baumgarten, Lothar, 'Status quo', *Artforum*, 26, no. 7 (1988).

Beck, Ulrich, *The Re-invention of Politics: Rethinking Modernity in the Global Social Order*, trans. M. Ritter, Polity Press, Cambridge, 1997.

Beilharz, Peter, *Postmodern Socialism*, Melbourne University Press, Carlton, 1994.

Benjamin, Walter, 'The Work of Art in the Age of Mechanical Reproduction', in *Illuminations*, trans. H. Zohn, Schocken Books, New York, 1973.

Benjamin, Walter, *Charles Baudelaire: A Lyric Poet in the Era of High Capitalism*, trans. H. Zohn, Verso, London, 1973.

Benjamin, Walter, 'The Task of the Translator', in *Illuminations*, trans. H. Zohn, Fontana, London, 1973.

Berger, John, *Success and Failure of Picasso*, Penguin, Harmondsworth, 1965.

Berger, John, *Ways of Seeing*, Penguin, Harmondsworth, 1972.

Berger, John, *And our Faces, my Heart, Brief as Photos*, Writers and Readers, London, 1984.

Berger, John and Jean Mohr, *A Seventh Man*, Penguin, Harmondsworth, 1975.

Berterame, S., 'Immigrants in Italy: Problems of Racism and Integration', unpublished Ph.D. thesis, University of Manchester, 1994.

Bhabha, Homi, 'Dissemination: Time, Narrative and the Margins of the Modern Nation', in *Nation and Narration*, Routledge, London, 1990.

Bbabha, Homi, *Nation and Narration*, Routledge, London, 1990.

Bhabha, Homi, 'Culture's In Between', *Artforum*, 32 (September 1993).

Bhabha, Homi, 'How Newness Enters the World', in *The Location of Culture*, Routledge, London, 1994.

Bhabha, Homi, *The Location of Culture*, Routledge, London, 1995.

Birks, J. S., I. J. Seccombe and C. A. Sinclair, 'Labour Migration in the Arab Gulf States: Patterns, Trends and Prospects', in Cohen, *Sociology of Migration*.

Blaschke, Jochen, 'German peculiarities – German Models: A Contribution to the Discussion on Migration and Ethnic Relations', conference paper, *Culture, Communication and Discourse*, Manchester, 9–12 December 1992.

Blaschke, Jochen, 'Introduction', *Globalization, Culture and Migration*, Eurofor Conference, Athens, October 1996.

Bottomley, Gillian, 'Anthropologists and the Rhizomatic Study of Migration', *Australian Journal of Anthropology*, 9, no. 1 (1998).

Brah, Avtar, *Cartographies of Diaspora*, Routledge, London, 1996.

Braidotti, R., *Nomadic Subjects*, Columbia University Press, New York, 1994.

Briggs, J. and F. David Peat, *Turbulent Mirror*, Harper & Row, New York, 1989.

Brittain, Victoria and Larry Elliott, 'World's Poor Lose out to Corporations', *Guardian*

Weekly, 22 June 1997.

Brunn, S. and T. Leinbach (eds), *Collapsing Time and Space*, HarperCollins, London, 1992.

Bull, Malcolm, 'Vision and Totality', *New Left Review*, 207 (September/October 1994).

Buroway, Michael, 'The Functions and Reproduction of Migrant Labour: Comparative Material from Southern Africa and the United States', in Cohen, *The Sociology of Migration*.

Calabresi, Massimo, 'Of Human Bondage', *Time* (February 1998), p. 26.

Camnitzer, Lois, 'The Whitney Biennial', *Third Text*, 23 (Summer 1993).

Carter, B., C. Harris and S. Joshi, 'The 1951–55 Conservative Government and the Racialization of Black Immigration', *Policy Papers in Ethnic Relations*, no. 11, University of Warwick, Centre for Research in Ethnic Relations, 1987.

Cassidy, John, 'The Melting-Pot Myth', *New Yorker*, 14 July 1997.

Castles, Stephen, *Here for Good: Immigrant Workers and Class Structure in Western Europe's New Ethnic Minorities*, Pluto Press, London, 1984.

Castles, Stephen, *Migrant Workers and the Transformation of Western Societies*, Western Societies Program, Occasional Paper no. 22, Center for International Studies, Cornell University, 1989.

Castles, Stephen, 'Contract Labour Migration', in R. Cohen (ed.), *The Cambridge Survey of World Migration*, Cambridge University Press, Cambridge, 1995.

Castles, Stephen, Mary Kalantzis and Bill Cope, *Mistaken Identity: Multiculturalism and the Demise of Nationalism in Australia*, Pluto, Sydney, 1988.

Castles, Stephen and Godula Kosack, *Immigrant Workers and Class Structure in Western Europe*, Oxford University Press, Oxford, 1973.

Castles, Stephen and Mark Miller, *The Age of Migration*, Macmillan, London, 1993.

Chambers, Iain, *Migrancy, Culture. Identity*, Routledge, London, 1994.

Christie, Michael, 'Germany Urged to Tackle Sex-Slavery', *Reuter World Service*, 1 December 1993.

Clay, C. and M. Leapman, *Master Race: The Lebensborn Experiment in Nazi Germany*, Hodder & Stoughton, London, 1995.

Clifford, James and George Marcus, *Writing/Culture: The Poetics and Politics of Ethnography*, University of California Press, Berkeley, 1986.

Cohen, Robin, *Frontiers of Identity: The British and the Other*, Longman, London, 1994.

Cohen, Robin, 'Introduction', *The Sociology of Migration*, Elgar, Cheltenham, 1996.

Cohen, Robin, *Global Diasporas*, UCL Press, London, 1997.

Corrigan, P., 'Feudal Relics or Capitalist Monuments? Notes on the Sociology of Unfree Labour', *Sociology*, 2, no. 3 (September, 1977).

Davidson, Alastair, *From Subject to Citizen: Australian Citizenship in the Twentieth Century*, Cambridge University Press, Cambridge, 1997.

Davidson, Donald, *Inquiries into Truth and Interpretation*, Oxford University Press, Oxford, 1984.

Debord, Guy, *Society of the Spectacle*, Black & Red, Detroit, 1983.

Deleuze, Giles and Felix Guattari, *Kafka: Towards a Minor Literature*, trans. D. Polan, University of Minnesota Press, Minneapolis, 1986.

Deleuze, Giles and Felix Guattari, *What is Philosophy?*, trans. G. Burchell and H. Tomlinson, Verso, London, 1994.

de Man, Paul, *The Resistance to Theory*, Manchester University Press, Manchester, 1986.

Derrida, Jacques, '*From* Des Tour de Babel', in *Theories of Translation*, ed. R. Schulte and J. Biguenet, University of Chicago Press, Chicago, 1992.

Derrida, Jacques, 'The Deconstruction of Actuality', *Radical Philosophy*, no. 68, Autumn 1994.

Derrida, Jacques, *Spectres of Marx: The State of the Debt, the Work of Mourning and the New International*, Routledge, New York, 1994.

Dicken, P., J. Peck and A. Tickell, *Unpacking the Global*, Manchester International Centre for Labour Studies, Working Paper no. 10 (February 1996).

Douglass, Mike, 'Culture and the City in East Asia: A Perspective for the 21st Century', in *International Conference on Cities in Transition: Towards a Creative and Co-operative Order* (Seoul Development Institute, November 1994).

Douglass, Mike, 'Global Migration – Beyond Multiculturalism', unpublished paper, 1997.

Durham, Jimmie, *The Bishop's Moose and the Pinkerton Men*, Exit Art, New York, 1989.

Durham, Jimmie, 'Cowboys and . . .', *Third Text*, 12 (Autumn, 1990).

Durham, Jimmie, *A Certain Lack of Coherence*, Kala Press, London, 1993.

Durham, Jimmie and Jean Fisher, 'The ground has been covered', *Artforum* (Summer 1988).

Durkheim, E., *Suicide*, Free Press, New York, 1951.

Durkheim, E., *The Division of Labour*, Free Press, New York, 1956.

Duval Smith, Alex, 'Foreign Bodies: Black Marketeers Trade in Women', *Guardian,* 13 June 1996.

Eagleton, Terry, *Exiles and Émigrés*, Chatto & Windus, London, 1970.

Elias, Norbert and John Scotson, *The Established and the Outsiders*, Cass & Co., London, 1965.

Emmer, P. C. and M. Morner (eds), *European Expansion and Migration: Essays on the Intercontinental Migration from Africa, Asia and Europe*, Berg, New York, 1992.

European Commission Conference on Trafficking in Women, 10 June 1996.

Featherstone, Mike, *Global Culture*, Sage, London, 1990.

Fisher, Jean (ed.), *Global Visions: Towards a New Internationalism in the Visual Arts*, Kala, London, 1994.

Fisher, Jean, Introduction, 'Some Thoughts on "Contaminations" ', *Third Text*, 32 (Autumn 1995).

Foster, H., 'The Artist as Ethnographer', in *Global Visions*, ed. J. Fisher, Kala Press, London, 1995.

Fraser, Nancy, 'From Redistribution to Recognition: Dilemmas of Justice in a "Post-Socialist" Age', *New Left Review*, 212, (May/June 1996).

Frederickson, George, *The Black Image in the White Mind,* Harper and Row, New York, 1971.

Freyre, Gilberto, *The Masters and the Slaves*, trans. S. Putnam, Knopf, New York, 1946.

Freyre, Gilberto, *The Gilberto Freyre Reader,* trans. B. Shelby, Knopf, New York, 1974.

Frisby, David, *Simmel and Since*, Routledge, London, 1992.

'Frontiers', *Oxford Literary Review*, 14, (1992).

Fusco, Coco, 'The Border Art Workshop/Taller de Art Fronterizo: Interview with Guillermo Gomez-Pena and Emily Hicks', *Third Text*, 7 (Summer 1989).

Gadamer, Hans-Georg, *Truth and Method*, Sheed & Ward, London, 1979.

Garcia Canclini, Nestor, 'Scenes Without Territory: The Aesthetics of Migrations and Identities in Transition', in N. Richard and B. Murphy (eds), *Art from Latin America: La Cita Transcultural*, Museum of Contemporary Art, Sydney, 1993.

Garcia Canclini, Nestor, *Hybrid Cultures,* trans. C. Chiappari and S. Lopez, University of Minnesota Press, Minneapolis, 1995.

Garcia Canclini, Nestor, 'Modernity after Postmodernity', in *Beyond the Fantastic*, ed. G. Mosquera, INIVA, London, 1995.

Garcia Canclini, Nestor, 'Re-thinking Identity in Times of Globalization', in *Art and Cultural Difference*, ed. N. Papastergiadis, Academy Books, London, 1995.

Gaulart, Claudio, 'Postcards on the Road', *Third Text*, 18 (Spring, 1992).

Gellner, Ernest, 'The mightier pen?', *Times Literary Supplement*, 19 February 1993.

Gibson-Graham, J. K., *The End of Capitalism (as we Knew it)*, Blackwell, Oxford, 1996.

Giddens, Anthony, *The Nation-State and Violence*, Polity Press, Cambridge, 1985.

Giddens, Antony, *The Consequences of Modernity*, Polity Press, Cambridge, 1990.

Goldsheider, Calvin, 'Migration and Social Structure: Analytic Issues and Comparative Perspectives in Developing Nations', in Robin Cohen (ed.), *The Sociology of Migration*, Elgar, Cheltenham, 1996.

Gomez-Pena, Guillermo, 'A Binational Performance Pilgrimage', Cornerhouse Communiqué no. 2, Manchester, 1993.

Greer, Germaine, 'An Englishman's Home is an Illusion', *Guardian*, 15 October 1993.

Guattari, Félix,*Chaosmosis an Ethico-aesthetic Paradigm*, trans. P. Bains and J. Pefanis, Power Publications, Sydney, 1995.

Gupta, A. and J. Ferguson (eds), *Anthropological Locations; Boundaries and Grounds of a Field Science*, University of California Press, Berkeley, 1994.

Habermas, Jürgen, 'Modernity – An Incomplete Project', in *Postmodern Culture*, ed. Hal Foster, Pluto Press, London, 1987.

Habermas, Jürgen, 'Struggles for Recognition in Constitutional States', *European Journal of Philosophy*, 1, no. 2 (August 1993).

Hall, Stuart, 'Minimal Selves', in *The Real Me: Postmodernism and the Question of Identity*, ICA Document 6, ed. L. Appignanesi, London, 1987.

Hall, Stuart, 'New Ethnicities', in *Black Film, British Cinema*, ed. K. Mercer, ICA Documents 7, London, 1989.

Hall, Stuart, 'The Local and the Global: Globalization and Ethnicity', in *Culture, Globalization and the World-System*, ed. A. D. King, Macmillan, London, 1991.

Hall, Stuart, 'The Question of Cultural Identity', in *Modernity and its Futures*, Polity Press, Cambridge, 1992.

Hall, Stuart, 'New Cultures for Old', in D. Massey and P. Jess (eds), *A Place in the World?*, Open University Press, Oxford, 1995.

Hall, Stuart, *Stuart Hall: Critical Dialogues in Cultural Studies*, ed. D. Morley and Kuan-Hsing Chen, Routledge, London, 1996.

Heibroner, R., 'Follow the Money', *Los Angeles Times Book Review*, 1 June 1997.

Held, David, *Democracy and the Global Order: From the Modern State to Cosmopolitan Governance*, Polity Press, Cambridge, 1995.

Heyerdahl, Thor, *The Ra Expeditions*, trans. P. Crampton, Allen & Unwin, London, 1971.

Hicks, Emily, *Border Writing: The Multidimensional Text*, University of Minnesota Press, Minneapolis, 1991.

Hirst, Paul, and Graham Thompson, *Globalization in Question: The International Economy and Possibilities,* Polity Press, Cambridge, 1996.

Hobsbawm, Eric, *Age of Extremes*, Michael Joseph, London, 1994.

Holmes, Colin, *A Tolerant Country? Immigrants and Minorities in Britain*, Faber & Faber, London, 1991.

Hunt, Ian, 'Walter Benjamin and "Qualitatively Distinguishable Times"', in P. Buchler and N. Papastergiadis, *Random Access*, Rivers Oram Press, London, 1996.

Hutnyk, John, 'Adorno at Womad: South Asian Crossovers and the Limits of Hybridity-Talk', in *Debating Cultural Hybridity*, ed. P. Werbner and T. Modood, Zed Books, London, 1997.

Hutton, Will, 'Sun, Sea, Wine and Loneliness Down Under', *Observer*, 2 November 1997.

Kaplan, Caren, 'Deterritorialization: The Rewriting of Home and Exile in Western Feminist Discourse', in *The Nature and Context of Minority Discourse*, ed. A. R. JanMohamed and D. Lloyd, Oxford University Press, New York, 1990.

Kapur, Geeta, 'The Center–Periphery Model or How are we Placed? Contemporary Cultural Practice in India', *Third Text*, 16/17 (Autumn/Winter, 1991).

Kefala, Antigone, *The Alien*, Makar, St Lucia, 1973.

King, Anthony D., *Global Cities*, Routledge, London, 1990.

King, Anthony D. (ed.), *Culture, Globalization and the World System*, Macmillan, London, 1991.

King, Russel, 'Migrations, Globalization and Place', in D. Massey and P. Jess (eds), *A Place in the World?* Open University Press, Oxford, 1995.

Korol, Alexandra, *Ukraine and National Identity*, unpublished Ph.D. thesis, Department of Sociology, University of Manchester 1996.

'Krauts', *Granta*, 42, (1992).

Kristeva, Julia, *Strangers to Ourselves*, trans. L. Roudiez, Harvester Wheatsheaf, London, 1991.

Kritz, Mary, Lin Lim and Hania Zlotnik (eds), *International Migration Systems: A Global Approach*, Clarendon Press, Oxford, 1992.

Kritz, Mary and H. Zlotnik, 'Global Interactions: Migration Systems, Processes and Policies', in M. Kritz, Lin Lim and Hania Zlotnik (eds), *International Migration Systems: A Global Approach*, Clarendon Press, Oxford, 1992.

Kukathas, Chandran, 'Are There Any Cultural Rights?', in Will Kymlicka (ed.), *The Rights of Minority Cultures*, Oxford University Press, Oxford, 1995.

Kwon, M., 'The Fullness of Empty Containers', *FRIEZE*, 24 (October 1995).

Kymlicka, Will, (ed.), *The Rights of Minority Cultures*, Oxford University Press, Oxford, 1995.

Landa, Manuel de, *War in the Age of Intelligent Machines*, Swerve Editions, New York, 1991.

Lash, Scott and John Urry, *The End of Organized Capitalism*, Polity Press, Cambridge, 1987.

Lash, Scott and John Urry, *Economies of Signs and Spaces*, Sage, London, 1994.

Lechte, John and Gill Bottomley, 'Difference, Postmodernity and Imagery in Multicultural Australia', in G. L. Clark, D. Forbes and R. Francis (eds), *Multiculturalism, Difference and Postmodernism*, Longman & Cheshire, Melbourne, 1993.

Lee Hansen, Marcus, *The Atlantic Emigration, 1607–1860*, Harper, New York, 1961.

Leigh Fermor, Patrick, *Roumeli*, Penguin, Harmondsworth, 1983.

Leuchtag, Alice, 'Merchants of Flesh', *Humanist*, 55 (March–April 1995).

Lotman, J. M., *The Universe of the Mind*, trans. A. Shukman, Tauris, London, 1991.

Lotman, J. M. and B. A. Uspenskij, *The Semiotics of Russian Culture*, trans. A. Shukman, Michigan Slavic Contributions, no. 11, Ann Arbor, 1984.

Lyotard, Jean-François, *The Differend: Phrases in Dispute*, trans. G. Van Den Abbeele, University of Minnesota Press, Minneapolis, 1988.

MacIntyre, Alasdair, *After Virtue*, University of Notre Dame Press, Notre Dame, 1981.

MacIntyre, Alasdair, 'Relativism, Power and Philosophy', in K. Baynes, J. Bohmen and

T. McCarthy (eds), *After Philosophy: End or Transformation?*, MIT Press, Cambridge, Mass., 1987.

MacIntyre, Alasdair, *Whose Justice? Which Rationality?*, University of Notre Dame Press, Notre Dame, 1988.

McLuhan, Marshall and Quentin Fiore, *The Medium is the Message,* Allen Lane, London, 1967.

McQuire, Scott, *Visions of Modernity*, Sage, London, 1998.

Mar, Phillip, 'Just the Place is Different: Comparisons of Place and Settlement Practices of some Hong Kong Migrants in Sydney', *Australian Journal of Anthropology*, 9, no. 1 (1998).

Marx, Karl, *Capital*, vol. I, Foreign Languages Publishing House, Moscow, 1980.

Massey, Doreen, 'Politics and Space/Time', in M. Keith and S. Pile (eds), *Place and the Politics of Identity*, Routledge, London, 1993.

Massey, Doreen, 'The Spaces of Community', in N. Papastergiadis (ed.), *Mixed Belongings and Unspecified Destinations*, INIVA, London, 1997.

Melucci, Alberto, *Nomads of the Present*, Hutchinson, London, 1989.

Menzel, Ulrich, *Globalization, Culture and Migration*, Eurofor Conference, Athens, October 1996.

Mercer, Kobena, 'Art that is Ethnic in Inverted Commas', *FRIEZE* (November/December 1995).

Meyer, Birgit, 'Beyond Syncretism', in C. Stewart and R. Shaw (eds), *Syncretism/Anti-Syncretism*, Routledge, London, 1994.

Miller, Donald, *The Reason of Metaphor,* Sage, New Delhi, 1992.

Milosz, Czeslaw, 'A Symposium on Translation', *Threepenny Review* (Summer 1997).

Minh-ha, Trinh T., *Woman, Native, Other*, Indiana University Press, Bloomington, 1989.

Miyoshi, Masao, 'Borderless World?', in R. Wilson and W. Dissanayake (eds), *Global/Local*, Duke University Press, Durham, NC, 1997.

Mosquera, Gerardo (ed.), *Beyond the Fantastic*, INIVA, London, 1996.

Mouffe, Chantal, 'For a Politics of Nomadic Identity', in G. Robertson et al. (eds), *Travellers' Tales*, Routledge, London, 1994.

Nandy, Ashis, *The Intimate Enemy,* Oxford University Press, New Delhi, 1983.

Nandy, Ashis, *Traditions, Tyranny and Utopias*, Oxford University Press, Delhi, 1987.

Nunes, Z., 'Anthropology and Race in Brazilian Modernism', in Francis Barker, Peter Hulme and Margaret Iverson (eds), *Colonial Discourse/Postcolonial Theory*, Manchester University Press, Manchester, 1994.

Olalquiaga, Celeste, *Megalopolis*, University of Minnesota Press, Minneapolis, 1992.

Panayi, Panikos, *Immigration, Ethnicity and Racism in Britain, 1815–1945*, Manchester University Press, Manchester, 1994.

Papastergiadis, Nikos, 'Reading DissemiNation', *Millennium: Journal of International Studies*, 20, no. 3 (Winter 1991).

Papastergiadis, Nikos, *Modernity as Exile*, Manchester University Press, Manchester, 1993.

Papastergiadis, Nikos, *The Complicities of Culture: Hybridity and 'New Internationalism'*, Cornerhouse Publications, Manchester, 1994.

Papastergiadis, Nikos (ed.), *Art and Cultural Difference: Hybrids and Clusters*, Academy Group, London, 1995.

Papastergiadis, Nikos, *Dialogues in the Diaspora*, Rivers Oram Press, London, 1998.

Parekh, Bhikhu, 'Superior People: The Narrowness of Liberalism from Mills to Rawls', *Times Literary Supplement*, 25 February 1994.

Patnaik, Prabhat, 'International Capital and National Economic Policy: A Critique of India's Economic Reforms', *Economic and Political Weekly*, 29, no. 12, 19 March 1994.

Paz, Octavio, *The Labyrinth of Solitude*, Allen Lane, London, 1967.

Pertierra, Raul, 'Counterfactual Conditions of Culture and their Implication for Integration: A Philippine Example', *Pilipina*, 25 (Fall 1995).

Phizacklea, Anne (ed.), *One Way Ticket: Migration and Female Labour*, Routledge, London, 1983.

Pick, H., 'World Refugee Crisis Spinning out of Control, UN Warns', *Guardian*, 21 November, 1993.

Piore, Michael, *Birds of Passage: Migrant Labor and Industrial Societies,* Cambridge University Press, Cambridge, 1979.

Piper, Adrian, *Adrian Piper*, Ikon Gallery, Birmingham,1991.

Pope, Victor et al., 'Trafficking in Women', *US News and World Report,* 7 April 1997.

Portis Winner, Irene, 'Some Comments upon Lotman's Concepts of Semiotics of Culture: Implications for the Study of Ethnic Culture Texts', in Morris Halle, Ladislav Matejka, Krystyna Pomorska and Boris Uspenskij (eds), *Semiosis: Semiotics and the History of Culture*, Michigan Slavic Contributions, no. 10, Ann Arbor, 1984.

Potts, Lydia, *The World Labour Market: A History of Migration,* Zed Press, London, 1990.

Pratt, Mary Louise, *Imperial Eyes: Travel Writing and Transculturation*, Routledge, London, 1992.

Prigogine, I. and I. Stengers, *Order out of Chaos: Man's New Dialogue with Nature*, Bantam Books, New York, 1984.

Pugliese, E., 'Restructuring of the Labour Market and the Role of Third World Migrations in Europe', *Environment and Planning: Society and Space*, 11 (1993).

Raphael, Max, *Proudhon, Marx, Picasso*, trans. I. Marcuse, Lawrence & Wishart, London, 1980.

Rattansi, Ali, 'Race, Class and the State: From Marxism to Post-Modernism', *Labour History Review*, 60, no. 3 (Winter 1995).

Rex, John, *Race, Colonialism and the City*, Routledge & Kegan Paul, London, 1973.

Rollins, Tim, 'Art in the Construction of Beloved Communities', in *Mixed Belongings and Unspecified Destinations*, ed. N. Papastergiadis, INIVA, London, 1997.

Rose, Gillian, 'Place and Identity: A Sense of Place', in D. Massey and P. Jess (eds), *A Place in the World?*, Open University Press, Oxford, 1995.

Rosenau, James, *Turbulence in World Politics: A Theory of Change and Continuity*, Princeton University Press, Princeton, 1990.

Rouse, Roger, 'Mexican Migration and the Social Space of Postmodernism', *Diaspora,* 1, no. 1 (Spring, 1991).

Rushdie, Salman, *The Satanic Verses*, Viking, London, 1990.

Said, Edward, *Orientalism*, Routledge, London, 1978.

Said, Edward, 'Culture and the Vultures', *Times Higher Education Supplement*, 24 January 1992.

Said, Edward, *Culture and Imperialism*, Chatto & Windus, London, 1993.

Said, Edward, 'Culture and Imperialism', *Times Literary Supplement*, 19 March 1993.

Sapir, Edward, *Culture, Language and Personality*, University of California Press, Berkeley, 1956.

Sassen, Saskia, *The Mobility of Labour and Capital*, Cambridge University Press, Cambridge, 1988.

Sassen, Saskia, *The Global City*, Princeton University Press, Princeton, 1991.

Sassen-Koob, Saskia, 'Notes on the Incorporation of Third World Women into Wage-Labour through Immigration and Off-shore Production', in Cohen, *Sociology of Migration*.

Sennett, Richard, *The Conscience of the Eye*, Faber & Faber, London, 1990.

Serres, Michel, *Hermes*, Johns Hopkins University Press, Baltimore, 1982.

Shanin, Teodor, *Defining Peasants*, Basil Blackwell, Oxford, 1990.

Sheldrake, Rupert, 'The Rebirth of Nature', in *Random Access: Ambient Fears*, ed. P. Buchler and N. Papastergiadis, Rivers Oram Press, London, 1996.

Shohat, Ella and Robert Stam, *Unthinking Eurocentrism,* Routledge, London, 1995.

Shonibare, Yinka, 'Fabric, and the Irony of Authenticity', in N. Papastergiadis (ed.), *Mixed Belongings and Unspecified Destinations*, INIVA, London, 1997.

Simmel, Georg, 'The Metropolis and Mental Life', in K. Wolff (ed.), *The Sociology of Georg Simmel*, Free Press, New York, 1950.

Simmel, Georg, 'The Stranger', in K. Wolff (ed.), *The Sociology of Georg Simmel*, Free Press, New York, 1950.

Sklair, Leslie, *Sociology of the Global System*, Johns Hopkins University Press, Baltimore, 1991.

Smith, A. D., 'Toward a Global Culture?', in Featherstone, *Global Culture*.

Smith, Nick, 'Charles Taylor, Strong Hermeneutics and the Politics of Difference', *Radical Philosophy*, 68 (Autumn 1994).

Solomos, John, *Race and Racism in Britain*, Macmillan, London, 1993.

Spivak, Gayatri, 'Can the Subaltern Speak?', in P. Williams and L. Chrisman (eds), *Colonial Discourse and Post-Colonial Theory: A Reader*, Harvester, London, 1993.

Spivak, Gayatri, *Outside in the Teaching Machine*, Routledge, London, 1993.

Spivak, Gayatri, 'The Narratives of Multiculturalism', Lecture at Manchester University, January 1995.

Spivak, Gayatri, 'Of Poetics and Politics', in Catherine David and Jean-François Cherier (eds), *Documenta X – the book*, Cantz, Kassel, 1997.

Spivak, Gayatri and Ranajit Guha (eds), *Selected Subaltern Studies*, Oxford University Press, New York, 1988.

Stalker, Peter, *The Work of Strangers: A Survey of International Labour Migration*, ILO, Geneva, 1994.

Sweezy, Paul, 'Center, Periphery, and the Crisis of the System', in *Four Lectures on Marxism*, Monthly Review Press, New York, 1981.

Tabouri, Paul, *The Anatomy of Exile*, Harrap, London, 1972.

Taylor, Charles, *Multiculturalism and 'The Politics of Recognition'*, Princeton University Press, Princeton, 1992.

Thomas, William and Florian Znaniecki, *The Polish Peasant in Europe and America*, Dover Publications, New York, 1958.

Thompson, John B., *The Media and Modernity*, Polity Press, Cambridge, 1995.

Tizard, B. and E. Phoenix, *Black, White or Mixed Race?*, Routledge, London, 1994.

Torrance, John, *Estrangement, Alienation and Exploitation*, Macmillan, London, 1977

Travis, A., 'Howard Promises Tough Immigration Bill', *Guardian*, 14 March 1995.

Virilio, Paul, *Lost Dimension*, Semiotexte, New York, 1992.

Walding, R., H. Aldrich and R. Ward (eds), *Ethnic Entrepreneurs*, Sage, London, 1990.

Walvin, J., *Black and White: The Negro and English Society, 1555–1945,* Allen Lane, London, 1973.

Waters, Malcolm, *Globalization,* Routledge, London, 1994.

Whorf, Benjamin, *Language, Thought and Reality*, MIT Press, Cambridge, Mass., 1956.

Wicker, H. R., 'From Complex Culture to Cultural Complexity', in P. Werbner and T. Modood (eds), *Debating Cultural Hybridity*, Zed Press, London, 1997.

Williams, Raymond, *Towards 2000*, Chatto & Windus, London, 1983.

Williams, Raymond, 'When was Modernism?', in *Politics of Modernism*, Verso, London, 1989.

Williamson, James, *New People: Miscegenation and Mulattoes in the U.S.*, Free Press, New York, 1980.

Wilson, Elizabeth, *The Sphinx in the City: Urban Life, the Control of Disorder, and Women*, Virago, London, 1991.

Wilson, Elizabeth, 'The Invisible Flâneur', *New Left Review*, 191 (January/February 1992).

Wolff, Janet, 'The Invisible Flâneuse: Women and the Literature of Modernity', *Theory, Culture and Society*, 2, no. 3 (1985).

Wollen, Peter, *Raiding the Icebox: Reflections on Twentieth-Century Culture*, Verso, London, 1993.

Young, Robert J. C., *Colonial Desire: Hybridity in Theory*, Routledge, London, 1995.

Zizek, Slavoj, 'Multiculturalism, Or, the Cultural Logic of Multinational Capitalism', *New Left Review*, 225 (September/October 1997).

Index